TERRACENE

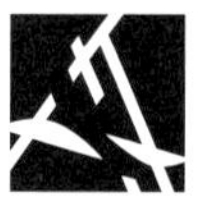

ANIMA: Critical Race Studies Otherwise

A series edited by Mel Y. Chen,
Ezekiel J. Dixon-Román, and Jasbir K. Puar

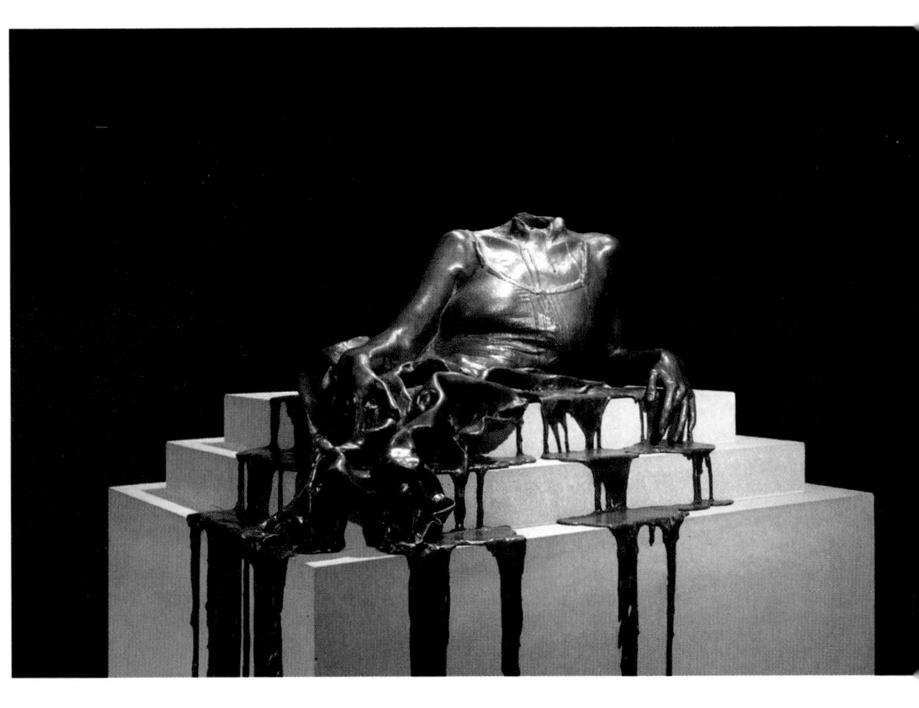

Terracene

A CRUDE AESTHETICS

Salar Mameni

DUKE UNIVERSITY PRESS
Durham and London
2023

Project Editor: Ihsan Taylor
Designed by A. Mattson Gallagher
Typeset in Utopia Std, SangBleu Sunrise, and SangBleu
Kingdom by Copperline Books

Library of Congress Cataloging-in-Publication Data
Names: Mameni, Salar, [date] author.
Title: Terracene : a crude aesthetics / Salar Mameni.
Other titles: ANIMA (Duke University Press)
Description: Durham : Duke University Press, 2023. | Series:
Anima | Includes bibliographical references and index.
Identifiers: LCCN 2022048888 (print)
LCCN 2022048889 (ebook)
ISBN 9781478025061 (paperback)
ISBN 9781478020066 (hardcover)
ISBN 9781478027041 (ebook)
Subjects: LCSH: Arts and society—Middle East. | Arts, Modern—
21st century—Political aspects. | War on Terrorism, 2001–2009, in
mass media. | Environmental degradation in art. | Human ecology
in art. | Terrorism—Environmental aspects. | War—Environmental
aspects. | Climatic changes—Social aspects. | BISAC: ART / History /
Contemporary (1945–) | SOCIAL SCIENCE / Ethnic Studies / Middle
Eastern Studies
Classification: LCC NX180.S6 M345 2023 (print) |
LCC NX180.S6 (ebook) | DDC 700.1/03—dc23/eng/20230315
LC record available at https://lccn.loc.gov/2022048888
LC ebook record available at https://lccn.loc.gov/2022048889

Cover art: Diana Al-Hadid, *In Mortal Repose,* 2011.
Bronze and cast concrete, 72 × 71 × 63.25 inches
(182.9 × 180.3 × 160.7 cm). Photo: Jason Wyche. Courtesy
of the artist and Kasmin Gallery.

*This book is dedicated to the sensoria of those enduring
war and environmental catastrophes.*

CONTENTS

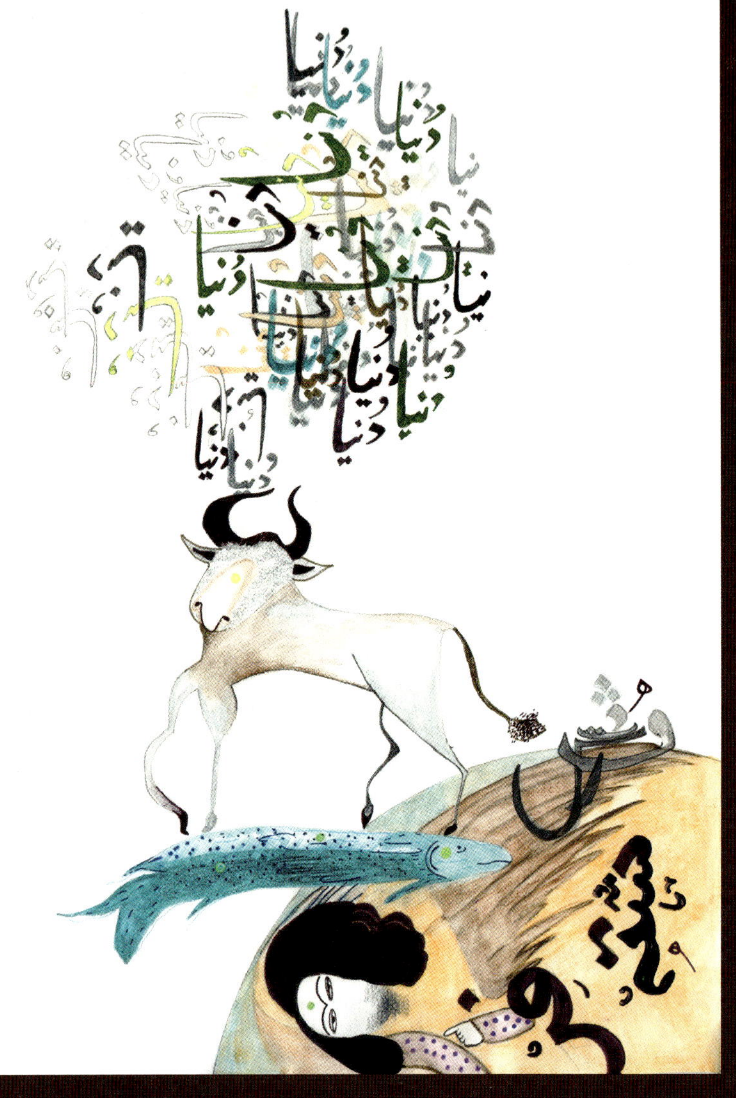

FIGURE CS.1 The world is balanced on the horns of a bull, who stands on a fish, who rests in the wings of an angel. Salar Mameni, *Creation Story*, 2022.

Creation Story

Creation stories bring worlds into being. I know a creation story narrated in Islamic poetic and visual arts that reads:

> *The world was once a flow that fused into a mass of rocks we know as mountains. The mountains rested on the two horns of a bull, who stood on the back of a fish. The fish, in turn, balanced on the wings of an angel.*

As transmitted knowledge, creation stories are told and retold by various speakers across generations, taking different formal qualities every time they are brought into the present through poetic, performative, or pictorial depiction. I rummage through my colored pencils, graphite, ink and ballpoint pens to draw an image of my creation story (see figure cs.1). I deliberately use what is available to me: the oil-based wax of my colored pencils and my ballpoint pens pressing colored ink mixed with Benzyl alcohol and phenoxyethanol onto my acid-free, postconsumer sketch pad. These are materials that bring the creation story into the present, a present shaped by the contradictions of merging synthetic microplastics and recycled paper on an earth overwhelmed by extractive economies that churn precious resources into cheap consumer products.

If my choice of contemporary materials seem at odds with the creation story I am recounting here, it is because we are habituated to the demands of historical thinking, which asks us to avoid scrambling the neat order of chronological time. Historiography asks us to plot every object into a fixed, allocated spot that does not deviate from the existing chronological schema. In the context of my creation story, the demand would be to provide accurate dates and regional specificity so that the story could be attributed to the thought systems of a particular people in time.

Complying with the demands of historiography requires the disclosure of the following facts: I can tell you that this creation story appears in different hand-painted copies of a manuscript known in Arabic as *'Aja'ib al-Makhluqat wa Ghara'ib al-Mawjudat* (Wonders of creation and the oddities of existence). The oldest existing version of the manuscript dates to the late thirteenth century and is currently housed in the Staatsbibliothek in Munich, yet many later copies exist in multiple archives (and languages) since the manuscript remained popular across the Islamic world until the nineteenth century.[1] As a cosmography, the manuscript is concerned with the nature of existence and is divided into two parts, the first concerning the celestial realm (of the planets, the heavenly bodies, and the fixed stars), while the second tells about the earth (the climates, rivers, mountains, vegetables, animals, and birds that roam alongside humans, demons, and jinns).[2] These are facts compiled by historians of medieval Islamic manuscripts, who have meticulously photographed, translated, and studied the folios of the multiple versions of *'Aja'ib al-Makhluqat* and who have commented on the shifting pictorial and rhetorical styles of the codex as well as the religious milieu and the professional ateliers that hired and trained the calligraphers who produced them.[3]

Yet historical contextualization goes against the grain of what creation stories ask us to do. Creation stories are neither bound to, nor derive their meanings from, particular historical moments. The creation story under discussion here, for instance, does not belong to the medieval Islamic period. Muslim writers in this period simply recounted a pre-Islamic creation story, many elements of which were indeed at odds with Islamic cosmographic perspectives of the time.[4] Muslim writers archived and transmitted pre-Islamic knowledge-systems within their manuscripts in a syncretic fashion. The historical data we produce about the manuscripts themselves minimize the function of creation stories as living knowledges that resist the very idea of historical time.[5]

As stories that are meant to convey the notion of "creation"—an event that by definition precedes us—creation stories defy the very idea of history. They rupture linear time and confront our attachments to logical schemas according to which historiography is organized. Furthermore, they compel us to contemplate our ongoing existence in relation to species and environments they conjure. Thinking alongside this creation story compels me to ask the following questions: What is the ecological imagination of this pre/Islamic creation story? How does it intervene into current scientific historiography, according to which we have entered the new epoch of the Anthropocene? How does engaging this story as a living knowledge-system disrupt the hegemonic secular scientific worldview?

These are some of the central questions of this book. As I outline in detail in part I, the notion of the Anthropocene proposes a new geological epoch in which humans are agents who shape the earth and cause climatic and geological change. The Anthropocene is a universalizing proposal that does not make room for multiple knowledge-systems and various modes of being human. Scientific proposals hold hegemonic status in the hierarchies of knowledge and are taken as facts based on the data they produce. The circular logic by which the criteria for what counts as data determines what counts as fact disqualifies knowledge-systems that have different standards for understanding and producing knowledge. This book engages numerous disqualified sites of knowledge as relevant to the environmental discourses of the Anthropocene. These include the ahistorical worlds of poetic ecological imaginations, syncretic spaces of Islamic cosmology and jinn possession, contemporary sense perceptions of war victims living in militarized zones, and the intelligence of nonhuman organisms. The data that such sites provide do not appear in graphs and time lines but ask that we question who intelligent actors are in a world thrown out of balance by the very data-collecting, historicizing, industrializing, secular humanity.

In order to launch us into the book's broader thesis, I want to think alongside the pre/Islamic creation story I have retold here and foreground some of the ecological insights it provides. One of the most striking aspects of this creation story is that its worldview does not revolve around the human. While it certainly assumes the existence of a human (by whom and for whom the image is created), it provides a set of relationships between physical and metaphysical entities that do not center the human. Living entities belonging to the terrestrial plain (the mountain, the bull, and the fish) are all held up in the wings of an angel, the invisible and the atemporal realm of the spiritual and the divine. In such a relationship, the living world is given a divine status and is offered to us as sacred. Within Islamic cosmographic traditions, the mountain referenced in this creation story is known as Qaf, beyond which is the realm of the unknown.[6] While there are a number of different physical geographic locations attributed to the mountain over time, what remains significant is that all mountains are understood to be connected to Qaf, hence endowing all mountains on earth with sacred status.[7]

I emphasize the sacred nature of Qaf (and by extension all mountains) in order to insist, at the outset, on the possibility for the coexistence of the sacred and the ecological, which contemporary scientific thought often disregards. Qaf's sacred status in creation did not pose a problem for premodern Muslim thinkers who explained phenomena such as earthquakes in relation to it. In one version for instance, Qaf is said to have spoken about how earthquakes are produced. Qaf says: "These mountains are my roots; there is no town in the world that is not connected with these mountains through some root ('irk). When God wishes to produce an earthquake, he orders me and I make this particular root vibrate, so that an earthquake happens to the grounds of this or that town."[8] In other versions, earthquakes occur when the bull tosses the earth from one horn to another or when the fish writhes underneath.[9]

Engaging with the sacred nature of natural phenomena, such as earthquakes, requires an entangled disposition toward the world. It requires that we move beyond a localized understanding of cause and effect toward a broader acknowledgment of the interconnectedness of all things. In part 2 of this book, I engage contemporary understandings of earthquakes in relation to explosions and oil-extractive industries. I show that the intensive military bombardments and extraction industries in the Persian Gulf region produce vibrations that are akin to earthquakes. This phenomenological conflation among war, industrialization, and climate is what I term *Terracene* in order to highlight the catastrophic ways in which the "natural" environment becomes a site of ongoing terror for those who inhabit militarized and (settler)colonial extractive sites. The result is weaponized ecologies that create zones of terror that are bordered off and distanced from the beneficiaries of military extraction.

Living in the Terracene requires a shift in thought: a shift from anthropocentric visions of the earth that see it as a site of resource extraction and militarized (settler)colonial occupations to one where the world is a sacred and intelligent site of interconnected beings. Our pre/Islamic creation story emphasizes this point by laying each figure on the back of another. Mountains are balanced on the back of a bull, who is balanced on the back of a fish, who rests on the wings of an angel. In such an image, the earth is not seen as a mere resource for the animal but is reliant on the bull to carefully carry the earth's weight on its horns. Indeed, if the delicate balance between the bull's horns and the mountains are lost, the earth is said to fall out of balance and shake (as in an earthquake). The inherent balance through which the cosmos is organized in the creation story is in direct contrast to extractive logics by which the earth becomes a provider of resources. The stacked image emphasizes instead the earth's reliance on the animal (and the fish and the angel in turn) for its existence.

The counterintuitive order in which the world is stacked in this creation story also asks us to contemplate the limits of rational thought and by extension human mastery over the workings of the cosmos. Not only is the human eliminated from having any central role in creation but is asked to understand positivist, verifiable knowledge to be at odds with creation. The thought of mountains standing on a bull's horns defies rational thought, as does the thought of a bull's weight being carried by a fish, not to mention the difficulty the metaphysical being of an angel poses for positivist understandings. By withholding the hubris of rationality, we acknowledge not only the futility of human mastery but, more importantly, that positivist reality is at odds with the sacred world we occupy. This is of utmost significance in a contemporary world in which solutions to anthropogenic climate change remain secular and anthropocentric, proposing more technological interventions through more advanced forms of data collection.

Our creation story refutes the human's ability to fully grasp the world through verifiable knowledge (by which a bull could never hold up a mountain). Instead, it appeals to our poetic, speculative, and imaginative intelligence through which we can grasp what is to be known about the world. It is our poetic intelligence, for instance, that allows us to fathom the significance of the gravitational reversal in this image and the ethics that such a reversal implies. While our verifiable reality tells us that heavier, bigger, stronger animals (such as a bull) can step over and kill a smaller one (such as a fish), our poetic capacities allow for alternate worldviews, which could—if taken seriously—change how power relations are imagined in the world. Taking this reading a step further, we might argue that the stacking of the heavier elements on the lighter ones emphasizes the unacknowledged significance of what positivist perspectives perceive as minor, small, or insignificant. Current mass extinctions of wildlife and shrinkage of biodiversity across the globe, for instance, are based in the diminished value of things whose absence or destruction are undermined or remain opaque to profit-driven economies focused on singular resources (such as oil). What our creation story makes apparent is that the elimination of any one element (a fish, for instance) can disrupt how the whole world is held up.

Why is it important to tell creation stories at a time of mass-scale planetary destruction? Today, epic narratives foresee planetary destruction in the form of climate disasters caused by war and industry. In the early 2000s, atmospheric chemist Paul J. Crutzen and marine biologist Eugene Stoermer proposed the term *Anthropocene* in order to name a new geological era marked by human industry. "Without major catastrophes like an enormous volcanic eruption, an unexpected epidemic, a large-scale nuclear war, an asteroid impact, a new ice age, or continued plundering of Earth's resources by partially still primitive technology," Crutzen and Stoermer wrote in a May 2000 newsletter, "mankind will remain a major geological force for many millennia, maybe millions of years to come."[10] The Anthropocene tells a destruction story. It argues that humans, as a collective species, have become a geological force with the power to destroy themselves and the planet.

Yet destruction stories are not all there is to tell. This book offers the term *Terracene* to hold space for other modes of planetary imagination. On the one hand, the term *Terracene* highlights the dystopian present—a world of *terror*—with multiple endings in war, disease, and ecological damage. On the other hand, it foregrounds creation—a world of *terra*—earthly beings generating lifeworlds. If there is to be an epic planetary story, it is best termed the Terracene so that (a) the emphasis is placed upon the *terror* brought about by specific militarized (settler)colonial industries, and (b) the narrative is told from the perspective of *terrans*: the creative multispecies inhabitants of militarized and extractive regions who bear embodied scars of terror and who also propose and practice resilient strategies for living.

I offer the term *Terracene* as a rebuttal to the scientific notion of the Anthropocene. In part 1 of this book, I tackle two specific shortcomings of the idea of the Anthropocene. First, I foreground its Eurocentrism. The notion of the Anthropocene equates a regional, European-industrial mode of production and its violent, colonial, and militarized expansion across the globe with the human (the *Anthropos*). This is a crude scientific generalization that cannot imagine—and more importantly refuses to see—other ways of being human. The second issue concerns the belatedness of the narrative arc of the Anthropocene. For those of us who have lived—and continue to live—in militarized and extractive geographic regions for generations, the novelty of the Anthropocene is incongruent with lives we have led, destructions we have witnessed, stories we have known. To our ears (and other sensorial modes of perception), the Anthropocene is not only an old diagnosis but simply a partial image of the planet.

This book joins a growing critical scholarship that challenges Eurocentric forms of knowledge-production that universalize planetary visions. My particular intervention centers contemporary artists and knowledge-producers from West Asia, a region that has been gutted and polluted by extractive industries (predominantly for petroleum production and refinery) backed by mass-scale military force. I think with artists concerned with the militarized ecologies of the Arab/Persian Gulf region—namely, Iran, Iraq, Kuwait, and Yemen alongside Syria and Palestine. I travel with them to wastelands, excavation sites, and toxic lands on fire in order to experience the Terracene sensorially.

In part 2, I listen to the Terracene with the Kuwaiti American musician Fatima Al-Qadiri, whose album *Desert Strike* (2012) builds on the sonic landscape of war in Kuwaiti oil fields. How do we hear the Terracene? What do we hear when we listen? Al-Qadiri's compositions occupy sonic spaces that blur the boundaries between explosions and earthquakes, oil and water, extraction and bombardments. In the aftermath of the massive fires in Kuwait, which were caused by Iraqi military bombing of oil fields in 1991, many expressed their experiences in silence. The German filmmaker Werner Herzog traveled to Kuwait in order to capture the fields of fire raging into the atmosphere in his film *Lessons of Darkness* (1992) and to talk to local residents. The film presents language as inadequate for articulating the social and political brutality that had led to that moment of geological disaster. How does one address the faceless drone designed to drop explosives from soaring heights? How does one put into words the dynamism of petrochemicals fueling orange flames into a receding blue sky? What is speech when lungs are filled with plumes of smoke, when the traumas of oppression and dispossession from land are generationally transmitted and felt? The two local speakers appearing in Herzog's film are mute, having lost their capacity for speech in the face of the magnitude of war and ecological violence. But silence can be a deliberate response to cruelty since the absence of speech does not signify a lack of meaning.[11] Voice, words, and speech are normative ways in which not only the human is defined, elevated, and separated from nonhuman animals but according to which an ableist hierarchical order of the human is achieved.

Parts 3 and 5 inquire about contemporary Iranian/Iraqi toxic sensoria produced as a result of geopolitical relations with crude oil. Literary, mythological, visual, sonic, and religious arts across cultures have proposed various aesthetic relations with crude oil that are far more diverse than the secular formulation of crude oil as fossil fuel. My task in these parts of the book is to map out a nonsecular mode of relating to crude oil by centering the works of contemporary Iranian artists such as Morehshin Allahyari, Gelare Khoshgozaran, and Reza Negarestani. I argue that contemporary Iranian artists have claimed crude oil as an Indigenous deity, whose powers can be conjured for developing new relations with climate change and the global war on terror.

The goddesses of crude oil, appearing in plastic forms, tell the story of Terracene in part 3, where I center the work of Morehshin Allahyari who replicates ancient Mesopotamian deities bombed and destroyed since the United States–led military occupation of Iraq in 2003. Allahyari's 3D plastic replications conjure ancient Mesopotamian knowledge-systems that have survived within oral, visual, and textual histories across contemporary Iran-Iraq borderlands. By examining her works alongside Reza Negarestani's fictional excavations of crude gods, goddesses, and jinns within telluric strata of the region, I read for a nonsecular geochronological story of the planet through the perspective of Indigenous Terrans.

In part 4, I follow a fictional resistance fighter known as the "Narrative Terrorist" in the work of the Palestinian artist Larissa Sansour, who confronts how territories are settled, policed, and resisted. Sansour's work is aware that settler colonialism is enacted through the disruption of multispecies lifeworlds and the production of uninhabitable environments. Her video titled *In the Future They Ate from the Finest Porcelain* (2015) follows the efforts of the Narrative Terrorist who utilizes carbon dating as a technique for drawing an alternative historiography of Palestine. For the Narrative Terrorist, carbon's chemical qualities can unsettle settler-colonial archaeologies of time by intervening in the earth's stratification. In my reading, the Narrative Terrorist offers a radical vision of being human, one that tackles the military occupation of Palestine through the lens of the earth's carbon cycle.

In part 5, I think with the material intelligence of crude oil. I speculate whether crude oil can theorize. Can it aestheticize? Can we allow crude oil to narrate the entanglement of our present geopolitical and geological relations? To pose such questions is to ask about the intelligence and sensibility of all Terrans. It is to propose that it is the earth's storage of complex carbon structures that has fueled the Anthropos claiming our new epoch. Scientific historiography and other forms of knowledge-production have long been understood as the domain of the Anthropos. Intelligence, speech, and creativity are indeed how the human has been demarcated from other earth-beings in Enlightenment philosophy. Aesthetic theory has a tradition of placing the human at the center of perception from whose perspective the world comes to be known.

In order to disrupt this genealogy, in part 5 I shift the domain of intelligence to crude oil in order to think aesthetics through crude oil's material intelligence. I do so by considering visual documentations of extractive industries, where explosions at oil-drilling sites claim the visual field. I examine a massive explosion at the Anglo-Iranian Oil Company's oil fields in southwest Iran, documented in *A Fire!* (1961), directed by the Iranian filmmaker Ebrahim Golestan. Following a distinct documentary film style, *A Fire!* is a poetic critique of the long history of British oil commission in Iran. Golestan's lens brings our attention to the formation of toxic landscapes in southern Iran and the pollutive bodies of Indigenous nomads living in the vicinities of urbanized oil towns. Despite the film's documentary frame, the director allows us to think with the agency of crude oil, whose explosive theater is the film's main visual element. In the film, crude oil is presented as an intelligent material that issues a refusal to those who attempt to drill it out of the ground. I use the term *petrorefusal* to name crude oil's sensibility toward humans it encounters at oil-extractive sites. Yet this is not the only possible relationship between humans and crude oil. When crude oil enters our bodies in the form of toxins, it transforms our senses, creating a radically shifted orientation toward the world.

While this book proposes the neologism Terracene as a useful term for thinking the present moment, I am also deeply aware of the limitations and inadequacies of language. As a writer, I am compelled to use words to create, formulate, and fashion new ideas, aesthetics, feelings, and states of life. Yet as a multilingual speaker, I am also aware of the limits of linguistic meaning (certainly monolingual writing and speaking). I do not hold language, voice, and speech to be the predominant (or even the most effective) mode of articulation. As such, I also guide you in this book with a number of drawings, poems, and creative prose.

I hence proceed with an acknowledgment of the crudeness of words in times of terror and the necessity for multisensory thinking, dreaming, feeling, seeing, and listening to the residues of extractive and militarized cultures who come to be known as terrorists within the geopolitical order of the globe.

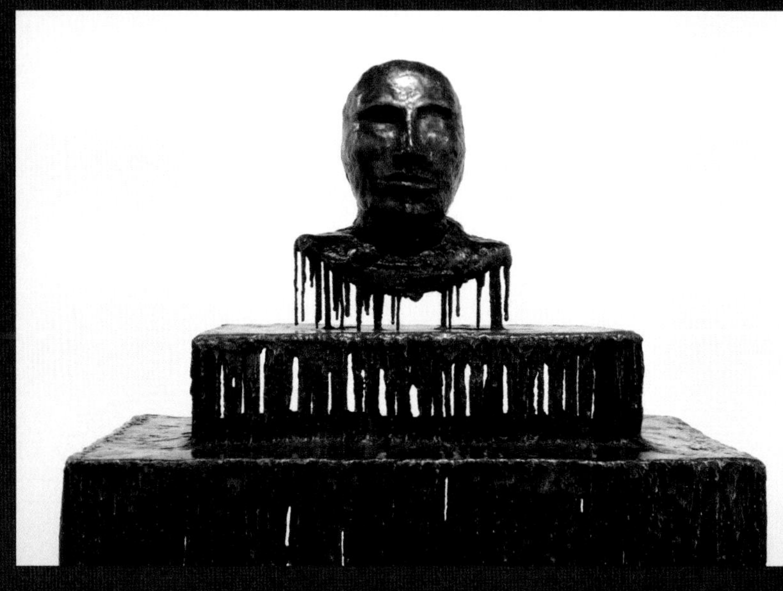

1

Terror and the Anthropocene

We are told that we live in the Anthropocene: the geological age of the human. Yet, many of us experience the present in ways that cannot be summarized through the notion of the "human" alone. We have lived with war, land dispossession, exploitation, and racialization, bringing us to question who the human is and how it is defined. The notion of the Anthropocene was coined in the early 2000s in order to name the problem of anthropogenic climate change by imagining a collective human species that had geologically changed the planet through industrialization. However, this scientific idea failed to account for sociopolitical disparities across the globe that had produced unequal access to industry. Some parts of the globe had higher concentrations of industrial machinery and were burning more fossil fuels. Other parts of the planet were more polluted and were accumulating waste at exponentially high rates. Some were building weapons while others were dying or surviving their explosions within rural and urban centers. Such disparities in the environment were the result of different histories of power and domination, different stories of the cosmos and different imaginings of being human.

The Anthropocene is a scientific story, and like all other stories, it was written in a specific historical time and place. I open the book here by bringing attention to the historical emergence of the concept of the Anthropocene in relation to the declaration of the global war on terror in 2001. While the scientific community, in the early years of the new century, was proposing a new geological timescale for the planet, politicians, journalists, writers, artists, and the general public were contending with a new geopolitical reality that was being described as a global state of war on terror. My task at the outset of this book is to attend to this historical conjunction that named the geological age of man alongside yet another war. In order to facilitate this conversation, I offer the term *Terracene* and ask the following questions: How do we think the Anthropocene through racialized wastelands of war and militarism? How can we understand the Anthropocene through sites, whose very subterranean fossils (in the form of crude oil and other extractive resources) have fueled war machines that destroy habitats, prompt mass migrations, and destroy ecosystems and biodiverse lifeworlds? How do we conceive of the Anthropocene through polluted and pollutive wastelands under terror?

At the most basic level, the Anthropocene must be interrogated from the vantage point of the war on terror because of the historical coincidence of the two terminologies in the early 2000s as frameworks for understanding a new world order. Since their conceptions, both ideas have proven discursively rich for envisioning the current state and governance of the planet. The war on terror was not the first time that "terror" was used to name a loosely organized enemy. Nor was the year 2001 the historical beginning of US-led militarism across the globe. Yet, September 11, 2001, has since served as a historical marker for the creation of what former US secretary of state Colin Powell referred to as the "Terror-Industrial Complex."[1] Despite widespread critique of the legal legitimacy, as well as social, economic, and ecological costs of this war, terror remains a symbolic diagnosis of our current mode of global governance. Indeed, as Junaid Rana notes, "Terror has become a keyword of the twenty-first century."[2]

The Anthropocene has not been studied in relation to the war on terror as they each belong to different disciplinary thought systems. Yet a closer look reveals many overlaps in how each term has conceptualized the planet. What is striking at first glance is the open-ended ways in which both the Anthropocene and the idea of terror are routinely defined. The Anthropocene is notorious for being an ambiguous concept for at least two reasons. First, the Anthropocene's ecological timescale cannot be readily sensed in our immediate surroundings. Imaging the Anthropocene requires thick data, historical mapping, and alternative temporalities to comprehend how capitalist industrialization across the globe has caused climate change on a planetary scale. While extreme heat, massive wildfires, seasonal hurricanes, and increased humidity are regularly experienced today, the gradual shift in climate patterns caused by collective industrial practices across wide-ranging locations and historical periods are more difficult to apprehend. As such, if humans are to be perceived as a geological force, changing the very chemical makeup of the planet, this can only be done by imagining a collective species who, unbeknownst to itself, acted geologically over a long period of time.

Conceiving oneself as part of a human species is the second challenge that makes the concept of the Anthropocene so ambiguous. As Dipesh Chakrabarty has noted, "We humans never experience ourselves as a species," since "one never experiences being a concept."[3] This is because the idea of being a part of the human species is an abstraction. To be the Anthropos of the Anthropocene requires the speculative exercise of becoming an abstract concept: becoming human. Being human is far from self-explanatory and arguably one of the most thorny philosophical ideas. Who gets to be called human is an open question for bodies who do not fit ableist, racist, and patriarchal visions. As such, identifying the contested category of the human species as the driving force of a new geological era is not as simple as the scientific notion of the Anthropocene suggests.

Similarly, terror has frustrated any clear definition, making it difficult to determine what or whom the notorious war is waged against. The terrorist, as Gayatri Spivak notes in a speech in 2011, is an "abstract enemy," one who can mutate and evolve in unknown ways.[4] This abstraction opens up the notion of terror to a substantial level of uncertainty so that being a terrorist becomes a slippery state of being. In his joint address to Congress and the nation in September of 2001, the US president George W. Bush designated a "collection of loosely affiliated terrorist organizations" as the enemy against whom "our war on terror begins."[5] This war, he continued, "will not end until every terrorist group of global reach has been found, stopped and defeated."[6] Much like the Anthropos, the terrorist is an abstract idea because it merges geographically disparate, heterogenous peoples into a single concept. As a term, *terror* attempts to collectivize unrelated peoples, actions, movements, and events into a coherent entity against which a "war" could be waged by the United States and its allies.

Both terror and the Anthropos are abstract concepts that collectivize heterogenous entities into a group. To say these are abstract concepts is not to undermine their rhetorical significance but to highlight that it is this very abstraction that has contributed to their discursive force. However, each concept approaches collectivization in a distinct way. While the Anthropos is meant to define *all* humans at a species level, *terrorist* is a name reserved for a particular human subcategory. The terrorist is, as such, a racializing concept that delimits the wide-ranging idea of the human. This is how racialization works. People are racialized when they are set apart from the universal category of the human based on abstract ideas about them. Darieck B. Scott explains blackness as a "patchwork of narratives condensed on the skin of the blackened and referenced in the images ascribed to them."[7] Following Scott's definition, we can understand terrorist as a "patchwork of narratives," accumulated on the body of the so-called terrorist. The terrorist is an abstraction built out of heterogeneous thoughts, actions, and images that Edward Said powerfully underscored in his notion of Orientalism. Said explained Orientalism as a "discourse with supporting institutions, vocabulary, scholarship, imagery, doctrines, even colonial bureaucracies and colonial styles."[8] Terrorism, much like Orientalism and blackness, is a racializing category gathering around bodies as a web of narratives and governmental practices.

Despite its reference to all of humanity, the Anthropocene is also a racialized concept. The notion of the Anthropocene gets thorny because it suggests that the whole of human species has unknowingly damaged the planet, making it uninhabitable for all. As I describe in more detail in the following pages of the book, the scientific proposal for the Anthropocene cites very specific practices of living in particular regions of the world as the driver of current climate catastrophes. Yet, it attributes climate change to the whole of human species. As Andreas Malm and Alf Hornborg have put it, "Steam-engines were not adopted by some natural-born deputies of the human species," rather "a tiny minority even in Britain, . . . Indeed a clique of white British men literally pointed steam-power as a weapon—on sea and land, boats and rails—against the best part of humankind, from the Niger delta to the Yangzi delta, the Levant to Latin America."[9]

As a concept, the Anthropocene generalizes scientific-industrial-military practices of *some* as the actions of *all* humans. This is how whiteness works. "There is no more powerful position than that of being 'just' human," writes Richard Dyer, "as long as race is something only applied to non-white peoples, as long as white people are not racially seen and named, they/we function as a human norm. Other people are raced, we are just people."[10] The human in the idea of the Anthropocene adheres to this conception of the "just" human, a collective that is racially unmarked but is universalized to claim the whole of human species.

The Anthropocene and the terrorist are both strong political concepts because they do not simply collectivize bodies into a generalized species or a racialized group, but they each also describe an *antagonist*. The age of the Anthropocene pays homage to a human who has interfered with the atmospheric and geological makeup of the planet. This human has caused a transformation in the earth's ecosystem in such a way that portents a danger to its own existence. Notably, the Anthropocene is "not a crisis for the inorganic planet" as such, but rather a predicament of the viability of human life in its current form.[11] The Anthropos is thus not simply the enemy of the planet but a threat to the well-being of all living species.

While the scientific notion of the Anthropocene names an epoch marked by species extinctions, desertification, ocean acidification, and further planetary damage to come, the unmarked "human" at the center of this idea undermines the inherent threat that the term aims to conceptualize. The terrorist, on the other hand, is the political name given to those who pose a danger to the current social, economic, and ecological order of the globe. Elizabeth Povinelli argues that the terrorist in the post-9/11 era has been "primarily associated with fundamentalist Islam and the radical Green movement,"[12] but the "terrorist is also the virus and the waste dump, the drug-resistant bacterial infection, and the nuclear fallout."[13] In Povinelli's assessment, terrorism is a multispecies assemblage that pulls together (some) humans, bacteria, events, and toxic wastelands.

Current discourses on terror, however, are never about the Anthropos. Terrorist does not name the human responsible for this damaged planet we currently inhabit. The term terrorist is not currently used to designate the human species at large. On the contrary, terrorism has been cut off from the Anthropos and is applied to any abstract condition that threatens the human from the *outside*. Instead of naming those who dump waste, the terrorist is the waste dump itself. Instead of naming the act of building nuclear weapons, terror is what ensues in the aftermath of their explosion. Terrorism currently does not name the Anthropos responsible for the damaged planet but the resulting wastelands, disease, and peoples threatening the Anthropos. Today, terrorism is not a term used for specific practices that have unraveled the ecological balance of the earth. Instead, it is used to bracket off the human from a multispecies assemblage that threatens it from an external, abstract danger zone. Terrorism today does not describe the dangers some humans pose to the planet through war and militarism but is a name given to viral dwellers of wastelands.

The terrorist thus falls outside of the category of the human and is an entangled fusion of the nonhuman (such as infectious disease or toxic landscapes) and the less-than-human (such as racialized bioterrorists). Terrorists do not build wastelands but are the virus that inhabit them. In Povinelli's description, momentous sites of the Anthropocene—the waste dump and the nuclear fallout—are offered as multispecies dwellings of hazardous chemicals and infectious-disease, which form geographies of waste and terror. The concept of terrorism thus creates a conceptual barrier to keeping the category of the human species intact. Terrorism creates a fissure in who can be perceived as human, producing a racialized domain that threatens the human externally.

Simply put, there is a paradox here. The thesis for anthropogenic climate change positions the human as the enemy of the planet. The human, and its drive toward industrial development, is proposed to be the reason for the melting of ice caps that expose ancient viruses. It is human industry that has caused sea levels to rise and threatens to engulf wetlands with toxic waste. Yet the discourse of the Anthropocene also envisions terror (peoples, viruses, and toxic landscapes) threatening the livelihood of the unmarked human. In relation to this terror, the unmarked human becomes a victim who must be defended. The Anthropocene is hence a political battleground between the unmarked human and the terrorist. "To be the Virus," writes Povinelli, "is to be subject to intense abjection and attacks, and to live in the vicinity of the Virus is to dwell in an existential crisis."[14]

When we consider the historical conception of the notion of the Anthropocene in relation to the declaration of the war on terror, we begin to see that the human has emerged as a militarized concept, one who must be defended from terror. "Definitions of terror and terrorism," as Anjuli Fatima Raza Kolb describes it, "shift from observable acts and events perpetuated by human actors to something more atmospheric and ontological, something distinctly at odds with the human."[15] For Raza Kolb, this "atmospheric" imaginary of terror follows virological and epidemic logics that, like a disease, can grip the human. "The epidemic thesis," Raza Kolb writes, "produces an 'inhuman,' natural enemy in order to negate political demands, and to justify a global security apparatus in defense of 'humanity,' a category that is constituted by its exclusion of phenomena perceived as contagious: like terror, like Islam."[16]

The virological logic of terrorism described by Raza Kolb contributes to the segregation of the globe into distinct dwellings of the racialized whose movement and migrations are governed, inhibited, and vigorously policed. A site such as Pakistan, for instance, is "a feeder state that produces terrorism to be exported abroad and that stands at the front lines of the War on Terror."[17] According to the logic of the war on terror, Pakistan is the site of "migrating terror," implying that terror is viral and infectious or a contagion that must be brought under security surveillance and control.[18] Jasbir Puar describes the virological notion of terrorism best when she writes: "With the unfurling, viruslike, explosive mass of the terrorist network, tentacles ever regenerating despite efforts to truncate them, the terrorist is concurrently an unfathomable, unknowable, and hysterical monstrosity, and yet one that only the exceptional capacities of U.S. intelligence and security systems can quell."[19] This conceptualization of terrorism as viral and subject to military eradication has a colonial history that has long associated racialized environments and their inhabitants as diseased, contagious, and a threat to public health.[20] To be the terrorist is to be perceived, in Raza Kolb's words, as a "public health crisis" and to be subjected to "ferocious military response and infinitely defensible surveillance undertaken in racial, ethnic, and religious terms as 'preventative' care."[21]

The slippage between a virus and a terrorist shaped the earliest visualizations of a virus under the microscope and its popularization in the public imaginary from the 1930s to the 1950s.[22] As Priscilla Wald explains it, "The language is familiar: viruses as enemies and invaders insidiously commandeer the machinery of the cell to reproduce themselves and, in so doing, damage or destroy the host."[23] Scientific knowledge thus has a history of defining the virus politically, as an enemy of the human against which the body must be defended. It is important to emphasize that comparing the virus to an enemy is not merely a metaphor within popular scientific discourse. The very idea that the body comes under viral attack is an importation of legal and political categories of defense into biomedicine according to which the immune system becomes the battleground for fighting infectious disease.[24] "Biological immunity as we know it," writes Ed Cohen, "does not exist until the later nineteenth century. Nor, for that matter, does the idea that organisms defend themselves at the cellular and molecular levels."[25]

The idea of the immune system as the body's defense mechanism is a military visualization of a scientific concept. "We generally presume that the immune system represents the front line in our incessant battle with the hostile forces of disease," writes Cohen. Faced with the unruly virus, the body needed a defense mechanism, an immune system, that could shelter and secure it against viral attacks. The human and the virus are thus codevelopments of political and scientific thought systems. The virus is an enemy of the human, whose body and vital force must be secured. This interdisciplinary history of the virus, and the human's immune response to it, is what allows these concepts to travel so swiftly across scientific and political landscapes and what has enabled the terrorist to be understood in virological terms.

The aim here, of course, is not to criticize interdisciplinary conceptual formations but to show that disciplines are porous and develop in relation to one another. The Anthropocene cannot be understood as a mere scientific concept without social and cultural resonances. Its proposal in 2000 was indeed a call, as Paul Crutzen and Eugene Stoermer put it, "to develop a world-wide accepted strategy leading to sustainability of ecosystems against human induced stresses."[26] The "Terror-Industrial complex" is among those institutions that have taken up this call, understanding "human induced stresses" as terrorism, against whom the unmarked human must be defended. As Robert Marzec describes it, since 9/11, "not only has climate change been accepted, but it has also been adopted by the U.S. military as a clear and present danger."[27]

The US military currently stands as the largest consumer of hydrocarbons in the world with a dependency on fossil fuels that drive continued investments in new infrastructures of energy.[28] Militarism has recently been closely linked to the Anthropocene by scientists who have identified the atmospheric trace of nuclear bomb tests as a synchronous stratigraphic signature across the globe.[29] While attention to militarism within the Anthropocene discourse is fairly recent, the US military has long contended with environmental issues and, according to Marzec, has in fact shown an increased attention to climate change in the aftermath of the declaration of the war on terror.[30] "The post-9/11 period (roughly 2004 to the present)," he writes, is a phase "during which climate change was fully adopted as a central military concern."[31]

Currently, the military understands climate change as "a threat multiplier," a form of imminent danger and a problem of national security.[32] In the language of the military, environmental disruptions are defined as threats. They may cause refugees and "destabilize borders," as in the anticipated case of rising sea levels in Bangladesh,[33] or they may be biosecurity threats initiated by perceived enemies, as in the case of the campaign against the weaponization of the variola virus by Saddam Hussein.[34] Brian Massumi has named this militarized response to the environment as the "war-weather continuum" whereby "large-scale weather-related disruption may well be enemy agitated."[35] Massumi's examples include the choice to dispatch the National Guard to New Orleans in 2005 after Hurricane Katrina flooded the city or the response of counterterrorism agencies to drought-induced fires in Greece in 2007.[36]

The examples noted above reveal that military responses to anthropogenic climate change are racializing practices that securitize "the human" against multifaceted notions of terror. The human and the terrorist are hence political coproductions that pitch multispecies bodies against one another. "The mode of being the 'terrorist,'" Massumi writes, "is wed to the potential of the unspecified threat" while being human is to be included within the domain of securitized bodies.[37] For the military, the Anthropocene is a site of terror, and the war on terror is the current military response to its ecological warnings. The reception of the Anthropocene by the terror-industrial complex has thus produced a racialized terrorist, a multispecies assemblage of bodies and wastelands that have come under security governance. Yet the Anthropocene is itself the production of the terror-industrial complex originating in European settler-colonial and imperial projects. In what follows, I turn to the colonial history of the Anthropocene and the European scientific productions that aesthetically produced the planetary environment we currently inhabit. I argue that the Anthropocene is a work of art produced by the collaborative efforts of scientists and the military.

2

Anti-Colonial Critique
of the Anthropocene

The concept of the Anthropocene, initially proposed by the atmospheric chemist Paul J. Crutzen and marine biologist Eugene Stoermer, holds that collective human industry on the planet must be recognized as having a lasting geological effect. "Now that humans—thanks to our numbers, the burning of fossil fuels, and other related activities—have become a geological agent on the planet," explains Dipesh Chakrabarty, "some scientists have proposed that we recognize the beginning of a new geological era, one in which humans act as main determinants of the environmental planet."[1] This new geological era known as the Anthropocene is proposed to follow our currently accepted epoch, the Holocene, that began approximately twelve thousand years ago. As the *Anthropos* portion of the term Anthropocene clearly suggests, this new geological era perceives of the Anthropos—the human—as a geological force. It proposes that humans, as a collective, have had a lasting effect on the material makeup of the planet and are active agents in the future form of its biosphere.

Since its advent around the year 2000, and perhaps due to its increasingly widespread usage, the term Anthropocene has been met with many objections and alternative coinages. Scholars have taken issue with the hubris of naming an epoch after the human, an alarmingly familiar move to any student of settler-colonial and imperial histories who is well accustomed to the human's desire for expansion and settlement across wide geographies at the expense of feminized, racialized bodies cast outside of the category of the human. With this civilizational record, the Anthropos of the Anthropocene is a reverberating echo of historical practices that have quantified and converted every aspect of the planet into the property of the human from whose perspective all others are perceived, judged, and managed. As Donna Haraway has aptly warned, "The myth system associated with the Anthropos is a setup, and the stories end badly."[2] Leaving the concept unchallenged is to fall for the "setup" and to tell yet another story where the human is the hero of a new era, this time colonizing more than just geographical territories on this planet (and dreaming of the next) but the very geological makeup of the earth itself.

As a concept, the Anthropocene follows a progressive narrative of technological innovation and development. The proposed date for the geological shift to the Anthropocene is the latter part of the eighteenth century and into the early nineteenth century, coinciding with the invention of the steam engine that marks the growth of hydrocarbons in glacial ice cores and biotic change in marine life.[3] According to this time line, the data for anthropogenic change intensifies in the mid-twentieth century, with the accelerated extraction and consumption of fossil fuels leading to high concentrations of atmospheric CO_2.[4] The narrative flow of the Anthropocene hence relies upon familiar benchmarks of technological innovation for the purposes of capital accumulation, prompting scholars to coin alternative terms such as *Capitalocene* and *Eurocene* to describe the planet's geological era.[5] Such terms are meant to highlight that it is not the general category of the human that is responsible for changing the planet's geology but rather a particular mode of humanity (European) and a historically specific form of economic production and expansion (capitalism) that has generated the industries causing climate change.

Feminist Indigenous and critical race scholars have proposed important interventions to show that the Anthropocene's conceptualization is inherently Eurocentric, lacking the capacity to account for settler colonialism, colonial expansion, and neocolonial development in postindependent nations across the Global South. "The complex and paradoxical experiences of diverse people as humans-in-the-world, including the ongoing damage of colonial and imperialist agendas," writes Métis scholar Zoe Todd, "can be lost when the narrative is collapsed to a universalizing species paradigm."[6] Instead, Todd and Heather Davis have argued for tracing the time line of the Anthropocene to "1610, or from the beginning of the colonial period," in order to name "the problem of colonialism as responsible for contemporary environmental crisis."[7] This is also one of the key points in Sylvia Wynter's work, who has emphasized not only the effects of colonialism but of neocolonial governance on the changing geology of the planet. Wynter writes,

> A 2007 report in *Time* magazine on global warming tells us two things: first, that global warming is a result of human activities; and, second, that this problem began in about 1750 but accelerated from about 1950 onward. Now, the date 1750 points to the Industrial Revolution. But the article, which builds on the expertise of the U.N. climate panel, fails to explain *why* global warming accelerated in 1950. What happened by 1950? What began to happen? The majority of the world's peoples who had been colonial subjects of a then overtly imperial West had now become politically independent.[8]

In Wynter's assessment, postcolonial nation-states, arising as a result of liberation struggles, inadvertently followed capitalist models of "development" in the hopes of bringing their impoverished economies into competitive relations with former colonizers. "The West" Wynter explains, "is now going to *reincorporate* us neocolonially, and thereby mimetically, by telling us that the problem with us *wasn't* that we'd been imperially subordinated, *wasn't* that we'd been both socioculturally dominated and economically exploited, but that we were *underdeveloped.*"[9] As Wynter demonstrates, climate change has a direct relationship to (neo)colonial governance. Land grabs, resource extraction, and economic exploitation of (settler) colonies did not only support industrial development but created a global economic imbalance that resulted in postcolonial uprisings and liberation movements across colonized regions. These are geopolitical events that register on the climate scientists' calendar as geological change. The rise of neocolonial governance across former colonies, as well as consistent and ongoing reinforcement of settler colonialism despite decolonial efforts, has left a thick atmospheric trace.

The 1950s is geologically memorialized as the beginning of nuclear bomb testing, visible today in atmospheric radiocarbon data,[10] atomic landscapes, and radioactive deserts on Indigenous lands.[11] By the late twentieth century, the rise of megacities and manufacturing capabilities of BRIC countries (Brazil, Russia, India, China) began to put pressure not only on the global configurations of power but the planet's geological makeup. The scientific designation of the Anthropocene at the turn of the century presented these geopolitical events in geological terms as migrant and Indigenous laborers and activists across the globe protested land appropriation, extractive economies, and the toxic landscapes enabled and supported by corporate war machines.

Naming settler (neo)colonialism and militarism as the driving forces for anthropogenic climate change is to pose a question about who represents the Anthropos in the concept of the Anthropocene. Anthropos is the Greek word for the Latin *humanus*, and the human is the common designator for the collective species. Yet, as Walter D. Mignolo puts it, "The question is not 'what is human and humanity' but rather who defined themselves as humans in their praxis of living and applied their self-definition to distinguish and classify and rank lesser humans."[12] Should the notion of the human be reduced to Eurocapitalist models of being human simply for their hegemonic enforcement across the globe? Is the current biosecuritized version of humanity the only way such a collective can be defined? If the spin-off of various forms of settler-colonial exploitation is the impetus for the recognition of a new geological era, why would the immense diversity of human expressions preceding proposed dates for the Anthropocene be obliterated from the definition of humanity?[13] For it is surely not the human who is memorialized in the notion of the Anthropocene—if we understand humanness as a process, a persistent and unfixed realization in multitudinous forms. What we see expressed in the notion of the Anthropocene is rather a specific "genre," as Wynter would have it, of being human.[14] "*Humanness*," Wynter writes, "is no longer a noun. *Being human is a praxis.*"[15] The notion of the Anthropocene forgets the "praxis" of being human, the multiple expressions of becoming rather a fixed being of being human.[16]

An anti-colonial critique of the Anthropocene requires deep engagements with diverse forms of humanity as well as cosmic imaginaries. How humans are webbed or split from their environments has a radical bearing on how we understand bioplanetary relations. "To be human," Gayatri Spivak writes, "is to be intended toward the other."[17] This "other" in Spivak's assessment is the life-giving force that can take names such as "mother, nation, god, nature."[18] How we web or split with these others depends on cosmological stories and traditions we adhere to. In her lectures given at the turn of the century, Spivak offered us "the planetary" (rather than the global) as a way of being with this other. "The globe," she notes, "is on our computers. No one lives there. It allows us to think that we can aim to control it. The planet is the species of alterity."[19]

I interpret Spivak's evocation of the planetary as a way of contending with alterity and the unknown, or what Elizabeth DeLoughrey defines as a "method of reading that defamiliarizes 'familiar space.'"[20] The globe is different from the planet in that it is a symbol, an image with measured longitudes and latitudes accessible via Google Maps. The globe is an early modern European visualization of the earth that aided the colonial science of cartography. "To imagine the earth as a globe is essentially a visual act," writes Denis Cosgrove, "such a gaze is implicitly imperial, encompassing a geometric surface to be explored and mapped, inscribed with content, knowledge, and authority."[21] Spivak proposes the planet "to overwrite the globe."[22] The planet is not an unexplored site of territorial expansion. It is not the function of the imperial gaze that aims to map, measure, settle, and control. The planet cannot be reduced to a single image, a single cartographic imaginary, a single spherical suspension visible via satellite. Planetary thinking holds possibility for multiplicity and plural relations that are in perpetual flux. "If we imagine ourselves as planetary subjects rather than global agents, planetary creatures rather than global entities," Spivak writes, "alterity remains underived from us."[23]

I contend that the Anthropocene is global thinking that reduces the earth to the function of (some) human's visualizing, designed, and technocratic impulse. In the next few pages, I provincialize this image of the globe as the particular vision of the European scientist.

3

Provincializing the Anthropocene;
or, Why Artists, Feminists,
and Yemeni People Have Much
to Say about the Cosmos

The Anthropocene is a scientific proposal for understanding a planet damaged by climate change. What can art and aesthetics offer climate scientists? What would compel us to turn to creative, speculative, and performative methodologies of contemporary artistic practices alongside data analysis and numerical representations of the Anthropocene? Why look to artists to understand climate change when even the truth-claims of scientific inquiry have failed to convey planetary crisis to the general public?

I want to begin my responses to these questions by first interrogating the categorical distinction between art and science, as well as artist and scientist, that these questions presuppose. In his literary analysis of scientific myth-making and storytelling, Nasser Zakariya offers the scientist as a nineteenth-century figure. It was in the 1830s, Zakariya writes, "in which in the English context the term 'scientist' was first hazarded."[1] In order for the scientist to become a coherent category of identity, it had to be distinguished from others who might have a claim to the same knowledges that the scientist was attempting to produce. The scientist had to be separated from other researchers who were learned, experimental, impassioned by curiosity, and were in pursuit of knowledge about the world around them. According to Zakariya, the production of the scientist was dependent upon the removal of the nonscientist from scientific truth. Who then became the nonscientist? Zakariya explains, "The nonscientist is enfigured as classically trained patrician, as literary critic and humanist, or more vaguely and problematically still, as non-Western non-truth-seeking subject."[2]

The nineteenth century is, hence, not simply the period in which the category of the scientist emerged in Europe but an era in which a whole array of knowledge-producers were cast outside of scientific inquiry. As Zakariya's description suggests, not only is the nonscientist understood in opposition to "literary critics and humanists" but centuries of knowledge-producers—a whole diversity of peoples, cultures, and languages existing outside of Europe—were designated as nontruth-seekers. It is such that approximately a century and a half after the conceptualization of the scientist, Banu Subramanian, a scientist and a professor of women, gender, and sexuality studies, opens her book titled *Ghost Stories for Darwin* (2014) with the following paragraph:

> Traversing liminal spaces, traveling the hallways of academia, at the borderlands of disciplines. . . . Almost there, but never quite. Meandering, half mesmerized, half muddled, always mumbling. Dare I speak? Almost there, but never quite. Almost a scientist, yet a feminist; almost a feminist, yet a scientist; almost a native, yet an alien; almost an alien, yet a native; almost an outsider; yet inside; almost an insider, yet outside. . . . Almost there, but never quite. A life held captive in oppositions. How did I get to this tantalizing, much celebrated place, the home of the oxymoronic feminist scientist, this magical place of perpetual motion . . . nowhere, yet everywhere all at once?

Subramanian's compelling representation of herself as a liminal figure, somewhere between a scientist and a feminist, somewhere between an insider and an outsider, is a result of the persistence of the nineteenth-century European construction of the scientist as one who includes neither a feminist nor a South Asian scholar studying the biological discourses of plant diversity in relation to politics of human diversity in the Global North. While Subramanian's book is one among many current studies in the expanding field of feminist science and technology studies, her introduction begins with a pause necessitated by the exclusionary institutional histories under which she labors, learns, and educates. Before she even begins, she is tongue-tied. She is "half muddled, always mumbling." She is a feminist scientist, yet she asks, "Dare I speak?"

The muddled mumbling that Subramanian begins with arises from historical practices of silencing that have shaped knowledge-production by non-European feminists and those bodies that have been racialized through European settler colonization and chattel slavery. Disciplinary silencing has created physical absences within institutions of knowledge-production. These are absences that are far too visible to women of color walking through the corridors of the university, where hallways, as Subramanian aptly describes above, become disciplinary borderlands that separate scientists from feminists. Chanda Prescod-Weinstein, a theoretical astrophysicist, reiterates Subramanian's liminal experience when she writes, "To be black in physics is to confront hard questions about whether and where you belong."[3] While a black feminist can find herself present within the hallways of physics, the absences of other black bodies will lead her to question not only "where" she belongs but "whether" she belongs.

These vexed reflections on their status as scientists penned by women of color are due to spatial organizations of knowledge that perpetuate science as devoid of feminism, racial discourse, and humanistic inquiries. Physical absences produce intellectual racism and sexism, where various modes of knowledge productions are held to be distinct, unable to merge, mingle, and coexist. Sara Ahmed describes racism as "an ongoing and unfinished history, which orients bodies in specific directions, affecting how they 'take up' space."[4] "Spaces" writes Ahmed, "are not only inhabited by bodies that 'do things,' but what bodies 'do' leads them to inhabit some spaces more than others."[5] For Ahmed, gender—along with race—is a bodily orientation in space, "a way in which bodies get directed by their action over time."[6] If science, since the early nineteenth century, has been a gendered action that has constructed those oriented toward it as male, then a feminine or feminist scientist can disorient the very enterprise of scientific knowledge. It is such that feminists become bodies out of place because science, and in Ahmed's case philosophy, is "shaped by taking some bodies and not others as its somatic norm."[7] Racist and sexist norms are what we inherit from institutional histories and practices that create borders and barriers between disciplines.

Occupying spaces that rely upon your absence is a political act. It is a refusal to accept racist and sexist truth-claims. It is a refusal to believe that knowledge-production begins and ends with nineteenth-century Europe. "The world is older than the idea of Europe,"[8] writes Prescod-Weinstein emphatically. So are methodologies of knowledge-production. For feminists of color working in the halls of science, how knowledge is produced is just as important as its contents, and many are concerned with analyzing the ways in which scientists are producers of racial and gendered concepts. For the scholar of genetic science Kim TallBear (Sisseton-Wahpeton Oyate), "science is in, not above, historical and linguistic processes."[9] Science is produced by social actors with culturally specific perspectives. TallBear asserts that "'science' and 'society' are mutually constitutive—meaning one loops back in to reinforce, shape, or disrupt the actions of the other, although it should be understood that, because power is held unevenly, such multidirectional influences do not happen evenly."[10]

The scientific notion of the Anthropocene, which launched this conversation, is also a gendered and racialized production. The Anthropocene is a scientific narrative that centers European industrialization as the first stage in the development of a new planetary epoch. According to the proposals forwarded by Paul J. Crutzen, Eugene Stoermer, and others, the Anthropocene emerged in two stages: the first stage "began in the '1800–1850 period,' with the breakthrough development of fossil-fueled industrialization in Britain,"[11] leading to the second stage dating to 1945 "associated with the first human-caused atomic detonations."[12] The Eurocentric origin story of this chronology is quite apparent and, as I discussed in previous chapters, forgets European settler colonialism as well as US military exploits that pre- and postdate this chronology. Here, I want to discuss the proposed origin dates for the Anthropocene (1800–1850) in relation to the emergence of the figure of the scientist.

In the context of my discussion here, what is most striking about the chronology of the Anthropocene is its coincidental codevelopment with the rise of the scientist as a professional knowledge-producer. Historians of science have pointed out that the term *scientist* arrived into the English language in the 1830s in order to distinguish a particular professional. Since science itself had become a common term by the early nineteenth century, "this created pressure for an alternative term to refer to practitioners of science."[13] An organization founded in 1831, known as the British Association for the Advancement of Science, expressed the need for a new appellation and found *philosopher* to be "too broad," proposing instead that "by analogy with *artist* they might form *scientist*."[14] While at the time of its coinage, the term *scientist* was controversial, since "the few professionals then in existence saw the term 'scientist' as implying that science was a business rather than the high-minded labour of love that they considered it to be," today, the term is common, ubiquitous, and almost without a history.[15]

So, what can we make of the current scientific proposal that the Anthropocene emerged at the very same time as the professional figure of the scientist, somewhere in Britain, sometime between 1800 and 1850? This uncanny and curious chronology leads me to make the following proposal: Could it be that it was the European scientist who kick-started the Anthropocene? The evidence is simple enough. It was indeed British scientists who gave us the steam engine and the concept of energy that fueled and powered the heavy machinery of industrialization. It was in the early 1800s that the "British coalfields had standardized equipment and method" that enabled coal mining, and it was the conceptualization of "energy" as fuel that drove the desire to drill the first commercial oil well in Pennsylvania in 1859.[16] Industry was reliant on scientific concepts and measurements that calculated the calorific potential of fossil fuels that set their automatons into motion.[17] "Energy was born in plumes of coal smoke, wafting from Glaswegian ship-building factories and the British steamships that corralled its Victorian empire," writes Cara New Daggett, adding, "With the so-called discovery of energy in the 1840s, scientists finally had an explanation for how coal was remaking the world."[18] This was the world of the Industrial Revolution that begot the Anthropocene.

When narratives applied to the whole human species are found to be generated on a small collective of islands in the North Atlantic in a short period of time, we become aware of the rhetorical strategies that turn geographically and culturally specific stories into scientific truths. "The region of the world we call 'Europe,'" writes Dipesh Chakrabarty, "has already been provincialized by history itself."[19] What persist are "the universals—such as the abstract figure of the human or that of Reason—that were forged in eighteenth-century Europe and that underlie the human sciences."[20] What resonates in Chakrabarty's assessment, is the significance of undoing the underlying assumptions of science in regard to what counts as knowledge ("Reason") and who can possess it (the human scientist).

Such an endeavor is crucial for provincializing science and the scientist who holds claims to universal truths.

It is puzzling that the professional emergence of the provincial scientist at the time of heavy industrialization in Europe is of little concern to the theorists of the Anthropocene. On the one hand, we might attribute this to the methodologies of science that remove the scientist from the knowledge that the scientist sets out to produce. Science, after all, has scientists look outside of themselves in order to observe only that which is visible, verifiable, and calculable to everyone. In his analysis of the emergence of natural history, Michel Foucault puts the task of the scientist in this way: "Confronted with the same individual entity, everyone will be able to give the same description; and, inversely, given such a description everyone will be able to recognize the individual entities that correspond to it."[21] As such, not only are scientists to refrain from producing knowledges that are not observable by "everyone" but to make tools and quantify knowledge in such a way that all who use their methods and instruments can come to the same conclusions. Foucault gives the example of the microscope, which addressed an important problem: that of the subjective nature of the eye, or what we might call the diversity of perspectives. Instruments such as the telescope and the microscope resolved the issue of perspectival diversity by limiting what the eye could see through "the maintenance of specific visible forms from generation to generation."[22] This idea can be summarized in a definition of science from 1830: "Science is the knowledge of many, orderly and methodically digested and arranged, so as to become attainable by one."[23]

The lack of reflection by the theorists of the Anthropocene on the arrival of the professional scientist on the scene of industry in the early nineteenth century can hence be attributed to the normalized absence of scientists from scientific theories. Donna Haraway describes this scientific perspective as a "conquering gaze from nowhere" that "claims the power to see and not be seen, to represent while escaping representation."[24] We might ponder then if there is not an anxious repression of the scientist's role within narrative developments of the Anthropocene. For what ethical ramifications would contemporary scientists have to face should their discipline be found to be responsible for (or at least implicated in) the emergence of the Anthropocene?

At this point, it is worth looking more closely at how scientists appear within scientific proposals for the Anthropocene. What histories do they narrate for themselves? What roles do they play? Consider a passage from a

2020 paper by Paul Crutzen delivered after receiving the Lomonosov Gold Medal in 2019 for outstanding achievement as an atmospheric chemist and climate scientist. In this paper, Crutzen ponders the intellectual life of the concept of the Anthropocene since he first proposed it in the year 2000.[25] This time, however, Crutzen does not wish to present us with yet another set of scientific data. Instead, he sets before us a theatrical stage upon which he walks in a particular costume: that of Galileo Galilei.

In the opening passage of his article, Crutzen quotes from literature, a play by the German playwright Bertolt Brecht. "This epic play," Crutzen writes, "is about the amazing life of Galileo Galilei,"[26] who Crutzen quotes as saying, "I am convinced that the only goal of science is to alleviate the cumbersomeness (Mühseligkeit) of human existence."[27] In keeping with narrative tensions of an epic play, Crutzen then poses a moral dilemma. As he tells it, while Galileo's only goal is the betterment of human existence, he is nevertheless plagued by the fact that he has to deliver "bad news."[28] Galileo's bad news is indeed "scientific news" since Galileo is tasked with the problem of revealing that it is the Earth that is moving around the sun and not the other way around. Crutzen describes it as follows:

> When the Earth is moving and not the sun (Die Sonn stet still, die Erd kommt von der Stell), contrary to centuries of a rock-solid earth-centric view, how can ordinary people and how can established power cope with this fundamental scientific finding that dispels their belief of their own central place in the solar system? Fear and anger emerge accompanied by denial ("solar system denial"). It has taken indeed many years to swallow this "bitter pill."[29]

Just as we begin to envision Galileo on the theatrical stage, convincing commoners and the elite alike that the Earth moves under their feet, Crutzen pulls off Galileo's costume, revealing himself underneath. He then turns to us and asks, "What about the 'Anthropocene pill'?"

The Anthropocene pill is of course no different. In Crutzen's text, "history repeats itself" because scientists are possessors of wisdoms (or, rather, pills) that others cannot digest (or even swallow). In the déjà vu-like epic narrative of the Anthropocene, the scientist embodies the altruistic desires of Galileo: the alleviation of human suffering. He writes, "The desire for a better life, adequate shelter, food, health, and avoiding suffering is in all of us and is accompanied by hope and positive thinking." Nevertheless, Crutzen has some bad news. He writes, "The scale, speed, the variety and the intensity of changes on our planet have become overwhelming.

There is a concern that it is running out of control."[30] What is to be done in the face of this bad news? Crutzen responds: "Scientists have a moral obligation to provide society with guidance to their very best based on their imagination, observation, experiments, knowledge, understanding, discussion and reporting."[31]

The scientist here appears as the guide, the ethical compass that orients humanity toward its own betterment. Significantly, not all humans can take on this leading role because, as Crutzen makes clear in a short passage, not all humans can truly claim title to human wisdom. He writes,

> This reaction of Homo Sapiens (Wise Human) stands for our innate positive nature to understand ever better our planet and beyond in order to improve life and lessen suffering; this is how we Humans are. How we should describe "Wise" is much harder. At the outset, we know from ourselves that we, each being a wise human, at times do things that are not so wise.

It is clear from Crutzen's text that neither the scientist, nor even the Homo Sapien, is implicated in the dawning of the Anthropocene. Rather, the "out of control" state of the planet is more precisely the problem of the not-so-wise who do not take scientists as their guide. In this narrative structure of the Anthropocene, the scientist does not appear at the scene of industrialization helping to fuel the wheels that run industry (or later on, in the second stage of the Anthropocene, administer laboratories that develop and design atomic explosives).[32] Instead, in a theatrical sleight of hand, the scientist embodies ethical wisdom and becomes an objective observer standing at a distance from the havoc wreaked on the planet by the exploits of the not-so-wise.

I have suggested above that the not-so-wise have a long tradition within scientific discourse, and that they have been seen not only as those knowledge-producers who fall outside the disciplinary boundaries of science but also, in Zakariya's words, as "non-Western, non-truth-seeking subjects." There persists a "somatic norm" for the scientist, as Ahmed put it, which not only continues to produce exclusionary institutional practices that become sharply visible when feminists of color navigate the halls of science, but which perpetuate worldviews that universalize provincial knowledge-productions. Today, scientists have given a name to our current geological age: the Anthropocene. This name memorializes the achievements of scientists since the early nineteenth century, and while scientists have some "bad news" regarding the outcomes of their profession, they continue to urge us to follow their lead, because "accepting the concept Anthropocene," Crutzen writes, "will help keep our planet and humanity on a sustainable track into the future."[33]

Anthropocene is hence not a naming practice that simply claims the past and the present of the planet but is also an explicitly future-oriented cosmology. This is a cosmology that delivers the "bad news" of species extinction and planetary depletion while designating the scientist as the solution to the problem. In a coauthored article with Christian Schwägerl, Crutzen writes, "To accommodate the current Western lifestyle for 9 billion people, we'd need several more planets. With countries worldwide striving to attain the 'American Way of Life,' citizens of the West should redefine it—and pioneer a modest, renewable, mindful, and less material lifestyle."[34] The Western redefinition that Crutzen and Schwägerl offer, however, seems to follow familiar paths already taken by the settler-colonial-military-industrial-scientific complex. They propose, for instance, monetary investments in what they call "green security systems" that match military spending for the securitization of an "intricate network of climate, soil, and biodiversity" as well as the development of "geoengineering capabilities in order to be prepared for worst-case scenarios."[35]

Crutzen and Schwägerl's proposals beg the following question: If the "Western lifestyle" requires "several more planets" to achieve, is it wise for climate scientists to continue to ask the "West" to envision sustainable human habitations? In other words, should it be Western science that envisions planetary futures? For it is clear that Western scientific definitions of the cosmos and the planet are limited and not so wise. These are visions that are provincial but repeatedly come to stand in for universal notions of wisdom and humanity at large. While Western science exists among a diversity of knowledges that precede and postdate European thought, it has become hegemonic. We need to think instead, as Kathryn Yusoff has suggested, "in terms of who gets to formulate, implement, and speak to/of the future."[36] We need to challenge, as Zoe Todd does, the fact that "not all humans are equally invited into the conceptual spaces where these disasters are theorized or responses to disasters formulated."[37] I want to conclude this section with the demonstration of challenges facing Indigenous and non-Western knowledge-producers in the face of hegemonic implementations of Western science.

In December 1996, the National Aeronautics and Space Administration (NASA) sent a pathfinder to Mars, which landed on the red planet in July 1997. NASA understood their pathfinder to be the "first-ever robotic rover to [land on] the surface of the red planet," which "carried scientific instruments to analyze the Martian atmosphere, climate, geology and composite of its rocks and soil."[38] Soon after landing, however, their mission was challenged by what NASA's news chief Brian Welch described as "a ridiculous claim."[39] In July 1997, three individuals—Adam Ismail, Mustafa Khalil, and Abdullah al-Umari—filed a lawsuit against NASA in a court in San'a, Yemen.[40] The plaintiffs argued that Mars is an ancestral star of the Yemeni people, handed down to them in oral histories by their ancestors known today as the Hymaritic and Sabaean civilizations.[41] They requested that "NASA refrain from disclosing any new astronomical information pertaining to Mars before receiving formal approval from them or until a verdict is reached."[42]

Before the case was heard, however, the plaintiffs withdrew their claim due to a threat by the prosecutor to initiate their arrest.[43] While the Yemeni claim to Mars as their ancestral land never received a verdict, the space lawyer Virgiliu Pop has contemplated the claim's legal standing. He argues that there can be no legitimate individual or national claim to celestial planets based on the 1967 Outer Space Treaty.[44] Opened for international signatures by the Russian Federation, the United Kingdom, and the United States, the treaty was penned as a legal document that provided frameworks for access and exploration of other planets.[45] According to the treaty, "the exploration and use of outer space shall be carried out for the benefit and in the interest of all countries and shall be the province of mankind."[46] For Pop, the legal standing of this treaty disqualifies any state or individual, including the Yemeni plaintiffs, a legal title to Mars. His findings reiterate the initial reaction by NASA's news chief Brian Welch who told CNN, "Mars is a planet out in the solar system that is the property of all humanity, not two or three guys in Yemen."[47]

Pop's dismissal of a case that never went to trial is based on his confidence that settler-colonial lawmakers speak for "all humanity" and that terrestrial laws inscribed by settler-colonial states of the mid-twentieth century is eternally applicable to celestial bodies. For Pop, there is no need to consider why, or according to whom, representatives from the United Kingdom, the United States, and the Russian Federation were assigned to draw up a treaty to set legal precedence for outer space in 1967. Where did such a legal authority come from? Who assigned it? Instead, he bases his conclusions on the taken-for-granted truth-claims of settler colonialism. Indeed, as recent assessments of the 1967 Outer Space Treaty show, there is much to question in the treaty's positions on current political issues such as weaponization and resource extraction on other planets.[48]

The legal system's inability to hear Indigenous claims to sovereignty is well known and rests upon assumptions regarding what counts as legal truth. As Jill Stauffer has put it, at stake in such cases are who decides between "settler colonial legal storytelling" versus Indigenous "stories, songs, feasts, and material objects."[49] For the question is not what is truly legal but rather what counts as truth within juridical settings. Scholars of Indigenous legal claims to unceded ancestral lands have repeatedly shown that settler justice systems set the terms for what constitutes as evidence. Even in the best of cases, justices have argued that "much evidence must be discarded or discounted not because the witnesses are not decent, truthful persons but because their evidence fails to meet certain standards prescribed by law."[50] Elizabeth Povinelli has called this "the cunning of recognition," whereby Indigenous claims can only be heard if they are put in the juridical language of the settler state. "This is an impossible demand," writes Povinelli, "placed on these [Australian] and other indigenous people: namely, that they desire and identify with their cultural traditions in a way that just so happens, in an uncanny convergence of interests, to fit the national and legal imaginary of multiculturalism."[51]

Oral narratives that gift the red star to the Yemeni people as an ancestral inheritance do not count as evidence in courts of law that accept the terms set forth by the Outer Space Treaty. Such claims, as Povinelli suggests, can only be recognized if they fit within settler legal and linguistic worldviews. In the case brought to NASA by the Yemeni plaintiffs, I would argue, the claim should also converge with what counts as science. For this is not simply a case about law, property rights, and land claims on Mars but rather a claim to science and scientific knowledge. At stake here is not simply "whether they [the Yemeni] have paid the appropriate inheritance taxes" on Mars, as noted by the CNN correspondent, but rather whether Yemeni nonscientists can be legitimately conversant with scientists analyzing data on Martian atmosphere collected by their rover.[52] The easy dismissal of the Yemeni claim, after all, has little to do with their illegal trespass on Mars; rather, the Yemeni plaintiffs are charged with offering a "ridiculous claim" that interferes with scientific knowledge itself. Yemeni mythologies are ridiculed on the grounds that they are nonscientific cosmologies offending scientific truths.

But what if science was nothing other than mythological fabulation itself? What if scientific cosmologies were no different than Yemeni oral narratives in which planets were sacred ancestral gifts that were to remain within provincial orbits of inheritance? Let us recall that Crutzen has urged us to accept his theory of the Anthropocene through an identification with Galileo, who was indeed a cosmographer preoccupied with planetary relations. As historians of Galileo's life have noted, Galileo was not a scientist as we understand the term today (since the 1830s). Rather, he moved through various cultural and economic settings in order to produce and disseminate his work. As Mario Biagioli describes it,

> At Padua he developed a thriving instrument-making activity by attaching it to his conventional academic post; at the Medici court in Florence he crafted a new persona for himself by borrowing from the roles and profiles to court artists and literati; and during the controversy with the Inquisition he cast himself as a theologian by grafting his defense of astronomy and Copernicanism on the discourse of his censors.[53]

Not only does Galileo's move across differential systems of thought and skill sets such as art, object-making, and theology sound jarring to our disciplinary habits, but the very semantic reception of his ideas puts pressure on how we understand science and scientific activity today. Galileo's telescope, for instance, was made in the company of artisans such as lensmakers and glassmakers who have urged contemporary historians to read the telescope "within literary and 'artistic' contexts which shaped the uses and the meaning of the telescope."[54]

Likewise, Galileo's cosmology is historically and culturally specific, bringing recent historians to narrate Galileo's telescope as "a European story."[55] As I read accounts of Galileo's life, I wonder if even "Europe" is too broad of a geographical designation for Galileo's cosmology. For it is well known that Galileo's telescope brought to view "the Medicean Stars," or what scientists today call the satellite of Jupiter. "The Medicean Stars," as Biagioli explains it, "were not discoveries in the modern sense of the term. Galileo constructed them as a kind of object that, while displaying some of the features of our notion of scientific discovery, also participated in the economies of artworks and monuments."[56] Galileo's naming practice was a gesture toward his patrons at the Medici court, a gesture that presented the celestial bodies visible through his telescope as a "gift" to Cosimo II de Medici, the prince and his patrons at the court.[57]

Mars is hence not the only planet that has historically been gifted to a specific group of people. Galileo gifted Jupiter—as a monument—to his patrons at the Medici court. If scientists today accept histories in which planets can be gifted to one or two people, why is the Yemeni claim to Mars a "ridiculous claim"? It would seem that a history of science that begins with a Galilean dedication of Jupiter to the Medici court could also allow for a dedication of Mars to the Yemeni people. Yet a difference is drawn today based on which acts of gift giving can be accepted as science and which are to be dismissed as unfounded claims. Scientists, it appears, are those who inherit the "Medicean Stars" rather than the Yemeni Mars as their ancestral mythology. For it is precisely such ancestral mythologies (as we saw in Crutzen's article) that bestow legitimacy on scientific declarations. In part 4, I present the work of the Yemeni Bosnian American artist Alia Ali's rendition of Mars gifted to the Yemeni people.

Anthropocene is a provincial concept. If we are to allow for multiple knowledge-systems to imagine cosmological existence, we must blur the disciplinary lines that separate art and science. Much like other forms of creative production, scientific thought is produced within specific cultural and historical moments. Science is situated and must be analyzed alongside other creative, speculative, and performative methodologies practiced by various knowledge-producers. If scientists today claim Galileo as their ancestral figure, then scientific ideas lend themselves to artistic analysis. In the next section, I bring an art historical lens to the study of the Anthropocene as a concept. I ask: Can the Anthropocene be read as a work of art?

4

The Anthropocene
Is a Work of Art

The earth bears the trace of human activity. Nature recedes into human fabrications. This is the thesis of the Anthropocene, the age of the human. Trees are laced and replaced by power grids. Cement protrudes into gulfs to form islands. Machines drill into shale. Petroleum forms fogs in the atmosphere. Glass and steel scrape the sky. Land and water are transformed for human settlement, transportation, and telecommunication. The earth has become a fabricated sculpture, a total work of art. "Is not the totality of all our endeavors, all our social relations, tending towards the making over of the planet," asks McKenzie Wark, "a total work of art?"[1]

Scientists call this planetary work of art the Anthropocene.

"*Fiat ars—pereat mundus* [Create art—destroy the world]," declared Walter Benjamin in his well-known essay "The Work of Art in the Age of Mechanical Reproduction," originally published in 1935.[2] Prior to the coinage of the term Anthropocene, Benjamin understood the rapid industrialization and militarization of his time as a total work of art. It was art—the European drive toward *techne* (art, industry)—that was shaping the modern world in which he lived. This was a world of factories, automobiles, and machine guns. This was a world in which European settler-colonial ventures and resource extractions across the globe—that had secured European industrialization—had culminated in military-industrial warfare and a continent between two World Wars. Benjamin's Germany was being shaped by Nazis in power for whom the human beneficiary of the industrial age—understood by eugenicists in terms of whiteness and purity—did not include Jewish populations. As a Jewish German philosopher, Benjamin witnessed the erasure of his body from the category of the human, an unbearable circumstance that led him to take his own life in 1940. A few short years after the publication of his "Work of Art" essay, Benjamin stood at the national border between France and Spain, holding a visa to the United States, where he was rejected entry, along with other Jewish refugees fleeing internment. Faced with the imminent danger of internment and transference to a concentration camp, Benjamin ingested a massive dose of morphine and took his own life.[3]

"The logical result of Fascism," Benjamin wrote, "is the introduction of aesthetics into political life."[4] In Benjamin's assessment, the politics of imperialism, war, and eugenics were best understood as aesthetic relations that shaped and defined the world. "Instead of draining rivers," he wrote, "society directs a human stream into a bed of trenches; instead of dropping seeds from airplanes," he continued, "it drops incendiary bombs over cities."[5] These were the aesthetics of a militarized planet, a work of political-industrial art that ventured to build trenches in riverbeds and sow bombs rather than seeds. What Benjamin saw were meadows trampled upon by militant boots with trees burning in the background. He was a witness to hilltops giving way to barricades and an atmosphere filled with smoke.

In order to drive his point home, Benjamin turned to the Italian futurists who, in 1935, were preoccupied with Italian military aggressions in Ethiopia. In their manifesto, the futurists aestheticized the destructive imperial forces in Africa. They praised its sights, sounds, and smells for its utter beauty. They declared,

> War is beautiful because it enriches a flowering meadow with the fiery orchids of machine guns. War is beautiful because it combines the gunfire, the cannonades, the cease-fire, the scent, and the stench

of putrefaction into a symphony. War is beautiful because it creates new architecture, like that of the big tanks, the geometrical formation flights, the smoke spirals from burning villages.[6]

The futurists demonstrated Benjamin's observations that the imperial military destruction of the world was an aesthetic endeavor. Flamethrowers, tanks, and heavy machinery were carving the earth into a geometric collage of molten metal and plastics. The earth was a sculpture, an anthropogenic fabrication mechanically reproduced and devoid of eugenically defined humans. The aesthetics of the Anthropocene were the scene of terror, a Terracene. "Mankind," Benjamin wrote, was once "an object of contemplation for the Olympian Gods, now is one for itself."[7] Humanity's "self-alienation," he continued, "has reached such a degree that it can experience its own destruction as an aesthetic pleasure of the first order."[8]

Create art—destroy the world: The beautiful destruction of the Anthropocene.

We know this work of art intimately. We know the aesthetics of the Anthropocene, the sublime assault on Earth and its inhabitants. What is compelling about Benjamin's essay is, of course, its insistence on the reproducibility of the mechanical age. This is an age of the copy, of the artwork that repeats itself ad infinitum. The anthropogenic work of art is not one blast, one smokestack, one wildfire. It is repetitive. It is a choreographed performance of settler colonialism, militarized mining, and manufacturing that shapes the tastes, sounds, and textures of planetary environments. In Benjamin's essay, the anthropogenic work of art was produced through the clicks of the camera's shutter and the machine gun. These were the technological devices of the 1930s that were copying and reproducing colonial relations that had been at work for centuries. In the twenty-first century, the repetition continues.

Benjamin took his own life in the 1940s, but his observations remained operative after his death. Representational devices—such as photographic and cinematic cameras, recording devices, and surveillance technologies—continued to be utilized for military purposes. As Rey Chow has put it, battlefields are "reconfigured as fields of visual perception," where, "preparations for war were increasingly indistinguishable from preparations for making a film."[9] This is because the eye is the guide in the battlefield, where weapons build upon visual apparatuses to deliver bullets and bombs at targets seen at a distance. "Seeing" writes Chow, "is destroying"[10] echoing Benjamin's declaration: create art—destroy the world.

By 1945, the aesthetic destruction of the world was not simply dependent upon seeing but weaponizing the energy of light itself. The two atomic bombs—one uranium, the other plutonium—that were dropped on the two Japanese cities of Hiroshima and Nagasaki in August 1945 by the United States brought the photographic mechanisms of light and speed to implode upon Japanese civilian populations. "In a flash," Chow writes, "the formula $E=mc^2$, which summarizes Einstein's theory of relativity and from which the bomb was derived, captured the magnitude of the bomb's destructive potential: one plane plus one bomb=minus one Japanese city."[11] Chow's summarization is devastating. It rethinks the abstraction of scientific formulas in their material enactment upon the bodies of Japanese people. While there is nothing inherently violent about the theory of relativity, the relations it enabled is one of destructive obliteration through military force. Chow elaborates on the formula further:

> The speed of light is supposed to be a maximum, the fastest anything could possibly travel. The speed of light *squared*, is thus clearly and easily perceived as a very large multiplier. Because of its simplicity and visual representability, the formula successfully conveyed the important messages that one bomb could create great terror and that one airplane was enough to destroy an entire nation's willingness to resist.[12]

In Chow's assessment, the science of light, defined in a mathematical formula, was first visualized into a memorable and representable formula and then weaponized against civilians. In his book *War and Cinema*, Paul Virilio takes this formulation a step further to argue that the atomic bombs were indeed "light-weapons."[13] For Virilio, the mass, energy, and speed of light that make visualization possible were made into weapons as atomic bombs exploded upon the two Japanese cities. He writes,

> The first bomb, set to go off at a height of some five hundred meters, produced a nuclear flash which lasted one fifteenth-millionth of a second, and whose brightness penetrated every building down to the cellars. It left its imprint on stone walls, changing their apparent colour through the fusion of certain minerals, although protected surfaces remained curiously unaltered. The same was the case with clothing and bodies, where kimono patterns were tattooed on the victim's flesh. If photography, according to its inventor Nicéphore Niepce, was simply a method of engraving with light, where bodies inscribed their traces by virtue of their own luminosity, nuclear weapons inherited the darkroom of

Niepce and Daguerre and the military searchlight. What appears in the heart of darkrooms is no longer a luminous outline but a shadow, one which sometimes, as in Hiroshima, is carried to the depths of cellars and vaults. The Japanese shadows are inscribed not, as in former times, on the screens of a shadow puppet theater but on a new screen, the walls of the city.[14]

The atomic blast had taken warfare into new heights. The world was no longer a simple target framed as an image to be destroyed; rather, in a flash, atomic light delivered a blast that turned the urban structure itself into photographic devices. Atomic light engraved images on buildings, pavement, and bodies. These surfaces visually registered the bomb like a photograph. Carol Mavor explains it in this way: "A woman's kimono burned into her skin in an unnerving pattern. 'Atomic light' has seeped through those parts of her kimono that were lightly colored, as if she were clothed, not in cotton or silk but in the transparency of a photographic negative."[15] In the aftermath of the explosion, the surface of the city and the bodies of its inhabitants became photographs visualizing what could not have been seen in the blinding light that had lasted for no longer than one-fifteen-millionth of a second.

"There can be no authentic photography of atomic war because the bombings were themselves a form of total photography,"[16] writes Akira Mizuta Lippit. The atomic bomb turned cities into cameras and bodies and stones into films registering the blast. "If the atomic blasts and blackened skies can be thought of as massive cameras," writes Lippit, "then the victims of this dark atomic room can be seen as photographic effects."[17] While the fabrics and flowers burned away, their ghostly image remained, engraved on bodily surfaces. In Mavor's description, a skin that had once worn a kimono became a film after the blast, holding the negative trace of its pattern. "Organic and nonorganic matter left dark stains," Lippit writes, "opaque artifacts of once vital bodies, on the pavement and other surfaces of this grotesque theater."[18] For Lippit, the atomic bomb cannot be represented in visual form because the photographed and the spectator alike are seared into the image itself. There is no standing back to look at this scene because the flash has absorbed all into its radiant light. "Nothing remains," Lippit declares, "except radiation."[19]

While Einstein's theory of relativity is a visualization of the bomb in a mathematical formula, Lippit urges us to see the blaze of the atomic bomb as a massive camera that photographs the event of its own explosion. The explosion of the two atomic bombs on Hiroshima and Nagasaki repeated the Benjaminian formula: Create art—destroy the world. The blast was an aesthetic event, a work of art, because it created a total, annihilative image. The bomb created a large-scale photograph that absorbed everything into itself.

Atomic photography has no observers because it blurs the boundaries between witness and participant, photographer and the photographed.

In 2015, the Anthropocene Working Group became the observers of the atomic blast when they proposed that the testing of the atomic bomb in July of 1945 should be understood as the origin of the Anthropocene.[20] This was a response to the residual trace of the atomic explosions that remain registered upon the earth. The radioactive trace has enabled data visualization and the historical periodization of the Anthropocene. The nuclear trace of the atomic bomb offers the Anthropocene an aesthetic production of the human, an epoch "in which the planet became (re)written by artificial light."[21]

5

The Terracene

In this book I ask that we give the Eurocentric industrialist Anthropos, which stands witness to its own immortalization within the Earth's crust, a name other than human. What name can we give to settler-colonial imposition and exploitation of lands, resources, and habitats? What name can we give to the militarized wreckage brought about through exploits that have created wastelands and disrupted biodiverse lifeworlds? If we follow the effects of war, extractive economies, and the geological and climatic disruptions already experienced by the Earth's biodiverse inhabitants, we might land on a word such as *terror* to give texture to this state of planetary devastation and mass extinction. What better word than *terror* can describe this global condition of being in danger? To be under terror is to experience the precarity of life, to be threatened by an abstract or unknown peril. As the Italian philosopher Adriana Cavarero explains it,

"Going by the etymology, the realm of terror is characterized by the physical experience of fear as manifested in a trembling body."[1] Terror might describe an individual's "fear of death in battle," according to Cavarero, or "those collective experiences in which terrorized masses flee from natural catastrophes like earthquakes, floods, or hurricanes."[2] Terror might be how deer flee wildfires to avoid asphyxiation or how corals respond to ocean acidification. Terror is how corn plants wilt during a drought and soil's microbial communities respond to erratic rainfall. The word *terror* is indeed semantically caught up and sonically heard in the word *terra*, meaning *earth*. As a number of commentators have discovered, the etymological linkage between terror and terra is triangulated through the notion of territory.[3] Terra has an associative chain from Latin "*torrere*, to burn, dry, of the same root as the Sanskrit *tars*, to be dry, to dry up," while terror is from the Latin "*terrorem, terrere*, to make tremble, which etymologists link to the Sanskrit *tras*, to tremble."[4] Connecting these two roots is that of *territorium*: "a place from which people are frightened, or where terror is exercised."[5] Terror is how the earth is turned into territory through settler (neo)colonialism and how its geological makeup, such as oil, coal, uranium, and other minerals, are extracted. Territory thus names contested relationships between peoples, lands, and sovereignty. As Stuart Elden has noted, territory is currently a legal term designating "an entity that has not attained statehood."[6] Examples include the occupied territories of Palestine; Western Sahara; Australia's Northern Territory as well as Canada's territories that operate differently in relation to the settler federal state; Britain's many overseas territories, such as Cayman Islands; and unincorporated US territories such as Puerto Rico.[7] Territories result from settler colonialism and ongoing resistances to them. They are not simply markers of occupation and dispossession but are sites of continual contestation, force, and dispute.

In the case of Palestine, for instance, occupied territories are maintained via infrastructural impositions that create racialized difference made explicit through unequal access to space and resources. Palestinian territories are fissured and made inaccessible through a racist geography of checkpoints, roadblocks, and restricted access. "While settlers could travel freely across the West Bank on the main roads of the Palestinian network and dedicated highways (built on Palestinian lands)," writes Omar Jabary Salamanca, "most Palestinians were forced to use long, winding, potholed, and in some cases, unpaved, secondary routes."[8] Infrastructures of settlement such as roads, electricity, water, and telecommunications are the materials through which settler colonialism is enacted. Settler infrastructures have been essential, Joseph Pugliese writes, "in reproducing the settler state's biopolitical 'elimination' and 'replacement' of the Indigenous people who have never formally ceded sovereignty of their lands."[9]

The term *Terracene* is meant to highlight the terror unleashed by the complex machinery of war, settler-colonial and industrial-resource exploitations on a global scale that have led to the formation of massive wastelands and ongoing climatic disasters. Terracene is also meant to direct attention toward terra (the earth) and Terrans inhabiting such wastelands. *Terran* is the name I give to the multispecies dwellers of the earth, or what Marisol de la Cadena terms "earth-beings."[10] Terrans are mountains, wetlands, viruses, smoke plumes, mutated cells, and crude oil. While de la Cadena uses the term *earth-beings* to describe "other-than-human beings," I use the term *Terran* to discuss amalgamations of humans and other-than-humans inhabiting toxic and militarized wastelands.[11]

Wastelands are sites rendered worthless through militarization and resource extraction for the purposes of capital accumulation. In accordance with Traci Brynne Voyles's formulation of Indigenous lands under settler colonialism, wastelands are sites where resources are extracted and pollutants are dumped. Lands become wastelands through active devaluation of life-forms and the breakup and dissolution of complex networks of earth-beings through violence and warfare. "The 'wasteland,'" writes Voyles, "is a racial and spatial signifier that renders the environment and the bodies that inhabit it pollutable."[12] Wastelands are not merely collateral damage of colonial and imperial histories but sites actively maintained in a state of toxicity and ruination far into the future. Indeed, as Eyal Weizman argues, climate change is too often seen as the "accidental and indirect consequence of industrial development, demographic growth, trade, and transport triggered by Industrial Revolution in Europe and North America."[13] Yet, is it hard to accept "the argument for collateral damage" within active war zones, he continues, "specially when the killing of civilians is predictable, predicted, and even legally tolerated."[14]

By proposing the Terracene as a viable concept to think with, my aim is not to enter a game of nomenclatures but to take language seriously in shaping the stories we tell. What narratives can the Terracene offer that differ from what the Anthropocene has been telling? In his diatribe against humanities scholars who choose to think further about the concept of the Anthropocene, Timothy Morton argues that charges of "colonialism" or "racism" brought against the concept are nothing but petty quibble "while global mega corporations frack in their [humanities scholars'] backyards."[15] By painting critical race, Indigenous, and anti-colonial scholars as silent bystanders to corporate capital and hence complicit in their activities, Morton uses an old political strategy of silencing dissent by flattening a multiplicity of voices into the convenient "Anthropocene lovers" versus "Anthropocene deniers."[16] Rather than quit worrying and learn to "love the term 'Anthropocene,'"[17] as Morton commands us to do, I aim to further agitate the stabilization of the concept by adding the term *Terracene* (humorously yet pointedly) to the mix of the current list of neologisms.[18] Settler colonialism has long practiced the suppression and eradication of native languages and cultures across the globe, replacing them with hegemonic languages of the settlers. New words, sounds, gods, and thought systems are essential to resisting the Anthropocene. "We need vocabulary that comes from many experiences, not only from Greek. There is no reason to continue privileging Greek and Latin sources," writes Mignolo. "Epistemic disobedience means to recognize them and denaturalize them at the same time."[19]

Epistemic disobedience is important. In the face of cruelty, war, trauma, and disaster, we can feel lost for words. We may not know how to express what we hear, feel on our skins, or sense in our stomachs. Offering neologisms is one way of accessing new perspectives on worlds, species, and matters that otherwise escape our capacity for reason and understanding. Artists understand the power of neologisms. The artist collective known as the Bureau of Linguistical Reality, for instance, has worked to compile a growing dictionary of words to address new feelings arising from living in a new world as a result of climate change, extinction, and loss of biodiversity.[20] Their dictionary includes terms[21] such as:

- *Quieseed*: "a seed that due to social trauma stays consciously dormant not out of oppression, but rather due to deep intuition which senses not to seed until it finds itself in a fertile, fecund environment." From *Quiescent* [Latin] for "being still" and *Seed* [old English *sǣd*, of Germanic origin *Saat*].
- *Chuco*헐*sol*: "The experience of seeing a brilliant red sunset blown up by manmade pollution and knowing you're not supposed to enjoy it but you do anyway because the colors are a brilliant bright orange red fire–intoxicating to the eyes." From *Chuco* [El Salvadorian] slang for dirty + 헐 [Korean] an expression of surprise + *Sol* [Spanish] meaning sun.

- *Koyaanisqatsi*: "1. Life out of balance. 2. Life of moral corruption and turmoil. 3. Crazy Life. 4. Life in Turmoil. 5. A state of life that calls for another way of living." From *koyaanis* [Hopi] prefix meaning "corrupted" or "chaotic" and *qatari* [Hopi] meaning life.
- *Ihlapnapan*: "An understanding that two seemingly disparate groups are perhaps intimately tied to each other in a way that is mutually binding for both parties' survival. A state of awareness in a time of great cultural rift that, whether we like it or not, we are wedded to the other side, as they are to us, and the feeling of not knowing how to move forward with that understanding." from *Apnapan* [Hindi] meaning kin, family and *Ihlap* [Yagan] meaning to be at a loss for what to do next.

The above terms coined by a variety of people working with the artist collective use prefixes, suffixes, and expressions from multiple languages to name, or call attention to, present conditions that may not have required an expression before.[22] This is a practice not dissimilar to the production of scientific knowledge that relies predominantly on Latin and Greek language roots to name, periodize, and diagnose present and past lifeworlds. The Anthropocene is itself such a word pulling together two disparate terms to form a compound noun deemed to be expressive of an idea for our times. Anthropocene combines *Anthropos* (Greek for human) and *-cene* (from the Greek root *kainos*, meaning new, recent, unprecedented) to formulate the new era of the human. The word itself suggests a novelty or recentness to this particular performance or "genre" of the human. Anthropocene is not an expression of human diversity interconnected with multiple earth-beings that make up the planet. It is in that sense a crude diagnosis of this new time or this recent experience of the planet. If we replace the Anthropos with terra, we pluralize the Terrans with whom we think on the terrorized and territorialized planet.

6

Sensing the Terracene

The Anthropocene is a work of art.
Pyrotechnicians paint the skies with pigments.
Atomic lights tattoo bodies with charred lines.
Clouds cry acid onto crabs and crawlers of the seas.
Petroleum swirls in oceanic currents.
The Anthropocene is a scene of terror: The Terracene.

In the previous pages, I have contemplated the author of this anthropogenic artwork. I have asked: Who envisioned this damaged planet? Was it
the Anthropos as suggested by scientists? Can this artwork be attributed to
the whole human species? I have proposed that the notion of the human
species in this case is fraught. Not all humans have shared this aesthetic
vision for the planet. Not all humans have conceptualized, practiced, or
performed the cosmologies of the Anthropocene. Furthermore, the politi-

cal present has inherited imperial and settler-colonial histories that have defined the human within a limited Eurocentric framework. The human of the post-9/11 era inherits racial schemas that define it through immunity and security. These are discursive practices that profile, surveil, and eradicate viral terror (understood in a complex assemblage of atmospheric and multispecies forms).

Here, I want to set aside the question of who produced the Anthropocene in order to consider how this work of art is aesthetically experienced. I ask: How is the Anthropocene sensed, known, and encountered? What does it mean to be beholders of the Anthropocene, to sense its sights and sounds, to vibrate with its tremors, to feel our way through its toxins, digest its chemical residues, and inhale its pollutants?

This book is dedicated to the sensoria of artists whose lives have been compounded by the double effects of the Anthropocene and the war on terror. I have named this reality the *Terracene*: a world in which the effects of war and climate change are inseparable. This is the world of toxic, contaminating, and viral Terrans, multispecies bodies that are targeted for elimination. To inhabit this world is to be cast outside biopolitical state protections. The Terracene is the world of drowned refugees and oil-streaked wetlands submerged in rising seas. It is the world of insects and moss interred in the ashes of exploding pipelines. It is the site of internment that quarantines humans, cattle, and viruses alike. These are the lived realities of the Terracene.

In the last two decades, countless refugees have fled warfare in Iraq, Syria, Lebanon, Afghanistan, and other places within the broader SWANA region (Southwest Asia and North Africa). Syria currently claims the highest number of refugees since the outbreak of the Syrian civil war in 2011. Images of refugees in lifejackets huddled on small rafts and inflatable rubber boats flood news media. These are men, women, and children who have paid smugglers to assist their harrowing journeys across Aegean and Mediterranean waters.[1] Others find strength in their desperate poverty, swimming out to Grecian islands in the dead of night to avoid surveillance.[2]

The onset of the Syrian civil war in 2011 has routinely been attributed to severe droughts that had gripped farmers, causing crop failures and mass migrations to urban centers.[3] Yet as more recent studies have noted, Syrian ecological problems cannot simply be attributed to climate change but must be understood in a more complex political setting, "an admixture of colonization, expropriation, exclusion and neglect," a convergence of climate catastrophe and ongoing warfare endemic to the region at large.[4] The images of refugees landing on Turkish shores from Afghanistan, Iraq, and Syria confront us, as Anne McClintock has put it, with the "illegal US wars of occupation that both caused, and converged with, the accelerating catastrophes of climate breakdown and mass displacement."[5]

Displacement—as a result of the disappearance of place, power, and subsistence—registers on the body. It becomes condensed in tissues like sore muscles forming in the limbs of swimmers traversing cold waters for hours on end. The following chapters of this books turn to a series of artworks by artists who draw on their muscle memories, on their embodied knowledges of displacement in response to the thick matrix of geopolitical and climatic events in the region, spanning from Iran to Palestine. I am drawn to these artists' aesthetic productions because I share in their histories and aesthetic education. I make my shared knowledges explicit in this book by elaborating on my own experiential relations with environmental phenomena—such as earthquakes and wildfires—alongside my sensory perceptions shaped by living in Iran as a child during the Iran-Iraq War. These narratives support my central thesis that the machinery of war has created and perpetuated uninhabitable lands for racialized bodies across the globe. Exposure to the terror of aerial bombardments as a child has calibrated my senses to the impermanence, mutability, and precarity of life. Yet, as a survivor, I know about the great deal of imagination required of people living at the cross sections of war and environmental degradation. To survive is not only to imagine a future but to create and collaborate within precarious settings.

Making art is about the process of learning through sensing. Our sensory apparatus is multifaceted and unpredictable. Seeing, hearing, and smelling are not consistent or applicable to all bodies. Tasting, touching, and orienting can vary depending on our sensual wiring and cognitive relations with our nervous systems. Our bodies take in the world around us in diverse ways, producing unique aesthetic concepts and relations with the world. There is no uniformity here. I understand art as a practice of building unique sensual relationships to environments and the material worlds that make themselves known to us, just as my early exposure to aerial bombardments continues to shape my cognition of the world. For instance, I have learned lessons about sound and how it travels through the gut, bypassing the ear completely. I have learned about acoustic vibrations of Sheetrock and glass. These are sensory knowledges that are not simply limited to one sense organ (such as the ear, for instance) but include the wholistic range of a body that can lose balance, smell chemical deposits, watch fear in the face of close relatives, and indulge in the euphoria that follows after the departure of fighter jets above urban roofs. These sensorial events are how I remain oriented to the world. I understand my aesthetic education to have begun at an early age during the Iran-Iraq War, which continues to shape how I understand and relate to the world around me today.

Centering trauma within aesthetic discourse is challenging because trauma is by definition an impairment of the senses. Within the Freudian tradition, trauma is the body's encounter with excessive stimuli, or, as he writes, "We describe as 'traumatic' any excitations from outside which are powerful enough to break through the protective shield. It seems to me," he continues, "that the concept of trauma necessarily implies a connection of this kind with a breach in an otherwise efficacious barrier against stimuli."[6] Freud's theories of trauma were indeed based on his observational studies of veterans of World War I, those who had developed neurosis as a result of shell shock, loss of limbs, and other catastrophic physical and psychic experiences.[7] Trauma is opposed to aesthetic experience because it results from being exposed to an overload of sensory receptions, to circumstances in which a body is caught in the midst of terror.

Aesthetic philosophy does not theorize trauma. This is because, by definition, aesthetic theory attends to how sense organs manage excess sensorial input. The aesthetic category of the "picturesque," for instance, was coined by Enlightenment philosophers to describe "the tension between man (the perceiver and shaper of his surroundings) and 'wild nature.'"[8] Aesthetic experience within this framework is preoccupied with one's ability to create an objective distance according to which "wild nature" becomes tamed in the form of, for instance, gardens and artificial lakes.[9] This distanciation of the senses from the traumatic encroachment of one's surroundings is further exemplified in the Kantian notion of the sublime. The sublime names a subject's capacity for "self-preservation" in the face of "threatening and menacing nature—towering cliffs, a fiery volcano, a raging sea."[10] The sublime is the aesthetic response to threatening phenomena that inspire intense terror.[11]

As feminist scholars have long noted, aesthetics was initially formulated as the cognitive capacity of European men who were purported to possess the ability to transcend the terror of natural phenomena. Kant's writings on the sublime and the beautiful explicitly excluded women, the "dandy," and most of the world's inhabitants.[12] The sublime allowed the heteronormative, Eurocentric man to overcome terror by armoring his body and his senses, making him immune to fear and pain. As Susan Buck-Morss describes it, for Kant, "the man most worthy of respect is the warrior" whereby "both statesman and general are held by Kant in higher 'aesthetic' esteem than the artist" because of their capacity for "shaping reality rather than its representation."[13] The ideal aesthetic response to environmental threat is shielding the body so as to manage its experience of the world. Christine Battersby confirms this observation when she writes that the sublime "is exemplified by kings and commanders discharging their terrible strength and destroying all obstacles in their paths, as well as by the grandeur of the Alps."[14] Aesthetics is understood within classical philosophy, to be the domain of the warrior who develops a cognitive buffer to protect his body against environmental terror.

It is my contention that Enlightenment aesthetic categories such as the sublime are not adequate for understanding traumatic experiences that I am concerned with in this book. This is because Enlightenment aesthetic categories rely upon a self-possessed, bounded individual whose body remains at a distance from the environmental catastrophes that the Terracene implies. Since the turn of the century, many scholars have mobilized the category of the sublime to describe both the Anthropocene and the war on terror. Christine Battersby's book *The Sublime, Terror and Human Difference* as well as Gene Ray's study *Terror and the Sublime in Art and Critical Theory: From Auschwitz to Hiroshima to September 11* are among the most elaborate readings of the collapse of the Twin Towers in New York City in relation to the eighteenth- and nineteenth-century developments of the aesthetic category of the sublime. These analyses are echoed in other scholarship such as Frances Ferguson and Richard Klein's readings of the nuclear sublime in order to link anthropogenic climate change with militarized projects of nuclear annihilation.[15] Understanding the Anthropocene as sublime has gained much scholarly attention, spanning from older studies such as Bruce Robbins's "sweatshop sublime"[16] that named the globalized, capitalist labor system to Ian Baucom's most recent usage of "Anthropocene Sublime" in his book *History 4° Celsius*.[17]

This prolific scholarship has much merit as it searches aesthetic philosophy for a category to describe a contemporary world inundated with terror. Yet, as many of these scholars themselves note, the sublime was coined to describe an encounter with a threat that the subject ultimately transcends. The sublime, for Immanuel Kant, was an "encounter between an 'I' and that which has the capacity to annihilate it completely."[18] The keyword here is *capacity*, not the actuality of such an annihilation. As Battersby describes it, "In the experience of the sublime the audience or observer was said to derive pleasure from being (temporarily or potentially) overwhelmed by an object or an entity that seemed infinite or vast, powerful or terrible, exceeding the capacities of the human to imaginatively grasp or understand it."[19] The sublime is hence a descriptor for a *temporary* or *potential* encounter with something horrifying, a threat or danger that the subject would soon overcome. This is why the image of the warrior is so central to that of the sublime since it is the warrior who will ultimately protect itself against imminent danger.

My formulation of the Terracene does not involve this pleasurable distanciation from terror. Neither does it center the military figure of the warrior. Instead, I think with Terrans, those bodies and lands that are contaminated, extracted, flooded, and burned. Those people and spaces whose livelihoods are targeted and annihilated are not distanced from the terror they experience. Terrans of the Terracene are not shielded soldiers visualizing targets from afar gasping at the sublime screen images of pyrocumulus clouds and chemical explosions. The sensory experience of Terrans inhabiting the Terracene requires a theorization that neither presumes the presence nor the homogeneity of sense organs for the purposes of aesthetic experience. Categories such as the sublime are utterly inadequate for describing sensory modes of being cast at sea, as Syrian refugees have, caught (or drowning) in the midst of churning currents. It cannot formulate the bursting of ear drums proximal to explosions or when monsoons blend in with bombs in psychic and physical environments. The sublime cannot describe the loss of speech in response to violence or the numbing of olfactory senses in toxic wastelands. These sensorial experiences of living in the Terracene (which will be explored in detail in the chapters that follow), require aesthetic analyses that are not based on the protection and immunity of sensorial perceptions.

The aesthetic experiences I am concerned with in this book belong to those whose sensory organs are terrorized by industrial, atmospheric, and geological changes of the planet. This order of aesthetics belongs, for instance, to those civilians, flora, fauna, rocks, and roads who registered on their skins the atomic light exploding over Hiroshima and Nagasaki, becoming sensually and sensorially entangled with the radiation. Aesthetics originates in the Greek word "Aisthisis," meaning "perceptive by feeling."[20] As Susan Buck-Morss describes it, the "original field of aesthetics is not art but reality—corporeal, material nature."[21] The experience of those present at sites of explosion belong to the field of aesthetics, which, prior to

Enlightenment thought, engaged sensorial input, material impact, and corporeal reverberations. In Buck-Morss's assessment, while aesthetics is first and foremost an engagement with the sensory field of perception, Enlightenment philosophy has long suppressed this definition within its disciplinary formation. The production of the liberal-humanist subject, as Kandice Chuh has further elaborated, has privileged "a discrete and self-possessed individuality" while subjugating sensibilities formed through "relationality and entanglement rather than individuality and autochthons as the grounds of human ontology."[22]

The aesthetic formation of the autonomous human relies upon the valorization of critical distance rather than sensory entanglements, corporeal separation rather than absorption, a framed image rather than an embodied experience. This Enlightenment version of aesthetics has been hegemonic to such a degree that sensory perception, so central to the notion of aesthetics, has been subsumed by controlled versions of sensory planning. The legacy of Enlightenment philosophy, in the words of Buck-Morss, has meant that "the term 'aesthetics' underwent a reversal of meaning" so that today we understand aesthetics as "applied first and foremost to art—to cultural forms rather than sensible experience, to imaginary rather than the empirical, to the illusory rather than the real."[23]

Theorizing how Terrans sense is challenging because it requires two important interventions in aesthetic philosophy. First, theorizing sensorial experiences of the Terracene requires a renewed understanding of sense organs and how they aestheticize. Second, it requires a multispecies formulation that does not center the human. I outline these two interventions here.

1. Sense Organs

Aesthetic theory forgets the organs of perception. When watching a wave or listening to its crash on the shore, the skeletal, biological, and fleshiness of the eye and the ear are subsumed under their functional capacity to perceive these phenomena at a distance from the body. Elaine Scarry is among scholars who have drawn a distinction between the disembodied experience of seeing and hearing versus an embodied apprehension of eyes and ears as organs. "Vision and hearing," Scarry writes, are "so exclusively bound up with their objects rather than their bodily location" that "through them, one seems to become disembodied."[24] This is "either because one seems to have been transported hundreds of feet beyond the edges of the body out into the external world," she continues, "or instead, because the images of objects from the external world have themselves been carried into the interior of the body as perceptual content, and seem to reside there, displacing the dense matter of the body itself."[25] What Scarry describes here is the classic understanding of aesthetic experience, whereby distal sense organs—such as eyes and ears, which do not require direct contact with their objects of perception—establish a disembodied experience with objects in the world. In vision, the eye itself is forgotten because it remains distant, intact, and unentangled from what is seen.

What disrupts aesthetic experience, for Scarry, is pain. Injury to sense organs result in pain because sensation has been shifted from an external object to the sense organ itself. We experience pain when a sense organ becomes sensate. In Scarry's words, "If one experiences one's eyes or ears themselves—if the woman working looks up at the sun too suddenly and her eyes fill with blinding light—then vision falls back to the neighborhood of pain."[26] Touched by the rays of the sun, the eye is no longer understood to have vision but "falls back" into something else, into the realm of pain. In Scarry's formulation, pain as well as blindness become limit points to aesthetic experience. If the eyes do not engage in vision, if they are blind or injured, they are no longer defined as capable of aesthetic cognition.

Such a formulation casts injured, impaired, and disabled bodies outside of the realm of aesthetics. It does not allow for multisensorial engagements or nonnormative sensibilities of varied bodies. It presumes seeing to be the singular function of the eye, forgetting that the encounter with the sun is a sensate retinal experience, akin to touch. I suggest that rather than seeing pain as falling outside of aesthetic experience, we engage it as aesthetic embodiment. Pain, in Scarry's example, is not outside of aesthetics but enables the eye to have a multisensory experience beyond the hegemony of vision. Such a reading not only re-centers sensorial perception within aesthetics but resists Enlightenment preoccupations with sorting people, as Kandice Chuh puts it, "into the fit and the unfit, the rational and the unreasonable, Man and other."[27] When we abandon such hierarchies that name those who see as "Man" while casting out the injured and the blind, we adjust our understanding of sensorial perception.

Limiting body organs to single functions (the eyes must see; the ears must hear) has been a scientific/capitalist/industrialist aspiration. Scarry's text presents us with evocative descriptions of the instrumentalization of body parts and their functions by technological industries. She describes eyeglasses, microscopes, telescopes, and cameras as "the lens of the eye being lifted away from the body and carried out into the external world."[28] Clothing and bandages, in her text, are duplicate skins.[29] The built infra-structures of houses and cities, such as water and oil pipelines, follow the shape and function of the pumping heart that take "water to waterless ter-rains" and extract "underground coal and metal mines."[30] The steam engine, Scarry writes, magnifies "the bodily capacity for movement" since "it is perhaps enough simply to know that, for example, at the moment the steam engine first burst forth into John Fitch's imagination, he was, by his own account, limping."[31] As it is clear from these descriptions, not only is the human body formulated in pieces with specific functions, but the world is an anthropocentric imaginary based on reductive partition-ing of the body and its singular functions. "Limping," for Scarry, leads to the corrective desire for movement, facilitating the discovery of the steam engine, the infamous machine of the European Industrial Revolution that launched the Anthropocene.

As media disability studies scholars have noted, the idea that techno-logical innovations have helped to correct bodies into normative functions ignores the productivity of impairments for technological innovations. "Histories of closed captioning, audio description, and subtitling," Mara Mills and Jonathan Sterne write, "demonstrate that users with disabili-ties are often at the forefront of innovation in media systems that make them more useful for everyone."[32] Some of these innovations have their origins in functionalist approaches that aimed to correct bodies into pro-ductive normatively. Jasbir Puar has called the functionalist partitioning of the body "piecing." Piecing, for Puar, emphasizes productivity, rehabil-itation, and cure.[33] Piecing is how disabled, queer, and trans* bodies are made productive, legible, and sensate through medical and other biopo-litical interventions. "While this partitioning of the body is not a recent emergence—there is a long history of bodily compartmentalization as a prerequisite for capitalist production," Puar writes. "This piecing is not only about enhancing productive capacities but also about extending the body experientially and extracting value not just from bodies, but also from body parts and particles."[34] Within this technologized culture, the body is made productive, value-producing, and properly sensate, through corrective technologies.

In Puar's discussion, biopolitical protection and productivity is neces-sarily racialized and not afforded to all bodies. Settler-colonial and military occupations target racialized bodies' abilities. Discussing the deliberate maiming of Palestinians by the Israeli security state, Puar identifies sense organs as sites of settler-colonial attack and injury. Maimed organs in Palestinian territories do not simply belong to human bodies (such as those who are "shot to cripple" by the Israeli Defense Forces) but also extend to animals, plants, lands, and urban infrastructures.[35] "Not only bodies," Puar writes, "but also crucial infrastructure are maimed."[36] Joseph Pugliese echoes this claim when he describes settler-colonial warfare in occupied Palestinian territories in terms of "the bulldozing of orchards, the contamination of aquifers, the poisoning of soil, and the military shooting of cows and sheep."[37] These are tactics of maiming that are not simply limited to human bodies but what Pugliese terms "the more-than-human."

If we think of maiming in an expanded multispecies sphere, we can describe polluting and poisoning as injuries to lands, oceans, and atmospheres as well as the bodies of humanimals and vegetations that breathe them in and metabolize them. These are geopolitically distinct ecologies of the Terracene, where the sense organs of more-than-human bodies come under injury and assault. As Puar evocatively puts it, "sensation racializes."[38]

While in Scarry's formulation injured bodies fall outside of aesthetic capacity, I read Puar's provocation as a need to think of racialized aesthetics. How do maimed bodies sense? What are the racialized aesthetics of more-than-humans with maimed organs? I turn to these questions here.

2. Sensing with Injured Organs

Bodies melt and drip like oil in the sculptural works of the Syrian American artist Diana Al-Hadid. Born in Aleppo and raised in the United States, Al-Hadid is known for her large-scale sculptural pieces that seem to be under collapse. While she uses rigid and sturdy materials—like bronze, steel, concrete, and fiberglass—her sculptural structures appear to be in dynamic states of disintegration. In her piece titled *In Mortal Repose* (2011), a bronze, headless figure rests atop a concrete plinth (figure 6.1). Her head is missing but her torso leans on the elbow of her left arm, holding her in a classic reclining position. Despite the confidence displayed by the upright torso, the rest of the sculpture's body melts away. Her hips dissolve into liquid, dripping down the stepped plinth. To the ground fall her dismembered feet, crossed at the ankles. They dangle off the body, somehow intact, below the dripping stream of her liquified limbs.

In another series of bronze and stainless-steel sculptures titled *Blind Bust, I, II and III* (2012), heads flood their metal bases with molten secretions (figure 6.2). Their earlobes melt away while their eye sockets hollow

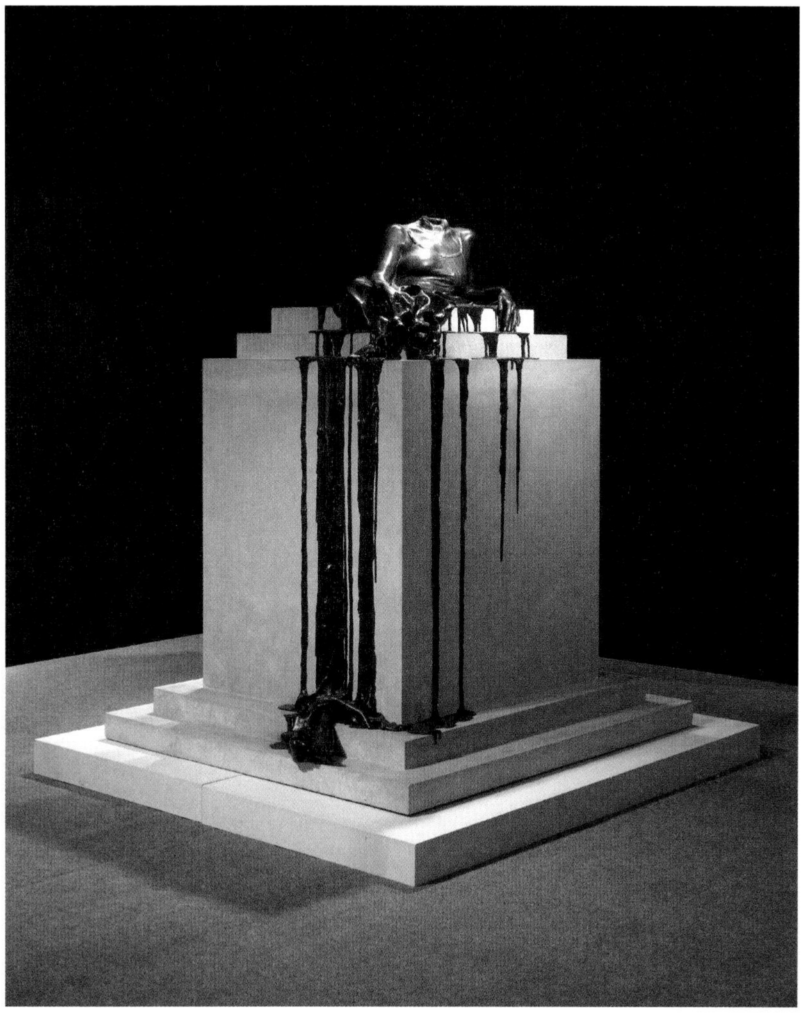

FIGURE 6.1 Bodies melt and drip like oil. Diana Al-Hadid, *In Mortal Repose*, 2011. Photo: Jason Wyche. Courtesy of Diana Al-Hadid.

like funerary effigies atop towering tombs. In a third, much larger sculptural structure titled *Phantom Limb* (2012), a headless torso dissolves from the hip into a multiladdered structure leading to a dismembered limb laying on the ground nearby (figure 6.3). As the title of this latter piece suggests, the figure has been amputated but the limb's memory persists like a ghostly remainder.

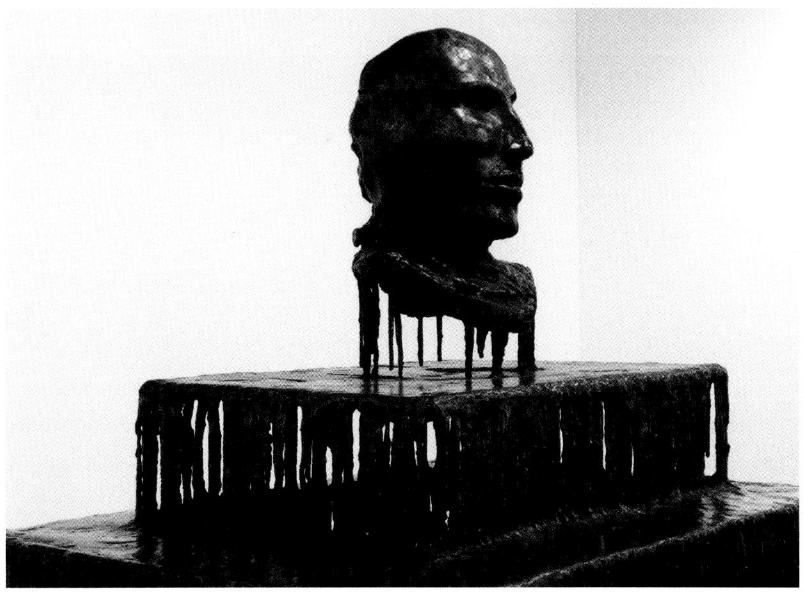

FIGURE 6.2 Heads flood their metal bases with molten secretions. Diana Al-Hadid, *Blind Bust II*, 2012. Photo: Jason Wyche. Courtesy of Diana Al-Hadid.

Over the course of time Al-Hadid was building these sculptures in her studio (the first one dating to 2011), Syria was undergoing social and political upheaval. 2011 is the year that brought Syria into the fold of the so-called Arab Spring, the consecutive protests that broke across the SWANA region in opposition to dictatorial governments in various countries such as Tunisia, Libya, Egypt, Yemen, and Bahrain. The conflict in Syria—and in Al-Hadid's native city of Aleppo—has since escalated into warfare on an international scale. While Al-Hadid does not directly link her practice to the war in Syria, her work has been understood as an evocation of "imminent—or recent—disaster."[39] As Sara Raza has noted, "Al-Hadid has been making work in this vein since well before the current Syrian conflict," pointing to the "omnipresent ghosts of tragedy and disaster that have migrated through history and time and are implicitly part of a repetitive cycle of grief and mourning."[40] Rather than reading Al-Hadid's work as direct representations of any specific events, I want to allow her sculptures to guide us in theorizing the aesthetics of the Terracene.

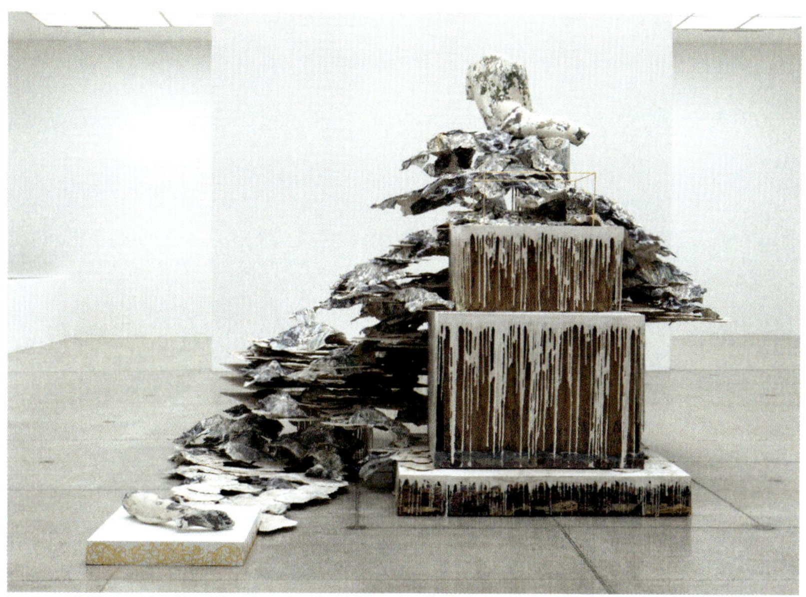

FIGURE 6.3 A headless torso dissolves from the hip into a multiladdered structure leading to a dismembered limb lying on the ground nearby. Diana Al-Hadid, *Phantom Limb*, 2012. Photo: Markus Woergoetter. Courtesy of Diana Al-Hadid.

Sculpture is meaningful in the context of Syrian art. Rich archives of ancient works, dug from numerous archaeological sites, reside in museum collections across the world in order to study political, social, and religious cultures of ancient Mesopotamia, including Syria's Roman period. This knowledge industry (of which art historians such as myself are a part) has become an active participant in the perpetuation of the current war in Syria. Like many other sites of ongoing warfare in the last few decades—such as Iraq and Lebanon—Syria's museums and world heritage sites have come under direct attack and lost valuable objects. Bullet holes have pierced through ancient walls and citadels while rockets and tanks have demolished archaeological sites suspected to house armed groups.[41] As the conflicts rage, residents prioritize food over history and, by extension, weapons over art. Knowledgeable of the market for antiquities, many have looted, dug, and traded ancient sculptures for weapons. "The rebels need weapons, and antiquities are an easy way to buy them," said a Syrian smuggler nicknamed Abu Khaled to a *Time* reporter in 2012.[42]

Sculptures and other artifacts have become tradable equivalents for weapons in an armed conflict that has disappeared and displaced more than just human populations.

Al-Hadid's bronze sculptures visually resonate with this historical and material cycle of art and arms. Bronze is one of the oldest products of Mesopotamian metallurgy used by metal workers to build both "prestigious objects" and "weapons."[43] In Al-Hadid's hands, bronze heads and torsos melt across their pedestals, visually indexing metallurgical transformations (or recycling) that can turn busts into arms. In pieces such as *Blind Bust* and *In Mortal Repose*, figurative sculptural pieces are shown to dissolve into the shapeless matter that gave them form, lending themselves to other uses. Despite their static nature as objects, Al-Hadid's pieces are visually dynamic, holding matter and form in constant tension. Each sculpture continually dissolves from representation into formless matter and back again. This is perhaps why her work is read as registering "imminent—or recent—disaster" because her figures do not hold their shape, falling constantly into the softness of the bronze alloy.

My use of the term *soft* to describe formless parts of these sculptures is of course figurative since the visual softness of dripping matter is indeed rendered in hard bronze—an alloy made "hard" in the technical process of mixing copper with arsenic perfected in Mesopotamia as long ago as the fifth and fourth millennia BCE.[44] The contrast between the softness that folds the flesh of these sculptures and the hardness of bronze out of which they are cast is precisely what produces the dynamism so apparent in Al-Hadid's sculptures. This is a dynamism that speaks to the malleability of metals that are not only capable of alchemical conversion but can be shaped into representational objects (both art and weapons).

Thinking about metals as dynamic and vital is paradoxical—more so in the current context where I have conjured weapons, those death-dealing instruments for which ancient artifacts have been liquidated. How lively are metals that bring death and destruction? How lively are sculptures exchanged for weapons that add to the death toll of humans, countless animals, and the more-than-human ecologies that support them? Mel Y. Chen's influential work on animacy has urged us to consider "gradations of lifeliness."[45] Are metals—such as lead in Chen's study—"dead" if they can activate toxic responses to what we understand as "living" organisms? Is lead "dead," as Chen writes, because it is "imagined as more molecular than cellular"?[46] In the case of metals such as bronze, can they be dead if they come to define the liveliness of human history, the societies and economies that they continue to enable in archaeological records? Are metals any less animate than the peoples who use them, both ancient and contemporary, both artists and soldiers? Bronze has been a vital actor in human history, requiring that we think with its deep materiality. As I discuss further in part 3 of this book, metals such as bronze interact with our bodies at a different scale such that industrial waste from ancient Mesopotamian metal mining and smelting sites continues to result in high concentrations of copper and lead in the plants and animals living in the surrounding areas today.[47]

"Who would choose metal," writes Jane Bennett, "as the symbol of vitality?" since "the association of metal with passivity or dead thingness persists."[48] When we consider the deep time of metals, it becomes apparent that metals only seem dead due to the divergent temporalities and temperatures that our bodies occupy. Bronze would indeed seem soft, liquid, and vibrant if we lived at its melting point of 1,675° F. Sculptures would come alive, moving their limbs and skins (like time-lapse animation), if our bodies occupied a temporality as long as the historical times through which they travel. But given that the temporality of metals is not afforded to our bodies, we associate them with immobility, with fixity, or, to use Bennett's words, with "dead weight."[49]

Metals are less speculatively alive when they act as instruments of war causing toxicity, impairments, and death. The ecological effects of high-tech warfare and extractive catastrophes can be immediate—they can pollute rivers, burn forests, and demolish cities—or they can take a long time to assess. Rob Nixon has called the length of time it takes for the effects of violence to show "slow violence," a form of trauma that may not be immediately apparent or get "counted."[50] This is how Nixon describes the slow violence of the Gulf War:

> Who is counting the staggered deaths that civilians and soldiers suffer from depleted uranium ingested or blown across the desert? Who is counting the belated fatalities from unexploded cluster bombs that lie in wait for months or years, metastasizing into landmines? Who is counting deaths from chemical residues left behind by so-called pinpoint bombing, residues that turn into foreign insurgents, infiltrating native rivers and poisoning the food chain? Who is counting the victims of genetic deterioration—the stillborn, malformed infants conceived by parents whose DNA has been scrambled by war toxins?

These are examples of multispecies bodies and ecologies of the Terracene, sites which, in Nixon's words, "convert the earth into a biological weapon."[51] My concern here, and throughout this book, is with how these sites are sensed, which I explore through the works of artists engaging multisensory responses to aerial bombings, toxins, viruses, explosions, fires, and earthquakes. The Terracene is a site of injury and trauma, disrupting the fantasy of an unimpaired, healthy subject who is centered within aesthetic theory. Such a subject is hypothetical and never truly existed but is held as an ideal within Enlightenment aesthetic thought. Living amid war and climate disruption not only puts pressure on the reality of such a subject position, but it also involves new impairments—as seen in Nixon's examples—for racialized bodies living under settler-colonial and military occupations that did not exist before.

Al-Hadid's sculptures tackle a range of such impairments, giving name to physical and psychological traumas in the sculpture's titles and visual renditions. The *Blind Bust* is a head with hollow sockets for eyes and no ears. *In Mortal Repose* is an acephalic torso, whose title brings attention to the sculpture's mortality. The *Phantom Limb* is a multilayered structure holding up a torso with severed limbs. The title *Phantom Limb* names the trauma of amputation and the psychological condition in which a severed limb continues to be sensate. The limb in question rests on a pedestal as part of the sculptural structure, resting behind the figure on the ground.

If disability is hard to notice at first glance in Al-Hadid's sculptures, it is because we are aesthetically calibrated not to see disability in art. As Tobin Siebers notes, the history of art does not "exclude" disability, but "it is rather the case that disability is rarely recognized as such, even though it often serves as the very factor that establishes works as superior examples of aesthetic beauty."[52] For Siebers, disability is everywhere in the history of art, from Roman Venuses to facial contortions in Picasso's paintings to deliberate wounding in performance art such as those of Chris Burden. Noticing disability, for Siebers, would mean attending to the rich archive of artistic practices that render "misshapen and twisted bodies, stunning variety of human forms, intense representations of traumatic injury and psychological alienation, and unyielding preoccupation with wounds and tormented flesh."[53]

In the case of Al-Hadid's sculptures, for instance, unseeing impairment takes the form of attributing missing body parts and sense organs to conventions of representation, whereby sculptural busts and torsos only render parts of the body or, alternatively, expecting that her work is referencing classical sculptures that have lost their limbs due to the passage of time or dislocation. This is indeed how her work is often received. Reindert Falkenburg, for instance, reads *Phantom Limb* as a "memory effect" whereby it "brings to mind memories of classical torsos such as the Parthenon sculptures in the British Museum" even though, he admits, "Al-Hadid's sculpture does not directly 'reference,' or 'cite' (let alone 'copy'), the Parthenon frieze, but triggers . . . memory of it."[54] Despite his own observation, however, Falkenburg goes on to write, "For me, however, there is no way back: I cannot 'un-see' my art historical background."[55]

Situating Al-Hadid's sculptures in the aesthetics of the Terracene not only necessitates "unseeing" through the ableist gaze of art history but requires moving outside the hegemony of the eye itself. For we can certainly place Al-Hadid's work, as Sara Raza does, in scenes of "imminent—or recent—disaster," according to which her sculptures become bodies maimed by bullets and covered in dripping oils and toxins. While such an interpretation is plausible, it also relies heavily on *visual* representations of impairment. In my assessment, visual renditions are preoccupied with how disabilities become visible to others, forgetting not only the broad spectrum of vision itself but the invisibility of many mental and sensory conditions. Furthermore, an emphasis on visuality privileges representation over multisensory complexities of sense perception.

It is apparent, for instance, that the sensation resulting from the psychological condition of the phantom limb, after which Al-Hadid's sculpture is named, is not equivalent to the visible presence or absence of limbs on a body. For the feminist media studies scholar Vivian Sobchack, who has explored her sensations in the aftermath of leg amputation in detail, "the binary opposition of 'presence' and 'absence' is itself a phantom constituted by a primarily visual logic."[56] This is a logic that equates "the sense of invisible presence with ghosts and phantoms, or absence with loss."[57] In contrast to this logic, Sobchack describes her shifting relationship to her whole body after amputation, and in particular to her nonamputated right leg. "Without either some corporeal problem or world contact to define its presence, and for all its fleshy solidity," she writes, "I sensed my right leg as little more than a generally vague and hardly weighty verticality."[58] While it was her left leg that was amputated, Sobchack writes of the changed perception of her right leg. "The supposed 'real' leg, the right one that was left," Sobchack writes, "visibly occupied space as some 'thing' objectively there that I barely felt here."[59] In contrast to the diminished feeling in her right leg, Sobchack describes occasional heightened sensations of pain or what she describes as "intermittent electrical 'zapping'" in her "phantom" limb.[60] This pain, in Sobchack's discussion, is a conundrum because it cannot be actually located. "The conundrum is," she writes, "that I do not feel it on or as my body—and yet I feel it."[61]

I include Sobchack's descriptions of "living a phantom limb" at length here because it moves us beyond the presumption that sensations solely reside in sense organs. Instead, her phenomenological experience conveys that acute sensations, such as pain, can exist without an embodied location while visibly present body parts (such as her right leg) can become indifferent to sensations. Sobchack's discussion has a far-reaching significance for aesthetic theory because it subjects all sense organs, such as eyes and ears, to the same condition. "This sense of the 'hereness' and 'thereness' of our body 'parts' is not limited to 'phantom limbs,'" Sobchack writes, but also applies to "the differently experienced modalities of the senses of vision and tactility, vision a distance sense ('there') and tactility a near sense ('here')."[62] In other words, some body parts (such as the tongue) require a hereness for them to sense, while others (such as the ear) rely on thereness.

Sobchack's interpretation of sensate embodiment places impairment at the origins of aesthetics, a philosophy dependent on displacements (hereness and thereness) of sense perceptions. Michael Davidson explains it well when he describes sighted artists' representations of blindness as ultimately conveying the limits of sightedness itself. He writes, "The artist in representing the blind represents himself in the act of feeling his way toward articulation and design."[63] Impairments here reside at the structural base of articulation and representation. As with Mills and Sterne's arguments above, Sobchack and Davidson theorize disability as central to aesthetics rather than lying outside of its orbit of sensations.

Aesthetic theory has long excluded experiences of trauma. As I noted at the outset, Freud's definition of trauma drew upon the experiences of veterans whose senses could not protect them from violent experiences on the battlefield. Trauma meant an overexposure of sense organs to stimuli that caused them pain and injury. While aesthetic theory has traditionally not held excesses such as noise, retinal strain, burns, or numbing within its domain of knowledge, a disability studies perspective allows for such an intervention. As artworks such Al-Hadid's sculptures remind us, traumatic sensing changes the very basis of representation itself. Her figures embody complex figurations and histories that do not simply visualize disabilities—despite their figurative forms—but bring us into displaced and invisible sensations.

I want to leave us here in the disformed drips, the mass of melted bronze within Al-Hadid's sculptures. These "soft" areas of her sculptures do not simply melt away the boundaries of what we might understand as coherent figures but loosen hardened ideas about aesthetics. The folds and ooze of these sculptures dissolve aesthetics into the messiness of matter and sensation. The dynamism of these sculptures, after all, does not reside in the figurative form (the "memory effect" of classical sculptures) but rather in such form's very material disintegration. In Al-Hadid's sculptures, form dissolves into matter and aesthetics becomes crude. Hers is a crude aesthetics.

7

Crude Aesthetics

We owe a huge debt of gratitude to the trees and animal groups in ancient times who led to the formation of these fossil fuel resources in the ground.
—Prose prayer (translated from Telugu) by industrial engineer Katta G. Murty, "History of Crude Oil Refining" (2020)

Dead organisms, in time, become oil due to heat and pressure from rock formations under which they are buried. "Crude oil" or petroleum (from Greek *petra*, meaning "rock," and *oleum*, meaning "oil") are names given to seepages that have leaked, oozed, and bubbled to the surface of the Earth in black, yellow, and white liquid pits. Extractivists came to Indigenous oil as latecomers. When they arrived, oil was already a participant in human life, collected by hand from pits "more than 4000 years ago in Babylon in the construction of walls and towers" and turned into "asphalt used to seal water tanks at Mohenjo-Daro" at the banks of the Indus River in contemporary Pakistan.[1] "For a very long period," writes the industrial engineer Katta G. Murty, "people in many different parts of the world have been noticing seepage of subsurface crude oil collecting in oil pits."[2] These seepages were put to many practical uses—such as building materials and adhesives—but were also vehicles for spiritual and aesthetic connections with the divine.[3] Zoroastrian priests built temples at the site of petroleum excretions, gathering worshippers around its eternal fires,[4] while the dead mummified in ancient Egypt were preserved using petroleum deposits gathered at Gebel El Zeit and the Dead Sea in Palestine.[5]

Industrial extractivists have long presented histories of petroleum—as well as the peoples, cultures, and religious practices that centered around oil—as "crude." The Iranian petroleum geologist Rasoul Sorkhabi describes his skeptical encounter with contemporary texts that read, "For thousands of years in the Middle East, it [oil] was messy and useless stuff, of interest mainly to a few Greek and Roman tourists,"[6] as impetus for his long-term research on the historical geography, records, and uses of petroleum (in all of its forms) in ancient Iran. I build my analysis here partly on his research in order to counter narratives in which the "Middle East" becomes an unchanging and static place for "thousands of years," with ecological relations that are incapable of perceiving oil as anything but "messy and useless stuff." In such statements, time, place, cultures, and religions, as well as the materiality of oil itself, are rendered crude. What can we make of this crude perspective, or rather crude aesthetic lens, that extractivists bring to the resources they desire?

My proposal: crude is an aesthetic category mobilized by extractivists in order to facilitate access to Indigenous resources such as petroleum. Macarena Gómez-Barris describes extractivism as "the colonial paradigm, worldview, and technologies that mark out regions of 'high biodiversity' in order to reduce life to capitalist resource conversion."[7] Extractivism is a global capitalist economy that has, since the 1500s, Gómez-Barris writes, "converted natural resources such as silver, water, timber, rubber, and petroleum into global commodities."[8] This process not only has impoverished resource-rich territories while accumulating capitalist wealth but has caused "dramatic material change to social and ecological life" of Indigenous populations.[9]

What is so crude about oil?

Extractivists understand oil to be crude prior to the distillation process that makes it refined. Within extractive oil industries, the term "crude" is used to aesthetically define the liquid fossils that are naturally produced within oil fields. Depending on the hydrocarbon mixtures of a given location, crude oil is classified into "light, medium and heavy" as well as "sweet" and "sour" depending on the sulfur concentration found within it.[10] These are aesthetic and evaluative languages of commodification that turn matter into capital.

Oil is not the only thing that is said to be crude.

Crude and refined are not only used to describe petroleum but are also racialized aesthetic categories that codefine the crudeness of matter alongside peoples, cultures, religions, and ecological practices that center them. Extractivists use heavy machinery to turn crude oil—the "messy and useless stuff"—into refined liquid that facilitate (settler)colonial urban cultures that have produced and continue to sustain racialized relations. The industrial refinement of oil at once constructs the category of the "refined human" who is separated not only from the messiness of crude oil itself but diverse histories of human relations with petroleum.

Observe, for instance, an 1873 account of petroleum production in Pennsylvania, written by J. T. Henry. While modern industrial drilling first began in Azerbaijan in 1848 and the first commercial oil well was drilled in Canada in 1858, the petroleum industry did not gain momentum until 1859 when the now well-known Edwin L. Drake drilled an oil well in Titusville, Pennsylvania, that fed the burgeoning US automobile industries.[11] A little over a decade later, J. T. Henry wrote *The Early and Later History of Petroleum*, describing the Pennsylvania oil region as "by far the largest field, [that] produces eight-tenths of all the Petroleum, now so largely entering into the commerce of the commonwealth, and of the nation, and has surely come to be an indispensable benefaction to millions of households, in every civilized nation upon the globe."[12]

Henry's historical sketch of petroleum production in Pennsylvania links oil with "civilized" nationhood, presenting a global industry that renders civilization possible. While the successes of the petroleum industry are the focus of Henry's text, he begins his account with an Indigenous prehistory to industrial drilling that, although in his opinion "accounted of little practical value," should nonetheless be cited. Henry writes,

> There is a tradition in Venango Co., P., that the oil springs on Oil Creek formed a part of the religious ceremony of the Seneca Indians, who formerly lived on these wild hills. The Aborigins dipped it from their wells and mixed it with their war paint, which is said to have given

them a hideous appearance, varnishing their faces, as it were, and enabled them to retain the paint for a long time, and token their skin entirely impervious to water. The use of this oil for their religious worship is spoken of by the French commander of Fort Duquesne in the 1750. "I would desire," writes the commandant to his Excellency, General Montcalm, "to assure you that this is a most delightful land. Some of the most astonishing natural wonders have been discovered by our people." "While descending the Allegany, fifteen leagues below the mouth of the Connewango, and three above the Venango, we were invited by the chief of the Senecas to attend a religious ceremony of his tribe. We landed, and drew up our canoes on a point where a small stream entered the river. The tribe appeared unusually solemn. We marched up the stream about half a league, where the company, a large band it appeared, had arrived some days before us. Gigantic hills begirt us on every side. The scene was very sublime. The great chief then recited the conquests and heroism of their ancestors. The surface of the stream was covered with a thick scum, which upon applying a torch at a given signal, burst into a complete conflagration. At the sight of the flames, the Indians gave forth the triumphant shoot that made the hills and valleys re-echo again. Here, then, is revived the ancient fire worship of the East; here, then are the children of the Sun." Tracing the course of the French commander down the Allegany river on our present maps, we find the spring spoken of, as evidently upon Oil Creek, and on marching half a league above that stream we will probably reach Rouseville, where Cherry Run flows into Oil Creek. The "gigantic hills" are still here, and the "thick scum" which the Indians gathered, and which careful, prudent men, now guard against conflagration, flows into peaceable tanks, and instead of lighting up the wilderness for exhibitions of uncouth savages, send joy and comfort into thousands of distant homes.[13]

Henry narrates the booming petroleum industry as built upon the lands and resources of Seneca Indigenous peoples, whose continued presence on the land is actively erased. "Elimination," as Patrick Wolfe writes, "is an organizing principle of settler-colonial society rather than a one-off (and superseded) occurrence."[14] The past tense of Henry's text not only erases the present violence of colonial settlement and resource extraction but presents an inevitable settler future of "joy" and "comfort" as results of the benefits of the oil industry and land appropriation. "In the eighteenth and nineteenth centuries," writes Kim TallBear, "the United States positioned itself—positioned 'Americans' or whites—as the rational agents capable of transforming nature into productive property, and Indigenous peoples as incapable of developing, indeed even surviving, in the face of the modern industrial state."[15] Henry positions himself as such an "American," building nationhood and industrial modernity upon Indigenous lands and resources. He mobilizes aesthetic language to justify settler futurism, transforming settler-colonial violence, as well as the toxic realities of extractivism, into the "joy" and "comfort" of settler homes, which in his language have already displaced "uncouth savages" relegated to the past.

Within Henry's account, Seneca religious ceremonies are in direct contrast to settler-extractivist relations with oil. The burning of the "thick scum" gathered on the surface of the stream by Seneca peoples is not only perceived to be of "little practical value" but understood as mere exhibitionism ("for the exhibition of uncouth savages") associating religiosity with "savagery," a term that produces a racialized subhuman category. In contrast, settlers are portrayed as "prudent men" who "now guard against conflagration." The spatial separation of settler homes from both the site of extraction and Seneca peoples is central to Henry's settler-extractivist logic. While Seneca peoples, in Henry's text, perform ceremonies at the oil stream, settlers extract oil from the stream, directing its "flows into peaceable tanks" in order to "send joy and comfort into thousands of distant homes." The oil pipeline here facilitates distance, a spatial separation not only between settlers and sites of oil extraction but between the "joy and comfort" of settler's homes and Indigenous peoples "formerly living in the wild hills." Henry describes the pipeline as "peaceable," using language to rewrite settler-colonial violence and toxic ecological productions from which the settler is both spatially and temporally distanced.

Henry's emphasis on "distance" points to ongoing histories of environmental racism that dump toxic by-products of industrial production within the vicinity of Indigenous and racialized communities. As Winona LaDuke puts it, "While Native peoples have been massacred and fought, cheated and robbed of their historical lands, today their lands are subject to some of the most invasive industrial interventions imaginable . . . threatened by environmental hazards, ranging from toxic wastes to clearcuts."[16] Extractive industries are major pollutants that not only extract matter from the land but produce waste products that need to go "away." The logic of "away," as Max Liboiron (Red River Métis/Michif) writes, assumes "infrastructural access to Indigenous land," without which "there is no disposability."[17] The oil-refining process alone releases chemicals into the atmosphere, dumps wastewater into waterways, and causes fires and explosions that cannot always be contained. This is why pollution and active dumping of waste products are enactments of settler colonialism.

Kim TallBear has noted the persistence of languages that assert "human agency upon the land" rather than "deep human-nonhuman relations *in place*."[18] For TallBear, the scientific view that humans have "agency upon the land" imagines two separate entities (land on the one hand and human on the other), creating a dichotomous relationship in which the category known as "human" comes to assert its agency *upon* the land. In TallBear's assessment, Indigenous peoples place an "emphasis on land-human co-constitutive relations."[19] This means that the notion of the human, from an Indigenous perspective, is coproduced with the land. This is a "human-nonhuman" relation that is produced "*in place*." Today, this view is politically asserted, as TallBear notes, in "the desire of indigenous peoples to emphasize their emergence as particular cultural and language groups in social and cultural relation with nonhumans of all kinds—land formations, nonhuman animals, plants, and the elements in very particular places—their 'homelands' or 'traditional territories,' for example."[20]

While Henry does not grasp the coconstitutive relations of humans "in place," and instead emphasizes extractive uses of the land through the distance and separation of "prudent men" from the "wilderness," his text nonetheless coproduces racialized humans in relation to oil and the lands on which it flows. Within Henry's settler-extractivist logic, oil's refinement (its "flow into peaceable tanks") is associated with "prudent" humans who pillage the land for its resources while the alleged usage of crude oil as paint by Seneca warriors is described as causing a "hideous appearance." Henry's aesthetic judgments here are at once racial judgments that produce categorically different humans in relation to oil.

Put simply, oil is racialized.

Crude is the name for the preextractive stage of a racially marked substance that becomes refined through commodification. Oil's crudeness and refinement are tied to who uses it and how. Oil is crude if it is used for "religious worship" yet refined if channeled into settler homes. Oil is crude if it facilitates Indigenous lifeworlds. It is refined if it is put in the service of settler futurisms.

Henry's conception of the use of oil within Seneca communities is further skewed by his Orientalist vision of Indigenous peoples in Pennsylvania. In his text, Henry cites the words of a French commander who, upon witnessing the Seneca ceremony in which the stream of oil is set aflame, exclaims, "Here, then, is revived the ancient fire worship of the East; here, then are the children of the Sun." From the Orientalist perspective of the French commander, Seneca practices are seen as continuous with "ancient fire worship of the East," collapsing Zoroastrian religious practices with those of Seneca "Indians."

Edward Said defined Orientalism as intertextual, one text citing another into a web of discursive practices. In Ali Behdad's words, "The Orientalist representation is always a *re*-presentation," whereby the "experience of the [Orientalist] subject is meaningful only in relation to the intertextual context of the discursive domain in which it participates."[21] The French commander's view of the Seneca ceremony is such a *re*-presentation, as he presents Parsee Zoroastrian practices in Southeast and Southwest Asia "revived" before him by Seneca "Indians." What links these disparate peoples and places together is the commander's colonial gaze rather than an uncanny "revival" or repetition of "Indian" religious practices. The commander's experience (or what he imagines he sees as he writes) draws on a history of Orientalist travel narratives that found oil pits at the center of religious life within European colonial geographies.

Zoroastrian fire temples appear alongside oil pits in numerous European travel writings. One is described by the German physician Engelbert Kämpfer in his *Journey into Persia and Other Oriental Countries*, written based on his travels to Persia in the 1680s:

> We went further and half an hour later came across a piece of land that was on fire; it was covered with a whitish gravel and ash dust. Many flames, wonderful to behold, issued from the numerous cracks. A few cracks were burning fiercely and the flames, shooting far out, filled the onlookers with dread; but they all consented to step quite near to the less fierce flames issuing from other cracks. Yet more of them gave off clouds of smoke or vapour which were hardly visible, but from which emanated a very strong smell of naphtha. The wonderful phenomenon extended to over ninety paces in length and twenty-six in width. The cracks were astonishingly small, split open to no more than a hand or foot's width. Some were shorter and semi-circular in shape, others were irregularly curved. . . . There we came across ten men or so, occupied in performing various tasks around the fire: some were cooking in copper and clay vessels, placed over one crack that was not burning too fiercely, the mid-day meal for their fellow-lodgers in the neighboring village Sroganni (Sarachany), which derived its name from this

fire. Others were burning lime on stones gathered from elsewhere and heaped together, and then separating the results into heaps which were to be taken away in small boats. Two Indian fire-worshippers, strangers from the tribe of the Parsees, were sitting quietly within a semi-circular wall which they had built, absorbed in watching and worshipping the fire that was leaping forth, and through which they adored the eternal divinity. From this naphtha there emanates a fine gas which has the power of causing the flames of a stove or lamp to blaze in no time, and which, once lit, burns away inextinguishably.[22]

As with Henry's text, Kämpfer's travel writing includes a great deal of observational detail in order to support the text's truth claims. Detailed attention to the size (ninety paces in length and twenty-six in width) and shapes (some shorter and semicircular in shape, others irregularly curved) of the cracks from which fire and smoke emanate appeal to a sense of realism in order to reduce the speculative and intertextual quality of Orientalist genres of travel writing. Accompanying observational details are aesthetic propositions that further contribute to Kämpfer's participant observations at the site. Kämpfer describes the look of "dread" on the face of onlookers confronted with the fierce flames and notes his sensitivity to the foul smell of oil (naphtha) mixed with vapor and smoke. These aesthetic and sensual descriptions provide an affective veracity to the text and his interpretations of the various uses of oil in Persia, whether in cooking for the lodgers in the neighboring village or by the Parsee travelers gathering in adoration around the fire.

Travel writing, according to James Clifford, preceded the professionalization of ethnographic fieldwork in the first half of the twentieth century.[23] "At the close of the nineteenth century," Clifford writes, "nothing guaranteed, a priori, the ethnographer's status as the best interpreter of native life—as opposed to the traveler, and especially the missionary and administrator, some of whom had been in the field far longer and had better research contacts and linguistic skills."[24] Prior to the twentieth century, it was indeed the travel writer, as seen in Kämpfer's text, who offered thick descriptions so as to position themselves as "the describer-translator of custom and the builder of general theories about humanity."[25] The professionalization of ethnographic fieldwork required a sharp distinction from "the earlier 'men on the spot'—the missionary, the administrator, the trader, and the traveler,"[26] yet anthropologists carried over the essential persona of the traveler as they pitched their tents and presented themselves "squatting by the campfire; looking, listening, and questioning."[27]

The historical continuity that Clifford draws between the missionary, the colonial administrator, the trader, the traveler, and the professional anthropologist—those "men on the spot" whose very arrival were facilitated by (settler)colonial desires for lands and resources—would not be complete without the addition of the extractivist, whose path to oil was paved and lit by the fires described by "men on the spot." This is vividly demonstrated in the 1907 travelogue titled *Across Persia*, written by Eliot Crawshay-Williams, an Englishman who traveled to Iran after resigning from his administrative post in India.[28] His travelogue devotes extensive attention to petroleum seepages in southwest Iran only a year before William Knox D'Arcy struck oil in the same region, founding the Anglo-Iranian Oil Company in 1909. In his travelogue, Crawshay-Williams foreshadows British extractivist wealth accumulations in Iran as he writes,

> Sulphuretted hydrogen combined with petroleum would convey some idea of its distinctive characteristic, and with feelings of mingled interest and disgust we awaited the explanation of the mystery. In a moment or two it came, when we rode up to a brilliant green stream running over slimy pink stones between crumbling yellowish-white banks. Dipping the hand into it, the water was warm. Despite the really terrible odour, we tracked the stream into its source. Some pools of hot sulphurous water bubbled out from among green slime and mud fringed with a yellow crystalline deposit. . . . As I passed thankfully back again to the track down a decrescendo of smell, I noticed black lumps of bitumen bobbling down the current. . . . Another stream, smelling less of sulphur but more of oil, burst from under the rocks a little further on, and it is near here that attempts have been made in the past to tap the petroleum reservoir which probably exists somewhere beneath the ground. Some day a happy man may hit the right spot, and then his fortune is made; but it is a speculative business. Half a dozen inches to the right or left, and you are, as Fate may decide, a pauper or a millionaire.[29]

As with Henry's text, Crawshay-Williams's self-described "interest" in oil is "mingled" with "disgust." The disgust is here attributed to the "really terrible odour" emanating from the warm, sulfurous pools bubbling with bitumen, yet this disgust is laced with an interested draw, a magnetic pull by the unknown location of a petroleum reservoir, which in his speculative assessment "probably exists somewhere beneath the ground." If, and when, such a reservoir is located, Crawshay-Williams speculates, the sensation of disgust will turn into happiness for it is a "happy man" who "may hit the right spot, and then his fortune is made." Crawshay-Williams's affective relationship to oil follows the same extractivist logic exhibited by Henry, for whom the "joy and comfort" of settler futurity on Seneca lands was dependent upon extortion and violent dispossession of land and resources. Here, Crawshay-Williams presents land as a "speculative business" for an individual who, with a single strike, may become "a pauper or a millionaire."

The extractivist says: land is a site of wealth accumulation for the lucky few. The rest can become dispossessed.

The lucky strike is the promise of good fortune that drives the extractivist, yet the "millionaire's" strike becomes death-dealing for those poisoned and eliminated in the process.

The extractivist says: oil is crude when it lies beneath bedrock. It becomes refined when it is distilled and separated into hydrocarbon molecules of varying weights that can be made into consumer products.

The material transformation of oil from crude to refined parallels the process through which aesthetic philosophers and anthropologists have attempted to transform the crude species into refined humanity. Aesthetic theory has long upheld this general distinction between the "crude" and the "refined," offering aesthetic education as the path toward proper humanity. In her reading of Kant's *Critique of Judgment*, Gayatri Spivak analyzes Kant's racialization of "the New Hollanders or the inhabitants of Tierra del Fuego" as those who cannot access proper humanity due to an incapacity for aesthetic judgment.[30] Spivak argues that the human is not an accessible category for all but is racially specific and by definition limited to European men. In Kant's work, Spivak argues, "the 'uneducated' are specifically the child and the poor, the 'naturally uneducated' is woman. By contrast *der rohe Mensch*, man in the raw, can, in its signifying reach, accommodate the savage and the primitive."[31] In other words, aesthetic education can bring the child, the poor, and the woman into the category of the human. Yet, the racialized "savage and the primitive"—the raw man—remains outside of aesthetic education and hence refinement and proper humanity. While the uneducated child, woman, and the poor can become refined through aesthetic educations, the "raw"—a category saved for the "savage and the primitive"—is the limit point for aesthetic education.

Anthropology shares in this legacy. Writing in 1901, the anthropologist Franz Boas attempted to explain the mental and sensory processes that distinguish crude from refined members of the human species. In his essay titled "The Mind of Primitive Man," Boas writes, "No matter how crude the standards of primitive man may be, we recognize that all of them possess an art, and that all of them possess an ethical standard."[32] While Boas urges us to recognize that the racialized "primitive man" is capable of producing art and ethical standards, he emphasizes the "crude" aspect of their judgment. For his assessment, Boas relies on a familiar formulation characteristic of aesthetic theory since the Enlightenment, in which ethics and aesthetics are closely intertwined. The human ability to make ethical decisions is linked to aesthetic perception, according to which the "crude" judgment of the racialized is determined. After a lengthy assessment, Boas concludes that "the mind of primitive man seems to differ from that of civilized man."[33]

The civilized man received an aesthetic/ethical education.

The civilized man made art/science.

The civilized man made the Anthropocene.

The civilized man colonized, settled, extracted, poisoned.

The civilized man created terror by turning terra into territory.

It is time to think with the crudeness of matter, form, and existence. For too long crudeness, as Kyla Tompkins writes, has signaled "the barbarism of base aesthetics: rough, rude, and blunt, lacking finish and maturity."[34] Crudeness appeals to Tompkins because "like the queer, it signifies so much that is Wrong."[35] Crudeness has accumulated the refuse of the civilized. It has come to signify, as Tompkins notes, the "everyday life of socially deviant peoples, people rendered deformed by capital, or simply understood as deformed within normative aesthetic frames."[36] Like the queer, crude is not "Wrong" but made "Wrong" through an Enlightenment-derived aesthetic education.

The Sounds of Terracene

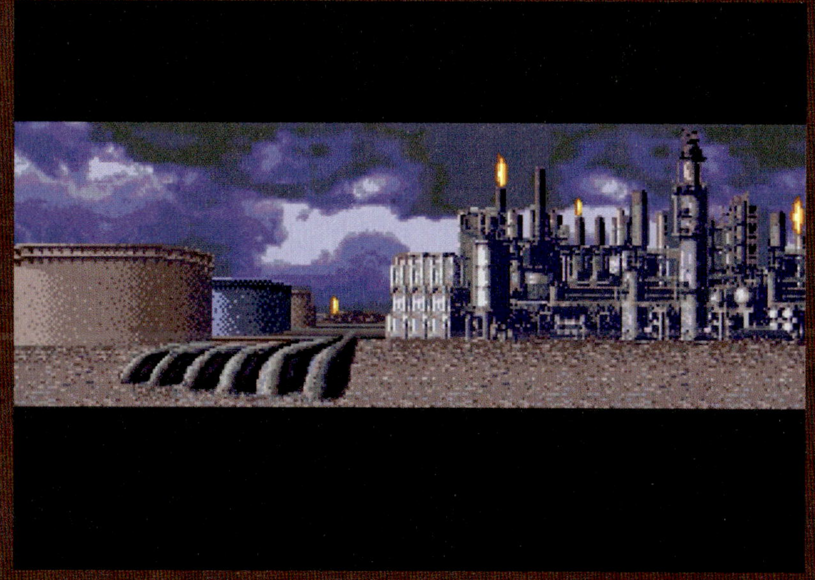

8

The Glass Shattered at My Feet

I have a recurrent vision of myself at the age of ten gripping onto the edges of my bed. I see my arms stretched long, fingers searching for the frayed borders of my bed sheet. My gaze is directed at the bedroom floor where the familiar patterns of a Persian carpet blur into new shapes traveling up alongside walls so unstable that they seem to hover in midair. The window, a short distance behind my feet, lets through the faint moonlight. Panes of glass rattle against their frame. I have been jolted from sleep by an earthquake, one of several I would come to experience over the course of my life. The earth rocked my bed into a raft sailing across waves surging up in every direction around my feet. My toes receded, my knuckles pressed white, moving in tandem with the torrent rushing through the ground.

There is something distinct about my memory of this earthquake that shook my room one early morning in the bustling city of Tehran. I retain it as a sketch, a series of pencil drawings zoomed onto my chewed-up nails framed by repetitive lines conveying walls resigning from their post. The image is permeated by sound, a high-pitched clink of a glass window that would shatter onto the floor only a short few months after the earthquake. On that early morning, the glass was resilient. It plasticized, shape-shifting from rigid matter into a pliable conductor of the Earth's vibrations. In a few months, that same glass would stiffen. It would crack and shatter into a thousand pieces, laying out the wave patterns of a bomb exploding nearby.

This was 1987. Political conflict between Iran's newly constituted Islamic Republic and neighboring Iraq had reached its zenith. The war's rhetorical abstractness had become increasingly material for civilians on both sides of the border. Land and aerial bombardment had come to transform our environments. Carrots wilted in pungent soils. Cats quivered under awnings. Nerve endings snapped. The sun became grapefruit in haze and smoke. Goats lacked calcium. Grocers shelved empty milk bottles, rationing eggs for those who carried coupons. Gasoline rushed in pipelines. Measles spread. Blush faded from peaches teetering on the tip of slanted branches in orchards. The war had left its mark.

The day my window shattered onto my bedroom floor was an ordinary day in early summer. I was home from school, alone with my mother. She was in the kitchen kneeling in front of the stove with a long stick, fishing out a utensil that had unexpectedly slid under. The bomb dropped onto this quotidian scene. A woman searching for a misplaced item, her hair draped onto one side, sweeping the ground as I flipped through magazines on my bedroom floor. On this day, the glass shattered at my feet. Small shards amassed—bright, translucent, sharp. A few months earlier the glass had endured an earthquake's tremor. Now it heaped into a pile.

9

Listening to the Terracene

I have offered the term *Terracene* as a way of thinking about the ecologies of war and the terror that ongoing warfare has extended on multiple Terrans and their habitats since the declaration of the war on terror. I have argued that the aesthetics of the Terracene are multifaceted and multi sensorial. Here I listen to a musical composition titled *Desert Strike*, released as an EP in 2012 by the Kuwaiti American artist and composer Fatima Al-Qadiri. Listening to Al-Qadiri's recorded compositions allows us an entry point into the sounds of the Terracene. How do we listen to war and the destruction of an environment? What are the audible sounds of disaster? As I have argued earlier in this book, the notion of the Anthropocene is notorious for its abstraction. It is a theoretical idea engaging long temporalities and wide geographies, obfuscating our ability to see, sense, and hear its workings within our surroundings. Knowing the Anthropocene sensually would require sensing ourselves as part of a multispecies environment across large stretches of time. Such an experience is difficult to fathom. We can think of ourselves as part of an entangled web of species whom we have never met, but we cannot readily experience our connectedness. We cannot physically sense our collective bodies shifting weather patterns or reducing biodiversity over time on a mass scale. The Anthropocene, in this sense, appeals to our intellect but not to our senses. It expects to garner an intellectual response but not an aesthetic one.

Perceiving the dual effects of war and environmental degradation is arguably just as daunting. How can we comprehend the massive scale at which chemical warfare has left its mark on the planet? How can we sense the psychic and physiological effects that work at slower scales than the timeline of combat, defeat, and victory? Al-Qadiri's compositions guide us through these questions.

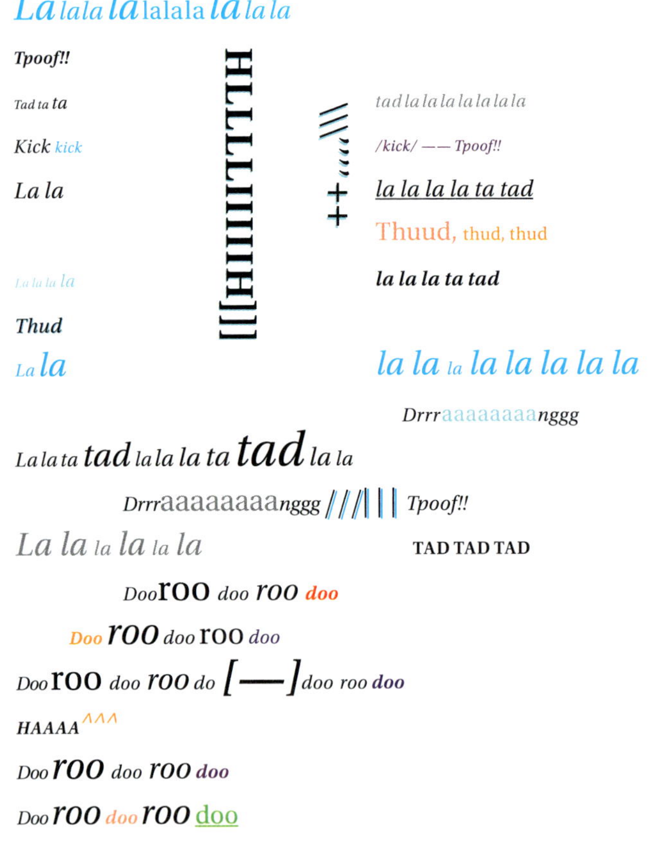

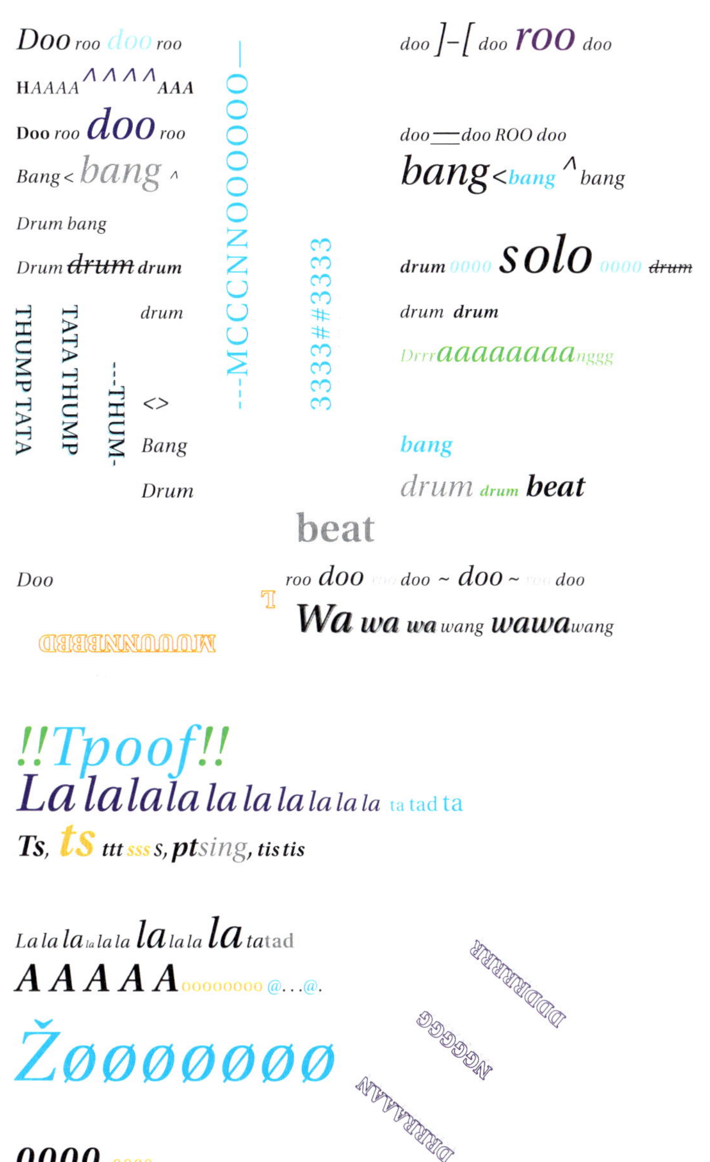

How to write in sound?

In my sonic approximation to Al-Qadiri's electronic beats for the track "Desert Strike," I have brought together alphabetic letters and symbols to convey my experience of the music in written form.

My text has become a poetic parallel, not a description of the sound.

Art History proposes the concept of ekphrasis. Derived from classical

Greek, ekphrasis is the practice of describing a visual image—such as a painting or a sculpture—in words. It dramatizes the visual in words for audiences who may not have the image before them but who can, through the orator's description, see that image in their mind's eye. Ekphrasis facilitates an imaginative relationship to a visual scene through the richness of language.

I am struck by the limitations of ekphrasis for sonic representation as I string together letters while listening to Al-Qadiri's music. The sound of these letters, as I read them out loud, fail at bringing the ambient electronic vibrations of Al-Qadiri's composition to the written page. There is little correspondence between what I am hearing and the letters I have at my disposal on my laptop's keyboard. Every beat I hear confirms my restricted repertoire of scattered letters and symbols. Can "roo" ring in your ear like a prerecorded sample on an electronic synthesizer?

I wonder about how you read the inscription above.

If you decide to read it out loud, you will make the music audible in your own pitch, on your own breath. Sounds will move through your lips, your throat, and your abdomen. You are the choreographer of the haptic sensation of every word in your body. "Doo roo doo" does not determine the sounds you will make but the muscular shapes your lips and cheeks are guided to take. Your tongue will avoid your teeth, it will tap the roof of your mouth then roll aside to allow some moisture to escape your throat in an aerial stream. Letters do not provide music as sound but music as muscular scores upon your body. The letters guide your muscles but the sound is entirely yours.

If you choose not to read the score out loud, if you ignore sounding out each line of the song I have provided, you will have a visual experience of my inscription of Al-Qadiri's composition. You will glance at the repetition of shapes and the inaudible symbols. You will tilt your neck and rotate the page. You will imagine a spatial flow of beats: continuity, break, flow, rupture, glitch. While my inscription is far from a score that can faithfully recreate the song, it does allow for a visual spatialization of her music. For the visual reader, I have included symbols that remain inaudible if you were to sound out the score. Symbols are indeed closer to capturing the untranslatability of music into words. They allow for improvisation with spatial and temporal configurations. They withhold the promise of bringing music to the page. They refuse fidelity and urge sensational intrigue and experimentation.

I hesitate to present metaphors for what I hear in Al-Qadiri's composition. Yet, within the practice of ekphrasis, the orator is free to develop a narrative, or even a distinct plot, from the painted image. If I were to follow suit, I would describe Al-Qadiri's composition as an action. I would say something akin to: *The drum beats at equal intervals urging forward the limbs of a thousand soldiers in tandem.* I would ask: *who is marching to the beat of this drum?*, prompting you to imagine a battlefield. I would say: *The drone hums in search of its target broken every so often by a brass piston firing at its aim.* Such a description would bring an interpretive angle to the music. While the soldiers and the aerial weapons are not present in the song, they are sonically available for extrapolation. The drums of a marching band, the monotonous hum and the sharp intensity of a brass instrument's pitch can be elaborated into an active plot.

The military scene I have presented you with here is not arbitrary. I was led into its semantic specificity through the titles provided by Al-Qadiri for each composition and the album at large. The tracklist for the EP *Desert Strike* is as follows: (1) "Ghost Raid"; (2) "Oil Well"; (3) "War Games"; (4) "Desert Strike"; (5) "Hydra." This list of track names provides a framework for an unfolding narrative across the sonic undulations of the EP. It tells the tale of raids and war games across a desert landscape rich with oil wells. The title song, "Desert Strike," aptly conveys a historical continuity between digging, extractive efforts to "strike" oil, and the military strikes on the desert raided for its resources. The titles provide a narrative flow, a temporal and historical progression that link the oil-bearing desert environment to the war games that follow. The final track on the album, titled "Hydra," is described by the artist as a song that "reminds us of a vast, toxic horizon revived by streams of liquid life."[1] This final song looks ahead into the future. It imagines a time as yet unreached. It looks toward a future moment of revival, when water flows across a landscape strewn with industrial debris and toxic waste in the aftermath of military-extractive practices.

Desert Strike

For Al-Qadiri, the framework for this epic narrative stretching across centuries and potentially millennia into the future is a video game after which she names her album. *Desert Strike: Return to the Gulf* is a Gulf War–era video game released in 1992 by the California-based gaming company Electronic Arts. The game is a thinly veiled scene of battle between US soldiers and the then Iraqi president Saddam Hussein dubbed "General Kilbaba." The game is a pixelated aerial view of a golden desert landscape adjacent to a blue stretch of water (figures 9.1–9.5). Warplanes and helicopters lift

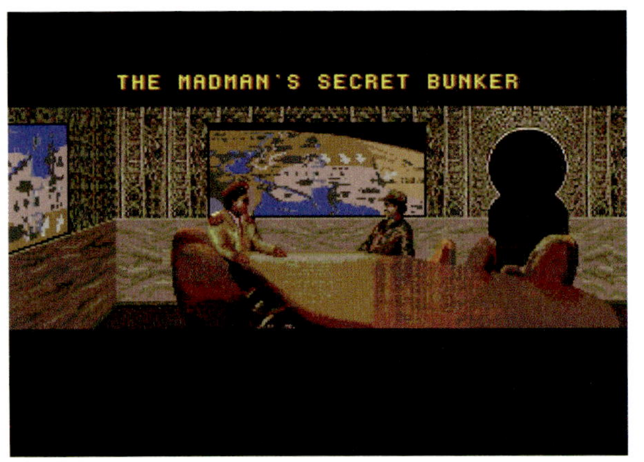

THE MADMAN'S SECRET BUNKER

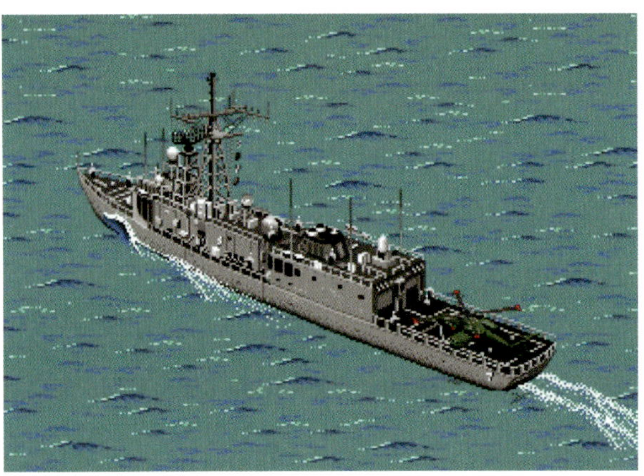

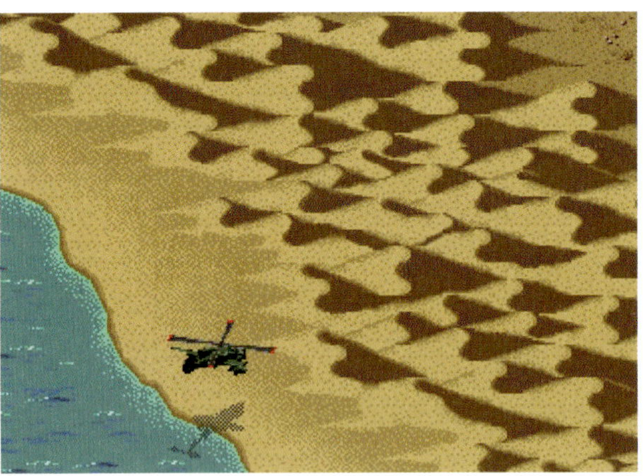

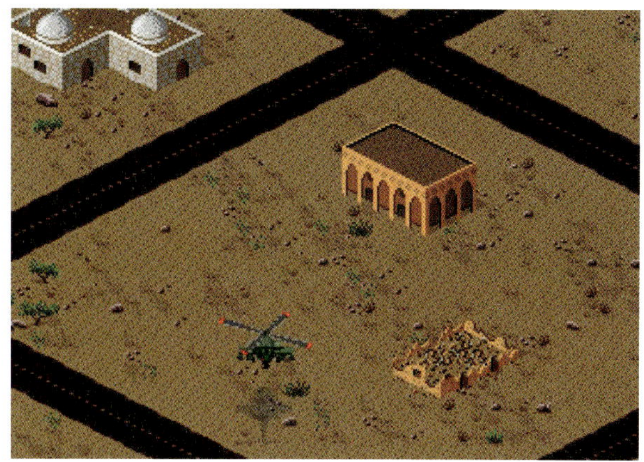

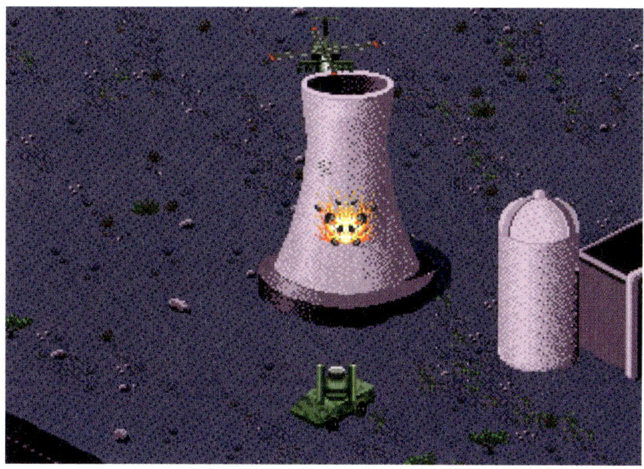

FIGURES 9.1–9.5 The video game *Desert Strike: Return to the Gulf* is a thinly veiled scene of battle between US soldiers and the then Iraqi president Saddam Hussein, dubbed "General Kilbaba." Stills from the game released by Electronic Arts, 1992.

off from military ships sailing in the choppy waves of the gulf. The land is strewn with oil refineries, nuclear power plants, hut encampments, watch towers, and a palatial residence surrounded by green gardens and arched structures reminiscent of Muslim architecture. Hovering above this landscape is a military helicopter whose point of view we are obliged to share as gamers. The action is provided by orange pixels shooting (da da da da da) from the helicopter's nozzle at the elements below. Each item on the ground struck by pixelated fires from the helicopter explodes into a grey cloud. Destroyed infrastructures and habitats disappear from the desert, leaving no residue but a gaping hole into the landscape.

The soundscape of the game is dominated by the propelling rotor blades of a helicopter and bullets firing at the structures below. The opening song, that gets repeated at the conclusion of every level of the game, is a multilayered digital composition with a fast, energizing beat. These are moments when the rationale for the war game is explained to the gamer on the screen. "Terrorist leader General Kilbaba," the game announces in a blinking yellow font dramatically lit against a black background, "stuns the world when he invades a small but wealthy Arab empire and takes over." The beat reaches a crescendo as General Kilbaba is shown capturing his opponents, hanging them on ropes, and descending their bodies into a barrel of boiling water. These scenes of torture build the ire of the gamer whose anger is celebrated by the music's intensity. We see General Kilbaba plotting the destruction of the world and journalists reporting on his evil plans. These scenes are accompanied by instructive vignettes where an officer in the US Army urges the gamer/pilot to "save the world from a psycho madman." These brief textual narrations provide a generalized political plot for the Gulf War. They tell the story of the ideological mission of the US military to "save the world" by intervening in Saddam Hussein's advances into Kuwait.

The game's cursory lessons in transnational politics match its crude aesthetic qualities. Visually, the game builds its scenes out of overlapping shades of colored pixels. Human figures seen from the gamer/pilot's point of view are blurry dots stretching out at intervals to form limbs that move the figure in various directions. Their actions are mechanical and repetitive. These digital figures are not individuated but are parts in a series of elements. All human characters, for instance, appear to be the same size, and all huts and fort structures are replicas of one another. The game's sonic composition follows a similar formal characteristic, where sounds of war are abstracted into beats. Throughout the game, synthetic noise is repeated at intervals, breaking up the cheer of victory with instrumental blasts that convey bombardments and explosions.

These minimalist visual and sonic informatics, that have since characterized video game aesthetics, are integral to the game's logic. Video games provide coarse outlines within their visual, sonic, and narrative structures so as to convey the "play" nature of their interface. In game studies, the lack of sharpness in video games follows the logical necessities of any game where a cardboard box can stand in for a fort and a stick can double as a horse. As David Myers explains it, "All forms of play transmit a self-referential message: 'this is play,' or, alternatively, 'this is not real.'"[2]

Yet, the formal and conceptual pixilation at play in video games also speaks to the political economy of gaming. The aesthetic qualities of *Desert Strike*'s digital interface present war as a game. With its reduction of complex transnational relations into "saving the world from a madman," the abstraction of sensory violence caused by explosives and artillery into a digital melody, and the diminishing of living organisms and their habitats into targeted outlines, the game simplifies lived relations into arbitrary rules and algorithms.

In her influential study *The Age of the World Target*, Rey Chow has elaborated upon the visual flattening of war into an image facilitated by the ocular-centric perspective of aerial bombing. She has argued that the development of aerial bombing is part of a process of flattening the world into an image with maximum visibility for targeted military practice. She writes, "In the age of bombing, the world has also been transformed into—is essentially conceived and grasped as—a target. To conceive of the world as a target is to conceive of it as an object to be destroyed."[3] This relationship to the world-as-target is heightened and facilitated by video games, which aesthetically reduce and simplify people and places into objects to be destroyed

Futurist Noise

Fatima Al-Qadiri was ten years old when the video game *Desert Strike* was released in 1992. The artist recounts a tale of her childhood encounter with the game at a time when populations living in Kuwait were experiencing massive "aerial bombings, air raid sirens and skies filled with smoke from black oil fires."[4] Al-Qadiri notes that in the midst of wartime violence, she and her sister Monira took refuge in play, developing an obsession with the video game *Desert Strike*.[5] Did the ten-year-old Al-Qadiri and her sister actually play the very game developed in California to parody their experiences as children during the Gulf War in the 1990s? Or was it the artist's later encounter with the game that prompted her to reimagine a scenario where two children living in Kuwait would play a game designed to develop their habitat as a target and subject to massive destruction? While the temporality of Al-Qadiri's encounter with the game is not the pressing issue here, it raises questions about the role of aesthetics in conceptualizing violence. How does Al-Qadiri's EP formulate an aesthetic encounter with the violence she, and her family, experienced in her childhood? How does her album reckon with the already existing aestheticization of her experience by game developers in pixels and digital sounds?

Central to Al-Qadiri's compositions on her EP is the use of noise: processed sound, repeated digital glitches, jarring overlays. These compositional techniques produce interruptions, rhythmic distortions, harmonic delays, and durational static that register as noise. "Noise," writes Steve Goodman, is "understood as intrinsically radical, as that which lies outside music."[6] Noise begins when music ends. It scratches and distorts meaning. Noise, Goodman continues, "is understood as a cultural weapon that attacks musical codes and networks in an audiosocial warfare of aesthetics."[7] We hear noise when sounds fail to follow a rhythm or semantic logic. Noise appears when communication breaks down and when we are recipients of unwanted sounds. In Goodman's assessment, the experience of noise is one of assault, one that signals "destruction, disorder, dirt, pollution,"[8] and an aggression toward aesthetic harmony.

Al-Qadiri's compositions utilize aesthetics of noise and its assault on the senses. She builds with noise to affectively wound the listener with sound and to iterate senselessness. It is perhaps the arbitrariness of war that registers as noise for civilians. After all, what is it other than noise that brings opaque political speeches and violent maneuvers to cities across the world? What other than noise can describe the complete transformation of urban settings—with their daily ambience of commerce, construction, congregation and commute—into zones of conflict? Aesthetically, noise is one way of sensing the sudden toll of sirens breaking the clamor of shopkeepers running to take refuge in a basement underground. Noise is one way to experience the senselessness of witnessing bombs falling onto schools, mosques, and hospitals on any given day. Noise is what is blurted out of the radio, the television, and other news outlets in the aftermath of explosions, justifying their continuous occurrence.

Noise is also one of the most effective ways of bringing war to a listener due to the crucial role that listening plays in zones of conflict. The experience of aerial bombardment that Al-Qadiri engages with is one where sound is the primary mode of apprehension. In times of war, civilians take refuge in bunkers and underground sanctuaries where warplanes are out of sight. Sonic and vibrational experiences of bombs dropped into the air get through these protective walls. Civilians sense the force of bombs releasing and exploding at various intervals. They hear artilleries of defense shooting up into the sky and sirens going off in the distance. Al-Qadiri's aural presentation of aerial bombardment is apt precisely because it proceeds from a phenomenological relationship to waves and airborne sounds that register as noise on the body.

The formal use of noise in Al-Qadiri's EP is also an intervention into a longer history of noise within aesthetic production. Using noise as an affront to an audience was prevalent in futurist, dada, and surrealist movements. Among these, the Italian futurists were the earliest artists to build a sonic engagement with aerial bombardment. Witnessing the weaponization of technological innovations by the military, Italian futurists issued a demand for artists to become physically incorporated into wartime aesthetics. The poet and author of the *Manifesto of Futurism* (1909), Filippo Tommaso Marinetti, proposed that artists (such as poets, performers, and musicians) were "supposed to receive and transmit vibrationally, to become a wireless observer of the grand panorama of the battlefield."[9] As Douglas Kahn explains it, Marinetti "had witnessed the first use of air-planes in modern warfare, and it was the whirling propeller of an airplane that had 'taught' him the destruction of syntax."[10] Faced with aerial conflict, Marinetti had proposed a physical transformation of the artist's body and its senses into an instrument of war. What else could an artist do than to be a transmitter of war's vibrational energies? What other vocabularies could an artist use when the latest technologies of destruction were the loudest instruments at work?

Rather than resisting the war's assault on the senses, the futurists proposed joining the war efforts, channeling its destructive energies into their artistic output. "Divert the canals so they can flood the museums!" Marinetti declared in his manifesto: "Oh, what a pleasure it is to see those revered old canvases, washed out and tattered, drifting away in the water! . . . Grab your picks and your axes and your hammers and then demolish, pitilessly demolish, all veered cities!"[11] Not only are these commands fired off at quick speed (Boom! Boom! Boom!), they order artists to do their part to destroy towns and with it their histories, cultures, and aesthetic productions. In this vision, artists are conduits of war. Their actions are in accordance with its destructive force, their speech is muddled with its commands, and their bodies vibrate in tandem with its violent force. It is in this context that Walter Benjamin condemned the futurists for their fascist politics. "'Fiat ars—pereat mundus [create art—destroy the world]' says Fascism," Benjamin declared, "and, as Marinetti admits, expects war to supply the artistic gratification of a sense perception that has been changed by technology."[12] For Benjamin, aestheticizing the technological assault of war on the senses was the height of fascism. Noise, in the context of Italian futurism, was not in defiance of established logics but an affirmation of state violence.

Italian futurism's engagement with aerial bombardment coincided with the Italo-Turkish War of 1911–1912, which historically is the very first military experiment with aerial combat. As a precursor to World War I, Italy declared war on the Ottoman Empire and occupied Tripolitania in modern-day Libya.[13] The Italian army dropped grenades, marking it the first recorded bombing on a town from above. From the start, aerial bombings were dropped on civilian populations, damaging buildings and military hospitals.[14] Marinetti's *Manifesto of Futurism* is clear about the orientalist specificity of the war on Muslim populations in North Africa. His text sets the scene in the very first few lines:

> My friends and I had stayed up all night, sitting beneath the lamps of a mosque, whose star-studded, filigreed brass domes resembled our souls, all aglow with the concerted brilliance of an electric heart. For many hours, we'd been trailing our age-old indolence back and forth over richly adorned, oriental carpets, debating at the uttermost boundaries of logic and filing up masses of paper with our frantic writing. Immense pride filled our hearts for we felt that at that hour we alone were vigilant and unbending, like magnificent beacons or guards in forward positions, facing an army of hostile stars, which watched us closely from their celestial encampments.[15]

Futurism is here declared as a movement consolidated "beneath the lamps of a mosque" and upon "richly adorned, oriental carpets." Marinetti presents the enemy's encampment as studded with the "stars" of the Ottoman flag. Standing at the front lines, the artist/soldiers are witnesses to the transformation of their own bodies into machineries with "electric hearts." As they continue to speak, their discussions become irrational, reaching "the uttermost boundaries of logic." Their texts become illegible, "filling up masses of paper with [their] frantic writing." Within these very introductory lines to the manifesto, Marinetti provides a vivid image for the Italian futurists' dissolution into senselessness. Noise here is an attack against the Muslim Ottomans of North Africa. Italian futurism presents an image of an artist who is plugged in, electrified, and transformed into a machine gun (da da da), spewing glowing bullets at the enemy.

Gulf Futurism

Much like visual technologies, such as the camera, electronic music has its genealogical origins in warfare. "Sound," Roshanak Kheshti writes, was "the ideal medium for covert surveillance and intelligence-gathering" in the first half of the twentieth century. "The unexpected result," she continues, "was electronic instrumentation."[16] Al-Qadiri's use of electronic music to render the sounds of war indexes the production of commercial technologies developed by the military. How can we account for not only the militarized histories of electornic music but also the racialized and militarized history of futurism as an artistic movement that precedes Al-Qadiri's interest in futurism? How do we study her cultural production within a lineage that has supported aerial bombardment on Muslim populations in Ottoman North Africa? It is indeed only against this historical background that we can fully engage the political resonance of Al-Qadiri's intervention into futurist aesthetics. In the larger context of her work, Al-Qadiri has engaged futurism head on. In an article cowritten with the artist Sophia Al-Maria, the artists describe the Persian/Arab Gulf region as the site of "Gulf Futurism."[17] The term "Gulf Futurism" describes the rapid urban development and technological enhancements brought about through petroleum economies that have led to cultural and environmental transformation. The Gulf, explain the artists, "has been hyperdriven into a present made up of interior wastelands, municipal master plans and environmental collapse, thus making it a projection of our global future."[18] "Over the past fifty years," the artists continue, "the Arabian Gulf has given to a very particular brand of futurism."[19]

Unlike Italian futurism, Gulf Futurism does not join the progressive, developmentalist futures of machines, metals, and monetary gain. Instead, Gulf Futurism indexes a "global future" that has already arrived in the Gulf. This is a future in which wastelands and depleted resources form the backdrop to unsustainable development and class stratification.[20] Italian futurism—coined a century prior to Gulf Futurism—advocated for the military/industrial project believing that the future was fast, sleek, armed, and armored. Gulf Futurism is the inheritor of that future. It is the aftermath of its dreary visions. Gulf Futurism is a present in which land and water have been shafted with metals. It is a present in which fossils have been extracted, habitats consumed and then bombed and burned into ashes. Unlike Italian futurism, which stood on the side of the aggressor, Gulf Futurism lives in the midst and in the aftermath of hostilities. In the words of Al-Qadiri and Al-Maria, Gulf Futurism confronts "the isolation of individuals via technology, wealth and reactionary Islam, the corrosive elements of consumerism on the soul and industry on earth, the erasure of history from our memories and our surroundings and finally, our dizzying collective arrival in a future that no one was ready for."[21]

Al-Qadiri's EP is the soundscape of Gulf Futurism. While the focus of the EP is on our arrival into a bleak future imagined by the modernist past, it nevertheless looks forward to other possibilities. The final track titled "Hydra" performs a conceptual departure from earlier compositions that deal with military, gaming, and extractive activities in the desert. Rather than the aerial view of the gamer/bomber or that of the pumping jack piercing beneath the Earth's crust, "Hydra" provides us with a new agential force ushering us into the future. Here we are thinking and listening with water flowing across sand dunes in the desert. Gone are the mechanical sounds and movements of cameras, snipers, and drills rotating in their metallic sockets. In this final track, the encounter is between water and sand dissolving into one another. "Hydra" presents us with a fluidity that is conceptually not present in the other tracks.

Thinking with water opens up new possibilities for sonic engagement. Water, after all, is a medium that muffles sound, making it hard for airwaves to vibrate our ear drums when we are immersed.[22] Water can protect us from noise. It can cushion our ears. Unlike the previous tracks on her album, such as "Desert Strike" or "War Games," the final track avoids the piercing sounds of explosions or the high-pitched bleeps of video games. "Hydra" is instead a slower track made mostly out of stretched sound waves that undulate and drag on. This being said, Al-Qadiri utilizes the same digital elements and sonic effects heard throughout the EP to create this flow. While "Hydra" introduces a conceptual departure from the previous compositions, it nevertheless remains within the same sonic repertoire as the rest of the EP. This is perhaps one way in which Al-Qadiri avoids sounding a utopian future that is removed from the realities of the present. Instead, she creates a coherent flow between our current processes of desertification and a rehydrated future to come. Rather than wishing for a radically different future that bears no resemblance to the present, the final song is a sonic continuation of our current moment and its material conditions.

One of the most interesting aspects of "Hydra" is its ability to calibrate our ears to the more fluid sounds in previous tracks that we might have previously missed. Every time I listen to the entire EP, I find myself looping back to the beginning to hear resonances of "Hydra" already present in layered rhythms of other songs. This exercise of relistening urges me to question the static nature of sound. If my own listening experience can change each time I listen to the record, how can listening be anything but dynamic across different auditors? Al-Qadiri's EP is indeed an invitation to consider the great diversity of listening practices. Her EP, after all, is presenting us with sounds of war as digital melodies. She is inviting us to listen to aerial bombardments through the ears of two ten-year-old girls lost in a video game. Her compositions lead us to consider listening as a performance, one that is acutely engaged with our environment and one that is subject to change and mutation across various bodies and listening practices.

Al-Qadiri's recalling of the sounds of war as musical compositions brings me to ask: What do civilians hear when they live in war zones and when their daily lives are punctuated by loud, screeching, buzzing, or humming sounds? In his ethnographic study of the sonic landscape of wartime Iraq, J. Martin Daughtry describes what an Iraqi dentist he names Tareq heard on a daily basis. Living in Sadr City in 2006, Tareq explains developing an expert knowledge of the range of sounds that he and his mother heard in their neighborhood.[23] Due to long exposures to sounds of gunfire, Tareq and his mother were able to distinguish between Iraqi and American snipers. In his description, Tareq likens the repetitive shots of the automatic rifle AK-47 to the Bedouin drum, the *zanbur*, noting the symphonic quality of their simultaneous and repetitive firings.[24] For Tareq and his mother, the battlefield was daily transformed into a symphonic orchestra led by *zanbur* players beating their drums. The two listeners became artists in their own right, arranging the noise of the battlefield into rhythmic compositions.

This form of deep listening performed by Tareq and his mother is the basis of any mode of creative practice in which the quotidian—or even the violent in the case at hand—become aesthetic. Daughtry offers the term *listening-as-poiesis* to describe this semantic conversion of instruments of violence into pleasurable symphonic performances outside the window in wartime Iraq. "This act of listening-as-compositions, of listening-as-poiesis," he writes, is "evidence of the resilience of wartime auditors, and their ability to cobble together some measure of agency within an extreme environment of violence."[25]

I want to take Daughtry's analysis further and add that listening-as-poiesis is an aesthetic act of production. It is a listening practice in which the auditor makes something entirely new than what was intended by the ambient sound's producer. "Poiesis," with its Greek root in the verb "to make," is about the creative act of bringing something into the world. Listening-as-poiesis, which I see at play in Al-Qadiri's compositions, is an agential participation in an event that may not have us in mind or may have even been actively orchestrated against our existence and well-being. Al-Qadiri's musical compositions are poetic renditions of strikes (both military and extractive) upon the desert. I have in turn made my own poetic rendition in response to her music. My visual poem, shared in the opening pages of this chapter, results from my own deep listening, a listening-as-poiesis that brings her composition onto the page. While listening is often perceived as passive reception, listening-as-poiesis turns listening into sound, both musical and textual.

I noted at the outset that art history provides ekphrasis as a literary device for engaging artworks. While writing remains the main medium through which art historians engage with artworks, we know that something (the aura, affect or aesthetic quality of the artwork) always escapes the written form. Michael Ann Holly puts it well when she writes,

> No matter how tangled and well-researched the web of words of those who write about art weave around a past work, something about it will always and forever resist capture. Its very autonomy ensures the pictorial that it will forever escape, even defy, textual delineation. Art historians know it, we feel it, but we choose very often to ignore it in the face of other kinds of knowledge.[26]

While Holly's concern is with the pictorial, the same is true of the sonic (along with other artistic media). There is always an excess that exceeds, or "will always and forever resist capture" by the written form. Yet, we can also rethink art history not as an attempt to "capture" a work of art—be it its aesthetic quality, political meaning or historical context—but rather as a practice of listening-as-poiesis, whereby we create our own artworks in poetic, visual or theoretical forms. I engage in this practice throughout the book, where I offer drawings and prose poems as a methodology of theorizing with artworks.

My relationship with Al-Qadiri's musical composition also exceeds my position as an art historian. I share with her the experience of aerial bombardments as a child, arriving at her work as someone practiced in the art of listening-as-poiesis in make-shift shelters during the Iran-Iraq War. "The Glass Shattered at My Feet" and "Shelter" (appearing in part 1 of this book) are two prose-poetics of listening to the embodied knowledges of that child, the wartime auditor.

Sounding the Terracene

In the vicinity of a battlefield, explosions can be too dangerous to hear. Their force and intensity create acoustic shockwaves too hazardous for our ears' soft tissues to handle. Curtis Roads has called such sounds "*perisonic* intensities (from the Latin *periculos* meaning 'dangerous')."[27] These are sounds that fall outside of our audible capacities. What civilians can and do hear in battlefields are at a much greater distance. "Very loud sounds (such as atmospheric thunder and other explosions)," Roads notes, "travel far."[28] These are sounds that reach our ears as low frequencies, as rumbling noise of what has struck at some distance away from where we stand. Al-Qadiri's compositions, have multiple sequences consisting of low-frequency drawls. The track "Oil Well," for instance, begins with the noise of a loud explosion but continues in prolonged drones that are punctured by sharp beats. Such sequences, that are consistent throughout her EP, urge us to ask what it is that we are hearing. Are these the sounds of explosions at an oil well? Are these thunderclaps? Are we hearing the noise of a dry desert cracking open under the baking sun? Are these bombshells snapping open in midair? Are these sounds of oil pumping out? Or are we hearing a rush of water streaming in to replace petroleum's viscous absence in bedrock?

These questions are difficult to answer because much of what happens underground, above us in the sky, or around us in our environment can be inaudible to us. We do not know what petroleum formation in bedrock sounds like. We hear thunder when clouds clash, when, in Karen Barad's words, "tenuous electrical sketches scribbled with liquid light appear/disappear faster than the human eye can detect."[29] Yet, we cannot hear clouds outside of their dramatic performances. We cannot hear them roll softly in the wind across the sky. We cannot hear the sun rise and set or earthquakes shake as a result of tectonic movements under our feet. Some sounds are too light for us to catch, such as a "caterpillar's delicate march," in Road's words "across a leaf."[30] Others are too vast, too slow or too fast, with frequencies beyond our timescale, for us to perceive.

Despite their imperceptibility, such sounds have been made audible and aestheticized by musicians and scientists alike. We know, for instance, of the American psychoacoustician Sheridan Dauster Speeth who developed a method for listening to earthquakes that differentiated them from atomic bombs.[31] Using digital technologies in the 1960s, Speeth trained musicians to listen to earthquakes attentively and to distinguish between the energy released in the lithosphere that moves the earth and those caused by nuclear testing.[32] Did earthquakes and nuclear explosions sound alike? People experiencing earthquakes have described them in many different ways. Some have likened earthquakes to a "deep booming noise, a dull heavy rumble, a grating roaring noise, or a deep groan or moan";[33] others have experienced them as a "fall of heavy bodies, the banging of a door, the blow of a sea wave on the shore";[34] yet others have drawn similarities between earthquakes and bombs, presenting the sensation of an earthquake to "explosions, distant blasting, the boom of a distant canon."[35] These descriptions aestheticize sounds that are barely audible. An earthquake can very well be an explosion or it can be waves crashing onto the shore.

While sound plays a significant role in the similarities people have drawn between earthquakes and explosions, it is no less important to consider vibrational movements felt by the body that are foundational to sonic experiences. Sound, as Nina Sun Eidsheim has aptly proposed, is "merely a trope" through which vibrational experiences are described.[36] This is not to say that sound does not exist but that it is only one way in which embodied pulsations are conceptualized. "Sound," Shelley Trower writes, is "a way of making manifest for the senses those vibrations that exist beyond the limits of sensitivity."[37] We use the figure of sound to convey the tremor of our limbs in the aftermath of an earthquake or when we are in proximity of an explosion. These are sensations more felt than heard. Seismic events run through our bones vibrating our organs and limbs. The ears are one site through which such vibrational experiences are registered on our senses.

In light of such vibrational overlaps between explosive and ecological experiences, I am fascinated by Al-Qadiri's attention to the intersection of war and petroleum extraction in her album. While she borrows the title of her EP from a video game, *Desert Strike* is semantically layered in the context of her work. The word *strike* has a dual meaning merging the geological setting of the Persian Gulf states with perpetual war that their underground fossils have enabled. The very puncture that found the earth to be rich with oil is repeated as air strikes drill further holes across oil fields. Her track "Oil Well" holds these tensions together. Composed as an undulating rhythm moving at the pace of a pumping jack, the song is punctuated by interruptions filled with explosions and sounds of coins being cashed in. These disparate layers of sound convey complex historical transactions that circulate around oil, money, and warfare.

Yet sound is only one way in which Al-Qadiri's music can be described. As an artist, she is attentive to vibrational dimensions of her practice and is known for sharing her music at clubs and on the dance floor. Clubs are indeed one place in which shaking, quaking, and pulsations are exaggerated within the architectural setting. "We can feel, hear and see a subwoofer vibrate," Trower writes, "and see its effects on other bodies or matter."[38] Our feet shake as they come into contact with the floorboards and our hands tremble as they lean against the walls of the club. Mirrors quiver, reflecting our blurred visions of ourselves back to us. Drinks spill. Bottles wobble and fall off the stage, shattering onto the dance floor. These are multisensorial dimensions of acoustic experience that register on our bodies. When Al-Qadiri plays her compositions at a club, she performs music as vibration. Here explosions move bodies huddled together as they do when civilians take shelter in basements. Walls shake and floors move as they do when a warplane goes by overhead. These vibrational experiences are energetic transformations of effected bodies and a reliving in the present of historical events.

I wonder, as I listen to Al-Qadiri's album, if what she has composed is the sounds of the Terracene. In Al-Qadiri's album, I hear sonic engagement with the Terracene at an aesthetic level. Her work moves our bodies in vibrations the way an earthquake would. It moves us the way an explosion would. The sensational palimpsest does not prompt us to parse out a cause for the vibrational sensations we feel. We are unclear whether it was an explosion at an oil rig, a bomb, or a seismic event that is referenced in her music. Yet, it is the overlay and accumulation of these events that are addressed to our senses, allowing us to confront our immediate being in the world.

10

Shelter

He is standing on the balcony. A pious man. Hi *aba* brown: a single cloth hanging long off his shoulders with two slits cut wide for his arms to slip through. He is a man of few words. His deep voice heard on occasion muffled under his breath, often in disdain expressing displeasure at the world. He stands with his voice caught in his throat in the dark night. No light but the faint rays of the moon traveling eons to reach the ridge of his brows.

Allah-O-Akbar professes a neighbor's voice echoing the chorus of *Allah-O-Akbars* dancing in the air.

Allah-O-Akbar

I want to join that chorus but I have no words at three years of age. Instead, I huddle in the basement with my elbows wrapped around my knees at the feet of more sensible adults, too young to gamble their lives away for the collective will of the Iranian people.

This war has no will.

Yet, he stands on the balcony swaying to the beat of *Allah-O-Akbar*.

How long can I hold my breath without asphyxiating? I entertain myself with this thought as we await the sound of the siren that tells us it is safe to come out of our shelter in the basement.

In the early days of the Iran-Iraq War, people shared their theories on which architectural features best served as shelters. Find a sturdy column: it will hold you up when your spine wants to collapse one vertebra at a time.

Find the hollow triangle under a staircase: it will be your canopy when glass and cement churn together into paste at your feet.

Find a basement perfumed with pickles and jars of jam fermenting as a futurist gesture.

If homes were always shelters from the rain, they now became origami as clouds cried bullets.

The column. The staircase. The basement: architectures of care.

Within their embrace rests the privilege of potential survival.

And the balcony?

where he stands listening to the sounds of *Allah-O-Akbar*.

Is the balcony for the pious or the reckless? How to explain the refusal to take shelter when the siren blurts out from the radio, the television, and the neighborhood mosque announcing with a prerecorded message that the siren we currently hear is declaring a state of emergency, meaning that you are to leave your current location and take shelter.

The embrace of the column, the staircase, and the basement is too cold for the pious, who dwell in the warmth of Allah's embrace.

Allah-O-Akbar

He called out his name.

11

Silence

First scene: She sits alone, anxious. She is tapping her foot on the ground. One hand holds her knee in place. The other hand flicks away a fly from her cheekbones. The paisley pattern on her scarf frames her face in shining silver. Her shoulders are rounded under her black veil that runs down to the ground to rest on her sandals. This woman's patient impatience is captured on screen in Werner Herzog's film *Lessons of Darkness* (1995) (figures 11.1 and 11.2). The film documents Kuwaiti oil fields burning in orange flames. Field after field of oil were set on fire in 1991 by Iraqi military as a departing gift to advancing Coalition forces led by the United States entering Kuwait. This woman is the first local we meet in Herzog's film. She greets us in silence. She sits facing the camera but her eyes are averted for a long moment of quiet anticipation. A metal chair has been placed in the middle of a courtyard for her to take her seat before the camera. The wall

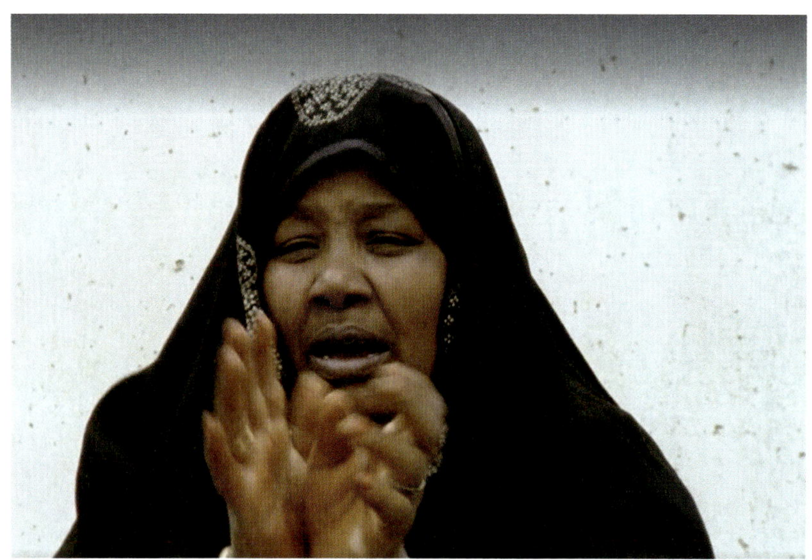

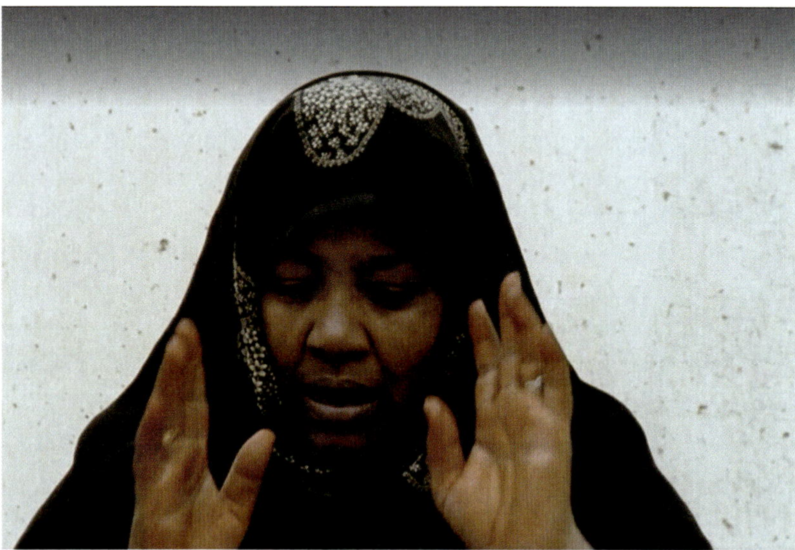

FIGURES 11.1 AND 11.2 She brings her inner wrists together, letting her palms fan out like a butterfly. Scene from *Lessons of Darkness*, dir. Werner Herzog, 1992.

behind her is chipped around patches of yellow and black mold. Pipes attach to a sink placed on the ground. Is this her house? Did she invite the camera crew into the courtyard of her home?

A voice-over, in the characteristic style of Herzog, assures us that the will of the camera is indeed matched by this woman's wish to speak. "We met a woman who wanted to tell us something," the voice-over begins: "She had been dragged away by soldiers along with her two grown sons and had to watch her two sons being tortured before her very eyes. This caused her to lose her speech. But she still tried to tell us what had happened." The camera's long shot that had framed her whole body in the courtyard now zooms onto her face. She communicates in her speechless speech by meeting the camera with gestures, with single words, with intonations. She furrows her brows and taps a finger to her upper lip. She brings her inner wrists together, letting her palms fan out like a butterfly. The context stops me from reading this gesture as a depiction of a bird in flight. Her palms are not winged creatures traveling up to the sky. Neither are they splayed out petals of a tulip bulb. She taps her wrists to convey just that—wrists coming together in a handcuff.

Her story rests heavy on her lips. She does not disclose it to us in any great detail. Her gesture of bringing her wrists together, which she repeats several times, is meant to convey the entire event. A handcuff was involved. We gather that much. Then she waves her hands away from her body. This is perhaps a motion of departure or walking away—handcuffed people going away. Her brief account, that repeats a few times, is each time concluded by a gesture up toward the sky. She looks up. "Ya Allah," she says and sends a kiss with her palms into the heavens. Her eyes guide us up, away from her, and into the sky. She brings her hands toward her temples, like a prayer, then holds one palm onto her chest. She leaves us at the end of her scene the same way she greeted us. She leaves us in silence.

Second scene: Another courtyard. Another woman. Kuwait. This woman is younger than the last one we met. She stands tall with a child draped over her shoulder. The child is two or three years old. He is silent. She is speaking in Arabic in a faint volume under Herzog's dubbed narrative. "Even the tears were black," he translates into English as she runs a finger from her eye down to her cheeks: "When my child wept his tears were black. When his nose ran it ran black. Even the spit in his mouth was black." She rubs the tips of her fingers together to give texture to the soot from the fires leaving their residue in her child's bodily fluids. She strokes her child's resting head against her shoulder. Herzog continues his dubbed narration of

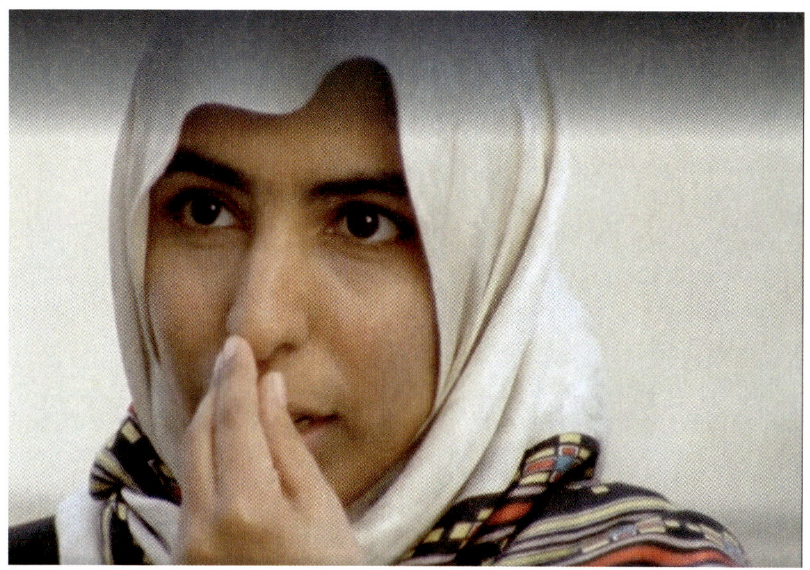

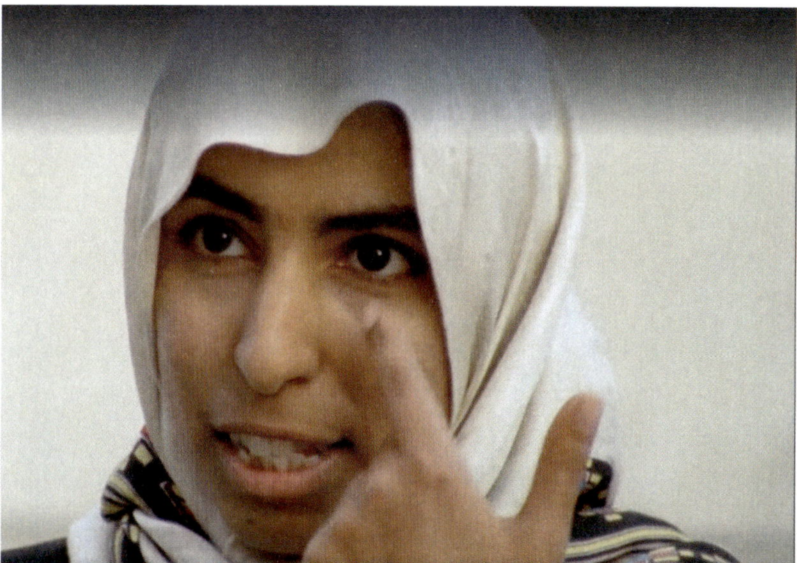

FIGURES 11.3 AND 11.4 "Even the tears were black," she says as she runs a finger from her eye down to her cheek. Scene from *Lessons of Darkness*, dir. Werner Herzog, 1992.

her story. A group of soldiers came into her house. One placed a boot on the child's head and squeezed. The child has since refused to speak. He has spoken once only to tell his mother that he does not want to talk anymore. He fidgets in his mother's arms and looks in silence at the camera (figures 11.3 and 11.4).

For the injured, the Terracene's sounds are muffled.

They get stuck in the ears and the throat.

The Terracene sinks into the ear drums, filling the ears' tubes and cavities.

The Terracene arrives at the larynx and the epiglottis.

It rests against the tongue.

The Terracene is loud.

The Terracene is silent.

Terran Deities

Oil, Fires, Fevers

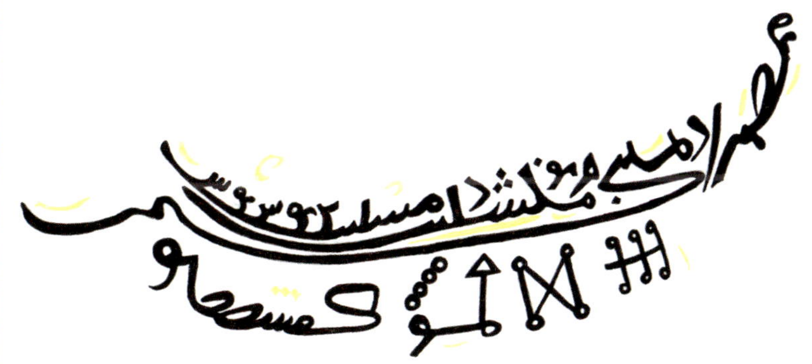

The Terracene requires that we think with ancestral knowledge. Some of these knowledges exist in ancient deities, who have protected, devoured, destroyed, or delivered life, disease, fires, earthquakes, floods, and cyclones. This part of the book is dedicated to ancient Mesopotamian deities: Lamassu, Huma, Homa, Pazuzu reanimated in the works of contemporary Iranian artists Morehshin Allahyari and Reza Negarestani and my own textual and visual conjurings. These deities appear here as creative and speculative knowledge-holders.

12

Lamassu

Monotheism has a long history of antagonism toward polytheistic deities. Islam's foundational stories speak of breaking idols purporting to be gods. Growing up Muslim, I learned about prophet Mohammad's heroic entrance into the Ka'ba in order to cleanse it of polytheistic idols. For many, this story has repeated itself numerous times over as contemporary expressions of Islam are performed through the destruction of statues representing polytheistic deities. One such instance occurred after the 2014 takeover of the city of Mosul in northern Iraq by ISIS (the Islamic State of Iraq and Syria) members, who disseminated audio-visual documentation of their entrance into several museums and heritage sites in order to topple, destroy, and deface sculptural objects.[1] As I discuss in more detail below, the international outcry regarding the ISIS destruction of sculptural objects revolved around the terror of Islam. The incident provided news outlets as well as cultural institutions, a renewed site for Islamophobic expressions. In these discussions, sculptural representations of ancient deities came to stand in for humanity at large—the unmarked Anthropos who needed to be defended and protected against Islamic violence.

The widespread appeals to protect museum and heritage objects in Iraq were based in long-standing institutional practices that believed in the removal of Mesopotamian deities from their sites for their protection. Archeological narratives represented such artifacts as part of a general human history rather than as sacred objects within specific cultural, religious, and historical practices. Outrage toward the toppling and defacing of museum artifacts failed to engage with conversations around decolonial struggles that questioned and resisted who such objects belonged to and what roles they performed in telling teleological histories of human civilizational developments. Struggles over Indigenous repatriations, historiography, and living practices were subsumed under broad institutional claims that purported to protect Mesopotamian artifacts as representative of human history at large.

In the following pages, I focus on the work of the Iranian American artist Morehshin Allahyari, whose research-based visual-arts practice offers renewed questions regarding conceptual, historical, and sacred roles that Mesopotamian deities perform in contemporary cultural life. Allahyari's practice offers creative, speculative histories based on oral and textual narratives that reorient our perspectives toward objects decontextualized within archeological and museological historiography. I situate Allahyari's work among others in this book, who mobilize history for anti-colonial ends. "Decolonization," Eve Tuck (Aleut) and K. Wayne Yang write, "brings about the repatriation of Indigenous land and life."[2] In their influential essay titled "Decolonization Is Not a Metaphor," Tuck and Yang urge us to refrain from using the notion of decolonization as anything other than ongoing Indigenous struggles for sovereignty, land claims, and repatriation.

I understand Allahyari's speculative historiography to be an anti-colonial practice for a number of reasons. First, much of her practice focuses on researching and understanding Mesopotamian deities who survive in sculptures, manuscript representations, and oral and textual cultures of the region. These are ancient deities who have come under erasure or who survive in syncretic religious forms. Allahyari's treatment is not to claim these deities as authentic signifiers of an untouched past but to engage them as part of living, present realities. Second, Allahyari recreates ancient

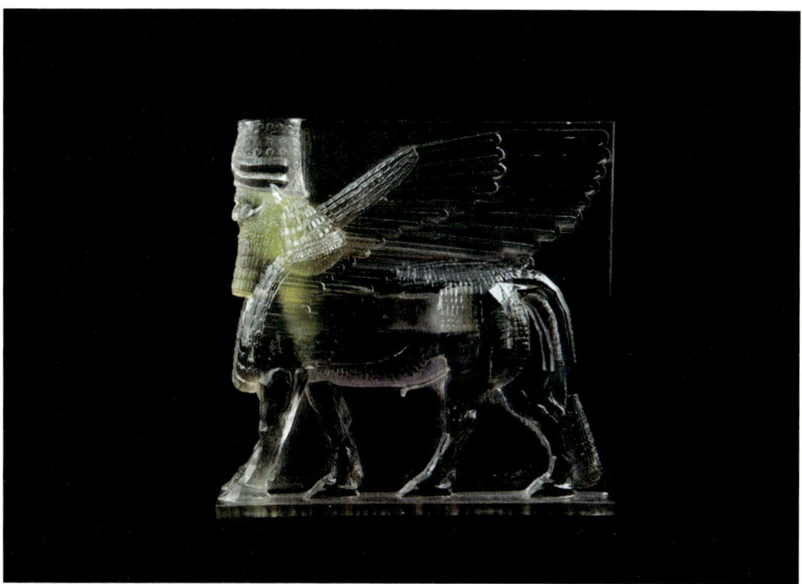

FIGURE 12.1 Looking at Lamassu's body closely, we can make out the contours of a winged bull with a lion's tail, who has fish scales on its chest and a bearded human head wearing a headdress wrapped with horns. Morehshin Allahyari, *Lamassu*, from the series *Material Speculation: ISIS*. 3D-printed resin and USB drive, 2015. Courtesy of Morehshin Allahyari.

Mesopotamian deities in 3D sculptural forms. Some of these have been destroyed by ongoing wars in the region. Others have long been removed and placed in museums in the Global North, whether in sculptural or flat representational forms within manuscripts. Allahyari's research and representation of these deities treat them as living culture, offering speculative historiography as a mode of engagement with cultural heritages that have become subsumed within archeological and museological narratives. I understand Allhayari's practice as one that reclaims material objects as well as histories, languages, and cosmologies that have come under violent colonial suppression. Artists such as Allahyari utilize archeological and museological records to not only critique the veracity of colonial histories but to offer alternate cosmologies and worldviews that enact and imagine anti- and decolonial futures.

In her sculptural series titled "Material Speculation," Allahyari creates 3D plastic replicas of ancient Mesopotamian deities that were destroyed by ISIS in 2014. Allahyari's replicas in this series belong to different periods in Iraq's history. They include, for example, a replica of the Assyrian deity Lamassu from the ancient city of Nineveh dating to the seventh century BC (figure 12.1), a winged Nike belonging to the Roman period of second century BC, and a priest holding an eagle from the city of Hatra dating to the first century AD. In order to create her replicas, the artist first digitally designs each destroyed object on her computer, based on found images prior to the object's destruction, then prints each figurine on a 3D printer. Once printed, each figurine is equipped with a memory card containing the artist's research, including historical information, provenance, maps, and email correspondence with art historians, archeologists, and staff at the Mosul Museum along with the video of their destruction circulated by ISIS members online.

The destruction of ancient Mesopotamian monuments by ISIS members in 2014 led to much upheaval globally and outraged calls for their protection. The director-general of the United Nations Educational, Scientific and Cultural Organization (UNESCO), Irina Bokova, initiated a social media campaign titled #Unite4Heritage, mobilizing scholars, archeologists, and historians to discuss the ramifications of the destruction of protected cultural-heritage sites in Iraq and Syria. In her opening remarks at a symposium on the topic held in Paris in 2015, she noted that "the attacks against Mesopotamia, which gave us writing, the wheel, the rule of law, are an attempt to obliterate the cradle of civilization and our common humanity."[3] Presenting ancient Mesopotamian Assyrian and Sumerian cultures as belonging to a "common humanity" was repeated by other archeological and art historical societies in the Global North. In Germany, a registered nonprofit organization known as Rashid International comprising international archeologists, cultural-heritage experts, and lawyers was instituted with the direct mission toward "research, assessment and safeguarding of the heritage of Iraq in danger."[4] As with UNESCO's invocation of a "common humanity" in relation to the region's ancient cultural production, Rashid International states, "Mesopotamia is more than a history of Iraq. Anyone who can read and write or who tills the soil, anyone who cherishes religion, practices law, or studies the stars owes a silent thanks to those who pioneered along the Euphrates."[5]

In the United States, the College Art Association released a statement in 2015 condemning the "senseless destruction" of ancient Assyrian sculptures, calling on transnational organizations to push for governmental protection of these monuments. They wrote,

The monumental works from this extraordinary ancient civilization had been preserved for over 2,500 years in one of the most important collections of Middle Eastern art, the Mosul Museum. CAA calls upon the Iraq and Unites States government as well as the ICOMOS, the World Monuments Fund and other international organizations to adhere to Hague Convention (1954), in concert with the public and the scholarly community, to develop and implement programs to protect ancient sites, monuments, antiquities, and cultural institutions in the case of war.[6]

These recent reclamations of Ancient Mesopotamia as the cultural heritage of humanity at large echoes ongoing reactions to cultural destructions in Iraq since the beginning of the Iraq War in 2003. For 2014 was, of course, not the first time that Assyrian, Sumerian, and Babylonian cultures had come under attack by ISIS. Indeed, the start of the Iraq War was marked by the massive burning of Iraqi national libraries and archives at various sites that not only turned some of the oldest records of human history into ashes but destroyed books and manuscripts documenting Baghdad's place as a major cultural center of the Arab world. Writing in 2006, American Studies scholar Wai Chee Dimock sounded a similar call for governmental protection of cultural sites, arguing that the lack of interest on the part of US-led coalition forces to preserve Iraqi cultural heritage had something to do with the status of the United States as a young nation. "The Coalition forces had in facji

t been protecting a number of selective sites, notably oilfields," she wrote, "but buildings housing ancient manuscripts were not on that valued list."[7] For Dimock, this negligence stemmed from the US military's inability to think beyond the national framework of a young nation for whom the span of time traversed in these records were simply unintelligible. In Dimock's assessment, the priorities of the marines would have been different had they seen these cultures as their own. Military personnel would have felt differently about the sites they watched burn to the ground had they considered the dense patterns of migration and settlements that connected human lives on the planet in overlapping circles of relations over long periods of time, a form of connectivity Dimock terms "deep time."[8]

Dimock's notion of deep time was in conversation with the emergent Anthropocene discourse in the early 2000s, a discourse that offered ancient Mesopotamia (where agriculture first emerged) as a key player in the development of anthropogenic climate change.[9] Dimock's theorization of deep time is an important move beyond nationalist historiography, holding us accountable to "phenomena with an extended life, longer than the life span of any biological individual."[10] Yet, despite her attempt to go beyond nationalist histories, Dimock holds onto protectionist narratives with which humanity at large and its cultural heritage are to be protected by the US military. Even as she offers the concept of deep time to "propose an extended duration" that is "planetary in scope," her examples are limited to placing recorded human histories in relation to one another.[11] This mode of argumentation not only centers an "Anthropos" in the form of a "common humanity" but undermines the terror of the Anthropos in the form of destructive military presence in war zones. Calling on the US military to protect the lands it has come to destroy overlooks the ongoing violence wherein attacks on heritage sites are only a momentary spectacle. Such calls for protection echo the succession of figures whose protection have justified the war on terror (a list most often including women, homosexuals, children, liberty, democracy, borders, etc.). Obscured under this cacophony is the fallacy of protection itself that works to incite further antagonism.

Here, I want to propose that the material objects from ancient Mesopotamia that have initiated calls for militarized protectionism have their own stories to tell, which can move us far beyond protectionist narratives we have heard thus far. As various Indigenous studies scholars and cultural thinkers have reminded us, what comes to be understood as "artifact," "museum object," or "heritage site" within settler-colonial, colonial, and imperial legacies are in fact sacred and vibrant actors in living relations with dispossessed peoples. In the words of Kim TallBear, "reference to indigenous thought by other traditions as 'beliefs' or artifacts of a waning time to be studied but not interacted with as truths about a living world—all of this is to deny our vibrancy."[12] When we look at Assyrian deities—such as Lamassu replicated by Allahyari (figure 12.1)—as silent relics of a bygone era in need of protection by UNESCO, international organizations, or the US military, we overlook and deny the presence of living knowledge-systems that continue to instruct and be vibrant in our lives today.

What would it mean to think with Lamassu, a protective deity within Assyrian and Persian oral and textual narratives? When not housed in a museum, Lamassu is a figure that stands tall at entrances to buildings, gates, or cities within ancient urban and architectural planning.[13] Looking at Lamassu's body closely, we can make out the contours of a winged bull with a lion's tail, who has fish scales on its chest and a bearded human head wearing a headdress wrapped with horns. Archeologists have surmised, based on Assyrian texts, that this hybrid, multispecies figure was a female deity named Lamassu, which translates into "vital strength."[14] Based on its semantic analysis, as well as its repeated appearance at gates and entrances in Assyrian and Persian sites, Lamassu has been interpreted as having had an apotropaic and protective role, "a benevolent spirit attached to an individual, a group, or a place."[15]

How might we interpret the notion of "protection" in this context? Does Lamassu's role as a protective deity offer nuance onto recent calls for her protection outlined above? What would protection mean if we did not engage Lamassu as an inanimate ancient artifact of a bygone era but a "vital strength" present and active today? Archeologists argue that Lamassu deities flanked entrances in order to "protect access."[16] They see these figures as guards, exerting masculinist strength to protect borders and to securitize a structure or a place. Such interpretations rely on preconceived beliefs in nation-state boundaries and a necessity for their securitization through force. I would ask: Are we not limiting our imagination when we automatically assume that all mighty figures standing at entrances are there to police access? Can we not interpret the meaning of Lamassu as "vital strength" in ways that do not follow masculinist performances of strength as force? What other knowledges can we glean if we read the idea of "vital strength" alongside Lamassu's transgender multispecies body?

Lamassu's body conveys a figure whose form is unfixed across lines of gender and species. Lamassu is identified as a female deity yet it wears a full beard that flows down to its chest, reaching over high cheeks to earlobes adorned with long earrings.[17] The bovine body (often called a bull) rounds into a hanging teat under its belly, queering its multispecies form. Visually Lamassu embodies multiplicity, indexing those who walk the Earth (human, lion, bull), those who swim in the waters (fish), and those who fly overhead with wings.

Lamassu's shifting form across both gender and species levels should give us pause regarding its designated role as a masculinist restrictor of access. Instead, Lamassu gains its power—or its "vital strength"—from its fluidity, from the fusion of multiple and open-ended life-forms. Such a form, I would argue, is not an embodiment of a boundary-maker; rather, it is a body that does not observe limiting parameters. Lamassu is not a protector of selective and isolated life-forms. While archeologists often refer to it as a "composite"[18] figure, we can also allow for dynamism by reading this deity in a state of transformation.[19] If we adjust our attention from seeing Lamassu as a static sculpture to one in performative movement, we can engage Lamassu in a state of shape-shifting and transition. Indeed, Lamassu's repeated appearance at entrances points to moments of transition from one place—or from one physical/psychic/gendered/species state—into another.

What Lamassu's figure can teach us is that restricting access and securitizing borders are not the only ways of understanding protection. If we are to care for Lamassu's existence, we need to think with its queer form and with the dissolution of boundaries that this queerness implies. It is in fact no coincidence that Allahyari selects Lamassu for digital and plastic reconstruction. My contention here is that it is Lamassu's protection—the apotropaic qualities of a benevolent spirit—that the artist herself seeks to summon. Allahyari's Lamassu printed in 3D plastic form is not only a deity animated into our presence but one whose very materiality is drawn from vital earthly matter. In her manifesto on 3D technologies, coauthored with Daniel Rourke, the artists contemplate the organic materiality of 3D manufacturing. They write, "Derived from petrochemicals boiled into being from the black oil of a trillion ancient bacterioles, the plastic used in 3D Additive manufacturing is a metaphor before it has even been layered into shape. Its potential," they continue, "belies the complications of its history: that matter is the sum and prolongation of our ancestry."[20]

With this statement, the manifesto ushers us into the figurines' deep time: the time of plastic molded from liquid oil that is itself composed of millions of ancient planktons. This is the deep time of petroleum, a substance that was once living matter and which continues to challenge our perception of what counts as life in petroleum-generated products. Plastic, in deep time, finds its genealogy in microbial life. Unlike its discursive resonance as dead and rigid matter, plastic, in Allahyari's manifesto, is a living agent within cultural and biological organisms. As mentioned above, Dimock offers the notion of "deep time" to propose a historiography that is global in scope, one that moves beyond the time/space coordinates of nation-states and individual actors. My use of the term deep time pushes this further in order to decenter the human altogether. What would it mean to think with deep times—such as those of crude oil—that set recorded human histories off-kilter? What if deep time did not simply mean "denationalized space," as Dimock proposes, but questioned the very centering of the human as the pivot of time?[21] What if we thought with Terrans who "do not do history," as Haraway puts it, but do instead "webbed, braided, and tentacular living and dying"?[22] How do we think, for instance, with the deep time of crude oil or with the webbed temporalities of oilfields that competed for the attention of US-led coalition forces in Iraq? What would the subterranean time of crude oil tell us that human desires for its extraction never would?

The time line I offer here is the deep time of petroleum, a once living matter fossilized and pressurized into crude oil. Crude oil comes to us through an expanded method of muck-making that presses the living and the nonliving together. We can envision its production as a time-lapse in which "fast-growing rushes and giant tree ferns grew in swamps in hot and humid climates hundreds of millions of years ago," and "as the swamps sank, so the organic matter became coal and petroleum."[23] The resulting mulch is a thick goo with a pungent smell, a formless matter with an energetic potential we call petroleum.

The geological process through which crude oil comes into being is not unlike what we observe on Lamassu's shape-shifting body. As noted, Lamassu is not simply a static sculpture but a deity in performative movement transitioning from one form into another. As with the deep time of crude oil's production, the temporality of Lamassu's shape-shifting body is vast. It is a time line in which carbon-based bodies of multiple Terrans (the terrestrial, the avian, and the aquatic) fold and unfold into one another. Rendering Lamassu's body in 3D plastic, as Allahyari does, takes the visual symbolisms of its shape-shifting into a material one. Allahyari's Lamassu is layered into shape from ancient microbial life, whose multispecies composition and temporal transition are visualized on the surface of its body. In its plastic form, Allahyari's Lamassu is a carbonic ancestor summoned into our presence.

Allahyari's manifesto offers crude oil—alongside petroleum-generated products such as plastics—as ancestral kin connecting us, biologically and spiritually, to this sacred matter. Plastic, in her work, is rendered as an ancestor, a deity, not unlike Lamassu, with "vital strength." Allahyari's manifesto asks us to do creative, counterintuitive, imaginative, and speculative work. She urges us to consider plastic as something other than heaps of dead matter piled up in toxic landfills. She asks us to trace our connectedness, through crude oil, to this symbolic object of anthropogenic climate change. Can we think of plastic not simply as vital but as sacred? Can plastic be thought outside of secular extractive logics? How would the knowledges of those dispossessed of their lands and material resources give renewed form to this matter?

Oil was arguably one of the most vital elements in the region to US-led coalition forces who prioritized its protection over others inhabiting the area. Protecting oil meant securing life for the US nation. As Stephanie Le-Menager has noted, "We experience ourselves as moderns and specially as modern Americans, every day in oil, living within oil, breathing it and registering it within our senses."[24] It is oil that enables the technological development, mobility, and the biopolitical protection that defines "modern American" identity. Securing access to oil is what brought the coalition forces to Iraq, to protect the extraction of a substance that fueled the very tanks and fighter jets that dumped chemical pollutants back into the land.[25] Living oil hence required militarized biopolitical protection that did not extend to the lives of those perishing in its vicinity. Oil and the wastelands it has produced last much longer than the current political conflicts over its extraction. These wastelands do not operate on the timescale of military history but stretch far beyond their calculations.

Thinking with the materiality of Allahyari's plastic figurines can guide us toward temporal adjustments. At the physical level, Allahyari's figurines replicate older sculptural materials, such as marble, limestone, and bronze, that were used to make the destroyed artifacts. Studies of mining practices in the ancient Near East show that metallurgical activity, such as copper mining for bronze production, continues to have ecological impacts in the region today. Ancient metal mining and smelting sites, such as Wadi Arabah excavated at the Israel-Jordan border area, show high concentrations of copper and lead contents in plants and animals living in the region today.[26] While such sites have long ceased to be active, their operations still resonate in the cultural objects they yielded, and their industrial waste persists in current living organisms.[27] According to the excavation team, "the vegetation within the study area has bioaccumulated both copper and lead from the ancient metalliferous smelting activity and these cations subsequently become available to the plants and herbivores in the area."[28] While art historians and museologists border off objects into distinct periods that may be far removed from us today, these objects' material residues live at the cellular level of living organisms. Historical periodization might set us apart from ancient artifacts but they live within us as toxins moving from one body to another through food, water, and respiration. Toxic wastelands hence live beyond historical periodization and across national boundaries.

If metallurgical practices from antiquity persist as pollutants today, what can we make of the temporality of militarized oil fields or what Rob Nixon calls the "ecologies of the aftermath" of warfare? Iraq sits among a concentration of oil-producing countries and has been the site of three major wars in less than fifty years: the Iran-Iraq War (1980–1988) as well as the first and second Gulf Wars of 1991 and 2003. The first Gulf War was the instigator of one of the largest oil spills in history when Iraqi military, "as a way to prevent any US marine attack and to furnish a carpet of fire, intentionally released an estimated 11 million barrels of crude oil into the Arabian Gulf" in 1991.[29] This was followed by repeated attacks since 2003 aimed at sabotaging petroleum infrastructures in Iraq.[30] These ongoing political conflicts add exponentially to pollutants released into the air, water, and soil by the day-to-day activities of the oil industry. While wars themselves can be segmented into distinct periods of conflict, their material effects last far beyond the decisive start and end dates on military time lines. While wars might end, hostilities continue in the geophysical structures of petroleum-saturated living organisms.

Oil, we can argue, produces different forms of life. Its extraction is key to the continuation of "modern American" living, but it is also the substance that creates wastelands across the globe. "Modern American" living, to be sure, is a life that neither extends to all who inhabit the Americas, nor those geographically bounded to the continent. "Modern American" living can extend across the globe in securitized zones—such as the one that hosted US troops at Camp Liberty in Baghdad's Green Zone (the International Zone of Baghdad)—but can withdraw its biopolitical protection in the United States as it did in 2010 when the Gulf of Mexico was flooded by the Deepwater Horizon oil spill. Oil is the substance that, on the one hand, supports biopolitical life contributing to feelings of "liveness" through mobility, connectedness, and cultural productions.[31] But it is also the substance that saturates wastelands. This is to emphasize that wastelands are not dead but sustain a differentiated form of life that fall outside of biopolitical protection. Oil produces geographies of terror, inhabited by toxins, viruses, debilitated bodies, and rebels alike. More importantly, oil contributes to the bordering-off and surveillance of wastelands creating zones of threat and conflict.

In Allahyari's work, 3D printing "is oil made digital."[32] It is hence used to summon (protective) deities such as Lamassu. In a published interview, Allahyari and Rourke contemplate the digital life of 3D objects before they go to print. Rourke points out that the preplastic, digital form of 3D prints has the potential to subvert surveillance at borders and checkpoints. He states, "Digital file can travel across borders and boundaries in a way that a physical object can't. You can seize Barbie dolls or dildos at the border, but the 3D.OBJ file will slip through and emerge out of a 3D printer."[33]

Amused by this elusive nature of digital files, he further notes, "The need is perhaps stronger than ever for creators, thinkers, makers, and activists who can themselves become that elusive."[34]

The question that Rourke tackles here is not a mere smuggling of objects through borders but negotiating power at a transnational scale. Surveillance technologies are currently at the forefront of border security practices. They support a form of governance that, as Brian Massumi notes, is based on "preemption." Surveillance technologies are designed to preemptively detect and eliminate potential threat by limiting movement across borders. Preemption, as Massumi explains it, controls the potential for a threat's future emergence. To further explain preemptive practices, Massumi provides the example of profiling. "What is profiled," he writes, "is a potential future."[35] Profiling is not based on evidence of past criminality but its potential advent in the future that power seeks to curb. Neel Ahuja clarifies this further when he writes, "Racial profiling acquires momentum through the public mapping of *uncertainty* in a globally interconnected world by asserting the *potential* for criminal motives among those world regions tainted by association with political Islam or communism."[36] Profiling is, in this sense, a process of racialization that maps ambiguity onto bodies that attempt to move across designated zones of terror.

It is against preemptive power that Rourke calls for fluid bodies that can move through frontiers and surveillance technologies undetected. Asking for "elusive" bodies, as Rourke does, is attractive in the context of a world where potentiality has become the site of policing. It speaks of a desire to critique preemptive profiling and the trampling of resistant life-forms before they even emerge. Yet we need to be careful when summoning elusiveness because the desire for soluble bodies that can dissipate into code has been a recurrent theme in posthumanist discourse. Posthumanism has long imagined embodiment as nothing more than the accumulation of data. The posthumanist notion of the body, as Katherine Hayles explains it, is one that "can become dematerialized into an informational pattern and rematerialized without change at a remote location."[37] In this posthumanist vision, data is separated from its specific gendered and racialized embodiment, leading to the assumption that data "is a kind of immaterial fluid that can circulate effortlessly around the globe."[38]

Imagining bodies as data occludes the material ways in which bodies are gendered and racialized at checkpoints. It forgets that it is data itself that produces differentiated bodies at the border. The production of racialized and gendered bodies through surveillance practices is best described by Simone Browne, who argues that racialization currently occurs through dematerialization of bodies into code. In Browne's assessment, bodily dissolution has not proven to be emancipatory for gendered and racialized bodies that have long been, and continue to be, objects of surveillance. Instead, surveillance technologies have racialized the body in algorithms and by "computational means through which the body or more specifically parts, pieces, and increasingly performances of the body are mathematically coded as data, making for unique templates for computers to then sort."[39] Fragmentation and dissolution allow digital technologies to create templates for profiling. Reduced to retrievable data, bodies under surveillance are made ontologically insecure. This means that bodies are racialized when made vulnerable to the truth-claims of technological apparatuses.

In light of Browne's discussion, Rourke's call for elusiveness cannot be naively taken up as a fantasy of disembodiment. Instead, it should alert us to the difficulty of upholding posthumanism as a radical dissolution of bodies in the face of racializing powers of surveillance and border control. Unlike the posthumanist dream of dematerialization expressed by Rourke— in which a body can disappear in one place and be remotely downloaded in another—Allahyari's Lamassu points to the very material connectedness of all things. As a deity with a queer body in a state of physical transformation, Lamassu brings attention to the arbitrariness of borders and boundaries in the first place. As a 3D figurine, Allahyari's Lamassu not only visualizes multiple species across its body but it is made from a substance that is itself multispecies: the viscous fossil of ancient life forms.

13

Huma

Allahyari's reclamation of ancient deities and their suppressed knowledges is fully apparent in another series of sculptural and video work titled *She Who Sees the Unknown*, which she began in 2016. This project reclaims, in the artist's words, "monstrous female/queer figures of Middle-Eastern origin, using the traditions and myths associated with them to explore catastrophes of colonialism, patriarchism and environmental degradation in relationship to the Middle East."[1] Similar to the figurines in her *Material Speculation* series, this project utilizes 3D modeling, scanning, and printing to animate these queer figures with a multifaceted approach. Allahyari presents each figure in a short video that narrates their mythologies and the logic of their contemporary conjuring.

A figure in this series is named Huma (figure 13.1), a jinn who, in Allahyari's video animation, is said to bring heat to the human body and

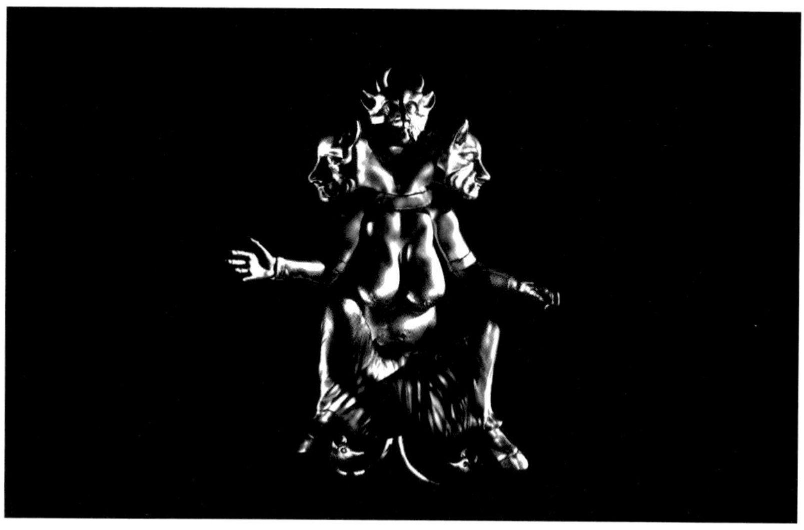

FIGURE 13.1 Huma resides in the deep, dark bowels of the earth. When summoned, Huma bubbles up in her oily black sheen. Morehshin Allahyari, *She Who Sees the Unknown: Huma*. Image of 3D-printed sculpture, 2016. Courtesy of Morehshin Allahyari.

is responsible for the common fever. Within Islamic traditions, jinns are invisible demons capable of possessing an individual's body. The Arabic root of the word jinn (j-n-n) is shared with the word *al-junun,* or madness, connoting possession by an invisible spirit.[2] Beliefs and practices of spirit possession have been prevalent in West and Central Asia and continue to animate religious, social, and psychological relations. Recent studies have argued for the continued presence of jinns within cultural practices that traverse the domain of the secular and the sacred. In Stefania Pandolfo's ethnographic work for instance, the jinn becomes the figure through which Muslim analysts and religious figures diagnose melancholia in accordance with the science of Arab medicine.[3] In Anand Vivek Taneja's study, jinns possess bodies in order to connect them to the historical past. "Jinns" Taneja writes, "are linked to deep time, connecting human figures thousands of years apart."[4] They are "figures of memory" who, in Taneja's analysis are antidotes to historical amnesia common to colonial and postcolonial statecrafts.[5]

Huma, the jinn conjured in Allahyari's work, appears on the planet as heat, a fever possessing the planet and its inhabitants. Huma is a figure residing in the deep, dark bowels of the earth. When summoned, Huma bubbles up in her oily black sheen. Much like Lamassu, Huma's body is a composite of humanimal forms. Three heads rise above full breasts hanging down toward two tails that gaze back at each other. Huma, in Allahyari's work, is the queer goddess of crude oil, a talismanic figure we can call upon to, in the artist's words, "make all temperatures equal."[6] Who other than the deity of petroleum could teach us about living on a heated planet? Working with oral historical narratives in which Huma can cast and heal the common fever, Allahyari conjures—literally animates and materializes—Huma into our world. Huma is here to intervene in the secularization of fossil fuels, extractive economies, and the rising temperatures that have gripped the terrestrial and the oceanic.

In her study of local knowledge within extractive zones of the Global South, Macarena Gómez-Barris offers Indigenous philosophies of relationality as those that can subvert colonial logics of extraction. Indigenous relationality, she writes, is "a relation to land, place, mountains, and the elements that assumes a profound sacred orientation and understanding that moves in registers that are not easily catalogued by the colonial project."[7] In this vein, I read Allahyari's material engagement with crude oil as an anti-colonial project that builds a sacred orientation toward crude oil in order to subvert colonial logics of extraction. Such an orientation is also necessarily queer in that it is speculative and futurist. In the words of José Esteban Muñoz, "Queerness is an ideality."[8] It is what lets us "feel that this world is not enough, that indeed something is missing."[9] Colonial extractive projects in Iraq and Iran have not simply dispossessed us of our relationality to land and its resources. They have also dispossessed us of our cultural, linguistic, religious, and symbolic modes of land-based knowledge. We have experienced disruptions of precolonial connections to crude oil that have today been replaced by nation-state-based discourses of oil sovereignty.

What Allayhari seeks instead is an attempt toward a new language, a new mode of relationality, orientation, and apprehension that build upon subjugated queer and feminist ways of knowing the world. For as Gómez-Barris argues, "Women of color feminisms have historically contended with precisely how to think beyond the colonial divide and place embodied knowledge as the source of a future-oriented imaginary of the planetary."[10] In Allahyari's artistic practice, the jinn, Huma, does the work of memory. Huma becomes the connection between the present and the deep time of petroleum that currently burns into our planetary presence.

14

Homa

There is a photograph of me in my personal archives at the age of nine visiting the ruins of Persepolis located just outside the city of Shiraz in Southern Iran (figure 14.1). I am wearing a woolen mustard jacket and I am standing in between my cousin and my younger brother. We stand still so that my mother can take our picture. My father seems oblivious to my mother's gaze behind the camera. With curiosity, he looks up at the back of the column stretching tall before him.

The column is crowned by a double-headed bird known in Farsi as "Homa," a mythological pre-Islamic figure indigenous to the Iranian plateau, dating at this particular site to 500 BC. My mother's photographic composition has much to say about Homa's role within Iranian cosmology. In her photograph, a horizon line formed by the desert plateau runs across the image, dividing the terrestrial and the celestial worlds. Below

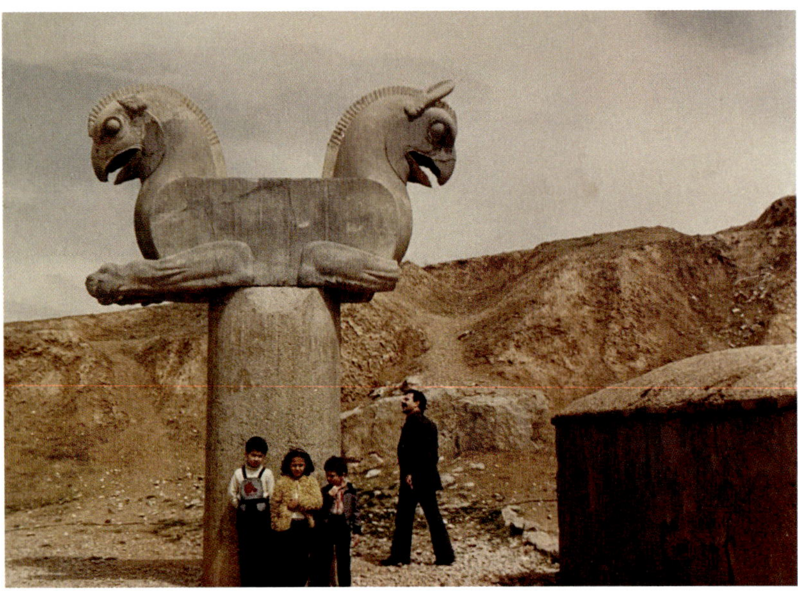

FIGURE 14.1 A horizon line formed by the desert plateau runs across the image dividing the terrestrial and the celestial worlds. Below the horizon line lies the land: the world of rocks, sand, and the human bodies that lean against a heavy column. Above is the vast stretch of a sky into which Homa begins to rise. Photograph from the author's archive.

the horizon line lies the land: the world of rocks, sand, and the human bodies that lean against a heavy column. Above is the vast stretch of a sky into which Homa begins to rise. This dividing (or, rather, suturing line) between the terrestrial and the celestial is indeed where my father's gaze is directed. He is looking up at the seam, at that point of separation/connection between the earth and the sky that the bird signifies.

There is a story my grandmother tells about the woolen mustard jacket I have on in this picture. Here I wear it over a white turtleneck, which, as my squinting eyes in the photograph may suggest, was overdressing for the warm day we had been blessed with on our day of sightseeing. We had taken a road trip from Tehran, where my family lived, to Shiraz. The reward was going to Persepolis, but as the day progressed I became ill, weak and shivering, asking for the jacket to keep me warm. By the end of the day, I had developed a fever, slowly infecting my brother and my cousin. Learning about my condition, a neighbor told us to burn some incense

(*Esfand*, which is the aromatic seed of wild rue) in order to cleanse ourselves from Homa's evil eye. "She can bring fevers to children," she said. The neighbor had also warned, according to my grandmother, to refrain from developing any photographs we had taken of Homa for possessing her in photographic form might continue to cast fevers onto our bodies.

Despite the warning, the photograph remains. It remains with a lingering anxiety about the effects of its presence in my childhood photo album. Has Homa caused all the fevers I have had since this photograph was taken? Has Homa caused the fevers of the COVID-19 pandemic, which broke out a short few days after I showed this photograph in a slide projection to a public audience (the last audience I engaged in person before the outbreak)? Did Homa cause the fever I had when editing this section of the book? And again, when proofreading this very passage!

It was my encounter with Allahyari's "Huma" that brought me back to this photograph. While writing about this photograph has not eased my anxiety toward it, I have learned that Homa standing tall behind me in the image is the pre-Islamic version of Huma that Allahyari conjures in her project. Within Islamic manuscripts the double-headed Homa acquires a third demonic head that grows horns twisting out if its cranial crown and tails elongating out of its pelvic cavity (figure 14.2). Islam, upon its encounter with Indigenous "pagan" religions in Iran (such as *Zartoshti* and *Asuri*), had to contend with various powerful deities. Such deities cannot easily fit within Islam's monotheistic schema and are hence reimagined within Islamic texts as demons and jinns. Huma is a syncretic post-Islamic rendition of Homa that continues to exert its powers. Homa/Huma today is a palimpsest that passes on oral knowledge across generations.

What Allahyari's work offers me is a queer futurist orientation toward my own archives and my own inherited oral histories. Such knowledge allows us to perform reclamations of our lands, languages, and resources. This is not a rematriation for "all of humanity" but a queer, speculative attempt at thinking the world otherwise. For Muñoz, "queer aesthetics frequently contains blueprints and schemata of a forward-dawning futurity" because "queerness is an insistence on potentiality or possibility for another world."[1] After all, isn't witchcraft, magic, and superstition the domain of queer, Indigenous, and feminized modes of effecting and changing the material makeup of the world?

As with my reading of Lamassu earlier, it is my contention that Allahyari's practice is a performative act of resacralizing the materiality of land in

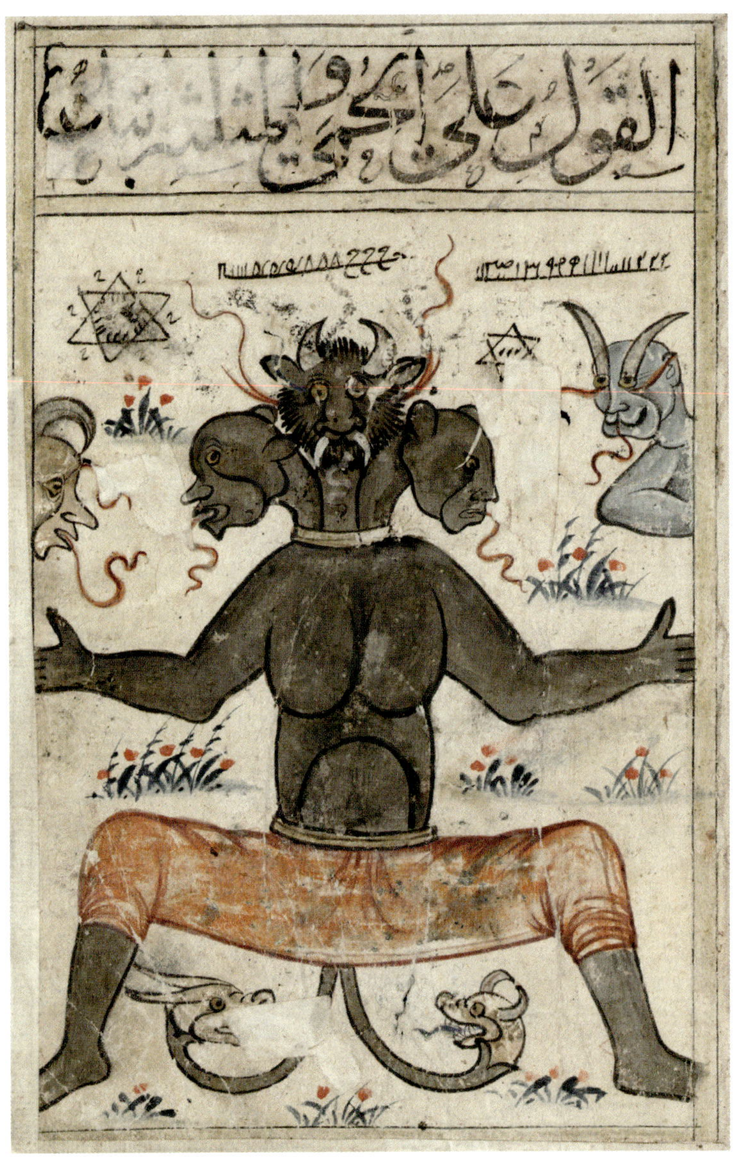

FIGURE 14.2 Within Islamic manuscripts the double-headed Homa acquires a third demonic head that grows horns twisting out if its cranial crown and tails elongating out of its pelvic cavity. Image from *Kitāb al-Bulhān* [Book of wonders] *and Other Works*, 1330–1450 CE. Bodleian Library MS. Bodl. Or. 133, fol. 30a. Photo: © Bodleian Libraries, University of Oxford.

the form of crude oil by calling upon oral knowledge carried within Indigenous deities. If crude oil, with its origin in microbial life, is to be treated as ancestral kin (as the artist urges us to do), then it has a sacred vital strength. Allahyari's work ushers us into a site of imagination, a speculative futurism in which the secular knowledge-production of the carbon-privileged give way to the sacred knowledge of the land itself.[2]

15

Pazuzu

Dust. Dust storms. Dust cyclones swirling in the four wings of a god said to be the bearer of epidemics: Pazuzu.[1] Its body is turbines spinning to the dance of dust particles, the smallest unit of the desert. Viruses go viral as Pazuzu passes by, lifting dust off the ground and throwing it into the wind, into a plague spiral (figure 15.1). How is a god to save us when it is itself fresh off a historical sleep that dreamed the present? This we do not know; yet Pazuzu is here, cloaked in the windstorm that leaves dust at the base of our doors that have shut us in and away from our kin whose breath will reanimate Pazuzu's dance.

2019 CE. 1440 AH. 1398 SH.

Pazuzu becomes powder. It dissolves into dust the very moment it is unearthed by the archeologist, her chapped hands remembering the last moisture of the lotion she caressed into every cell a few hours be-

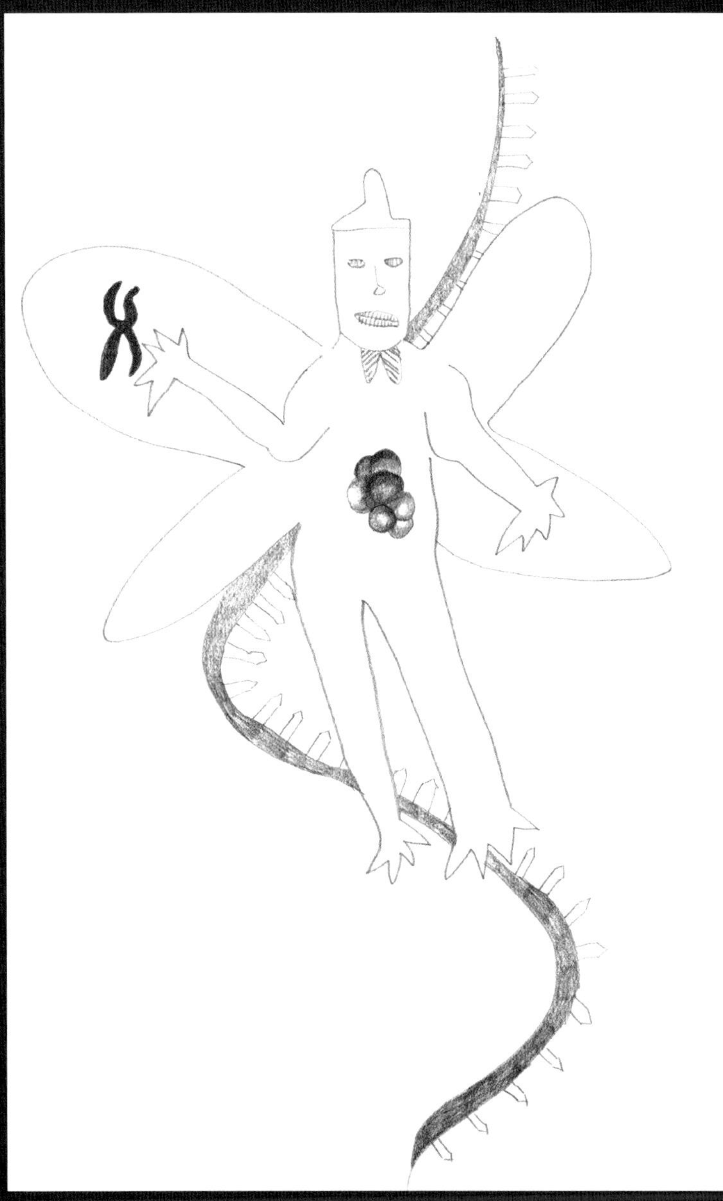

FIGURE 15.1 Its body is a turbine spinning to the dance of dust particles, the smallest unit of the desert. Viruses go viral as Pazuzu passes by, lifting dust off the ground and throwing it into the wind, into a plague spiral. Salar Mameni, *Pazuzu*, 2020.

fore she had to walk back into sunlight drumming down onto the sand dunes.

Pazuzu becomes powder. Its cylindrical body could not bear the pressure of the unpressure left by the removal of layers of earth that had held it snug in the planet's crust for thousands of years since the days it had rested there under the bed of the first human host to a virus that now, upon its unleashing by the archeologist, would become released into the dusty air of the Lut Desert.

Pazuzu becomes powder before it can cast its upturned eyes at the archeologist to comprehend why a human on this year of 2019 CE, 1440 AH, 1398 SH, would find herself at its burial site where it had held the RNA weave of a virus taut against the curves of its wings. Had there been a single drop of moisture in the air, it would have trapped the viral escape back into the earth to shelter it once again from its venture into the flesh of the demos across the globe.

The jinn released by Pazuzu's unearthing enters her body. Her convulsions begin at her dig site. She collapses onto the ground. Thirty seconds. She regains her posture, gets back up, and continues to dig. She attributes her nausea to the heat from the sun and kneels down to pick up what's left of the disintegrated dust of Pazuzu. She cups a handful of earth and gravel before a scream escapes her lips, an audible shout from the edge of her throat where her neck meets her collarbone. She feels a spasm and rubs the side of her neck. Now her shoulders begin to vibrate to an unknown rhythm along her spine. She begins to dance. The rhythm moves her arms like long snakes lashing against her shoulders, urging her hips to fall in line. She begins to twirl, her legs moving in jagged lines, in ways that muscle and bone would never obey. She leaps, she takes flight now laughing, now screaming, now uttering sounds and words that respond to the new shapes her tongue muscles can take. Pazuzu's dust settles onto her moist tongue, causing the pink organ in her mouth to dance, a dance to internal music arising from Pazuzu's dust stinging her heart. The jinn is in possession, exploring her inner worlds, moving from cell to cell like an amoeba setting sail across oceans.

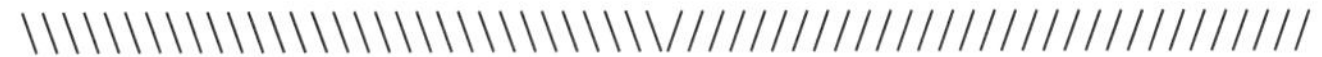

Pazuzu is held, like a relic, in the leaves of Reza Negarestani's *Cyclonopedia: Complicity with Anonymous Materials*, a book written to conjure gods moving through the atmosphere and telluric elements. *Cyclonopedia* is apotropaic, written to ward off the evil that it calls into being through the mouths of archeologists (figures 15.2 and 15.3).

Myths are bodies of knowledge that move from one mouth to another like a virus through the breath, similar to art but different in that sounds and mud and paint and words called art can only become myth if they change as they move through lips and become contaminated with the saliva that spits them out onto the next person.

When myths arrive into our present, what we sense is the gap between now and then. Time becomes stretched like the tongue that delivers the myth. When you learn about dog-headed demons, three-headed snakes, and towers and stones that no longer exist, you wonder how these stories might have changed, even incrementally, as they passed from neighbor to neighbor, changing turbines into electric power plants and gods into vaccines. When the past erupts into the present, magic happens. Walls crack, letting jinns walk through battlefields.

But time alone does not make myth. Myths need to be woven from hairs, nails, and skins of the living. Pipelines and war machines spin myths in *Cyclonopedia*. They fly overhead, drones atop oil droplets leaking into the bone-dry desert landscape. Myth here is the act of remembering votive figures, such as Pazuzu, unearthed to reconcile ancient bacteria with the contemporary Axis of Evil. What is myth if not an opening into the present of a past that is more closely akin to a possession, a possession that becomes a shape-shifting performance that animates the body through a demon, a jinn?

The Arabic correlation between jinn (spirit) and *junun* (madness), between the possessive spirit and insanity, cannot be known by secular knowledge, a form of knowing that expels gods from the world. Gods disappear because they are inexplicable in scientific language that searches only the body itself, its base matter, for evidence to explain the agitations of the convulsive body. Seizures, stutters, and the irregular and repetitive movements of heads and limbs, the ecstasy of being and possession appear as symptoms of an unstable mind, the toxins and chemical dysfunctions of the grey muscle within the skull.

The sacred becomes secular when a jinn is cloaked. The sacred moves through you like heat. It is dust. It is color. For the anthropologist Michael Taussig, the sacred is like a beautiful blue substance that appears across the sky before our blurred vision when ingested psychedelic plants take hold of the stomach, churning into nausea, bringing on the blues.[2] The sacred is like a song whose rhythm is harmonic and convulsive, seductive and

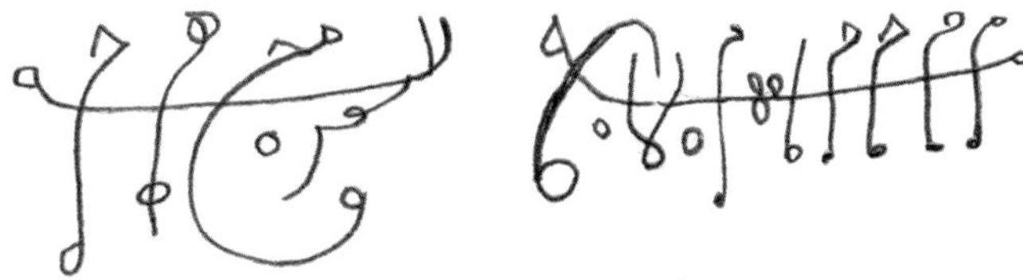

FIGURE 15.2 Apotropaic text written to ward off the evils called into being. Drawing by the author rendering footnote (82n) in Reza Negarestani's *Cyclonopedia*.

FIGURE 15.3 Apotropaic text written to ward off the evils called into being. Drawing

ecstatic. The sacred is unknown unless it moves the body in jagged lines that wrap limb over limb. It is unknown unless it is experienced as heat gathered from fire to move the fog off the surface of the eye. The sacred is what brings vision, what brings sound, what gives the body its aesthetic movements that carry the muscular into cosmic dimensions. Taussig calls the sacred "a polymorphous magical substance,"[3] one that burns orange into the forehead and out of the navel. The sacred is the line that connects the organic and the inorganic, turning carbon into that magical substance that binds me with a stone.

Narrative Terrorism

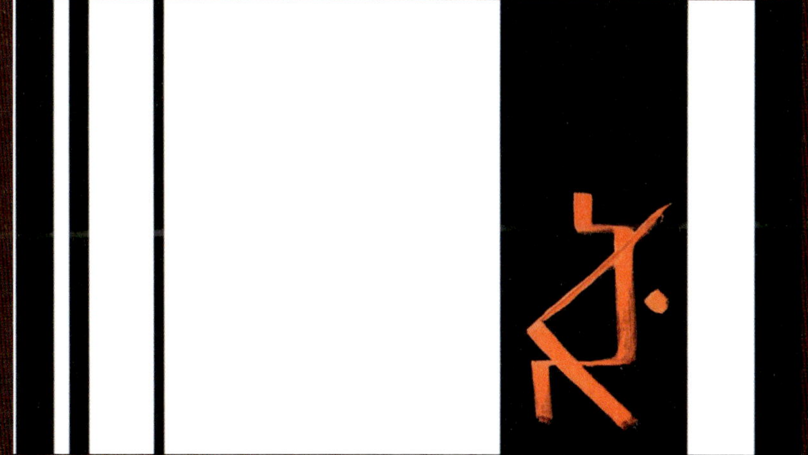

16

The Red Star

Yemen lives in the Red Star.

The Yemeni Bosnian American artist Alia Ali writes of her inheritance: "As children we were told of لنجم الأحمر (roman: al-najm al-ahmar), the Red Star, which was gifted to Belquis, our ruler, the Queen of سباء (roman: Saba'a/Sheba)."[1]

The Red Star: Mars: Yemen.

Mars was gifted to Queen Belquis and to the Yemeni people.

Ali visualizes her inheritance in a multimedia installation: A deep-blue room painted over with red Arabic calligraphy. Sounds overlay. Images overlay. Time shrinks and expands in a pixelated video projection.

Piercing. Abrupt sounds collected by NASA on Mars screech and blend into Yemeni beats. I pause on a video screen: a thousand dots of light, flickering. Suns. Stars. Planets. Promised lands. Futures. Dreams. The cosmos bleeds into the earth to join a group of men in dance. The men move in unison, keeping beat to Yemeni music. Circles form around their hips, their fists rise into the air (figures 16.1 and 16.2).

"If I dream of النجم الأحمر," writes Ali, "it is a sign that I exist not only here in the present, but also there in the future."[2] Ali's body expands and shrinks, traverses temporalities so vast that the mythic time of Sabean inheritance bleeds, like liquid color, into future Martian existence.

Let us pose a question about the materiality of the future. What is the future built out of? Will it be chemically the same as the present or will the future require different lungs and limbs for planetary habitation? What are the histories of the future? Who narrates them and in what languages? It is not controversial to believe that the future will be unrecognizable to us today. "In the age of climate change," writes the anthropologist Hugh Raffles, "the future is deeply marked by the inevitable eruption of non-predictable phenomena on startling scales."[3] "We know catastrophes are coming," Raffles continues, "and we know they'll take us by surprise."[4]

Who imagines the future and how remains deeply political. While the radical alterity of the future is inevitable, how we narrate it (whether it is catastrophic or utopian, for instance), depends on how we understand ourselves historically.

"While Western narratives of the apocalypse place the catastrophic earth-ending event in the future," writes Lou Cornum (Navajo), "Indigenous stories often cast the end of the world as something that has already happened, the effects of which continue to reverberate throughout Indigenous lives."[5] For Cornum, the temporality of catastrophe is a matter of perspective. It is dependent upon how we imagine and represent catastrophes. "The crisis imaginary," Cornum writes, is "representational form that obscures how the increasing collapse of ecosystems has been ongoing for hundreds of years for colonized peoples both in the Americas and around the world."[6]

In part 1 of this book, I discussed Yemeni claims to Mars as illegitimate within legal and scientific systems of the secular West. For the legal and scientific systems that ridiculed Yemeni oral narratives, there was no Yemeni future on Mars. Ali's treatment of this claim in her artistic practice takes a different stance. Ali posits Yemeni cosmologies into the future,

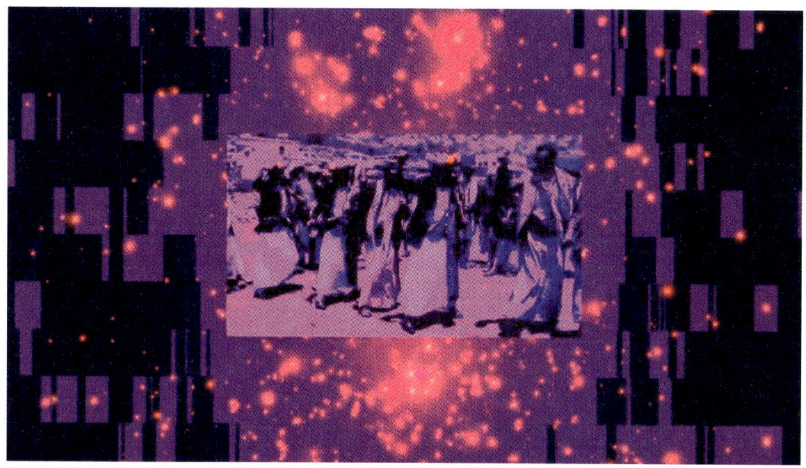

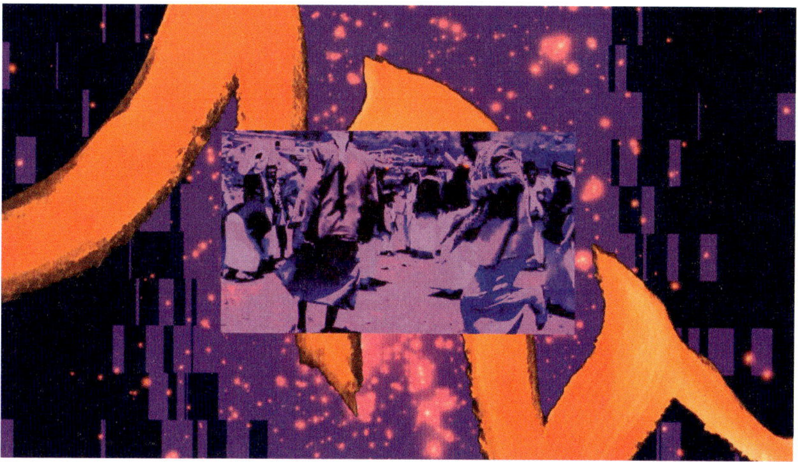

FIGURES 16.1 AND 16.2 The cosmos bleeds into the earth to join a group of men in dance. "مهجر//Mahjar," stills from video by Alia Ali, 2020. Courtesy of Alia Ali.

allowing a mode of time travel that preserves Mars for ongoing Yemeni habitation. In the next few pages, I contemplate contested claims on lands and cosmologies through the artistic practice of the Palestinian artist Larissa Sansour. In particular, I focus on the term "narrative terrorist," a term Sansour uses to describe how Palestinians are perceived when they stake a claim to their occupied territories.

17

Narrative Terrorism

Conjure a team of future archeologists excavating a site from our present moment. Imagine this team coming across fine shards of porcelain painted with the black and white grid pattern of the Palestinian keffiyeh. Imagine this team also uncovering the bones of a community of people who, over time and across generations, crafted and ate from this fine porcelain. Imagine this group of archeologists confirming, based on their findings, that an industrious people existed and prospered on this land. This group of future archeologists is anticipated in the work of Larissa Sansour. In her video (made in collaboration with Søren Lind) titled *In the Future They Ate from the Finest Porcelain* (2015), Sansour narrates the story of a woman who creates a fictional civilization by depositing porcelain fragments and bones from her own body into the earth, so as to alter the history of the land in the future. She has a warrant for her arrest because she has been identified as a Narrative Terrorist.

Larissa Sansour's speculative-futurist video considers the texture of the future within the context of Palestine under settler-colonial, military, and environmental siege.[1] Her video offers us new ways of thinking of the earth as a participant in life-making. Perceptions of the earth have been central to Israeli occupation of Palestine. As with other settler colonies across the globe, the occupation of Palestinian lands has been premised upon the evacuation of its inhabitants physically, legally, and imaginatively. The settler state of Israel, established between 1947 and 1949 through Jewish migration, relied upon the legal concept of *terra nullius* (empty land) in order to "present lands belonging to no one, emptied of sovereignty, ownership, or long-term possession rights."[2] Representations of Palestinian lands as empty, as uninhabited wastelands, supported Zionist claims to territorial settlement. Such claims were fortified by archeological knowledge-production. "Archeology," Nadia Abu El-Haj writes, "did far more than dig in search of evidence of an ancient Israelite and Jewish past embedded in the land." Instead, "the archeological record was understood to contain remnants of nations and ethnic groups, distinctly demarcated archeological cultures that could be identified and plotted across the landscape."[3]

Sansour's work intervenes in the futurity of archeological knowledge-production by revealing its fictive nature and the terror of its narrative constructions. Sansour is a London-based artist born in East Jerusalem in 1973 and raised in Bethlehem until her family left for the United Kingdom after the First Intifada in 1988.[4] The film I focus on here is part of a series of related video works (often called a trilogy) that include *A Space Exodus* (2009) and *Nation Estate* (2012). As a group, these works are exemplary of Sansour's larger artistic practice that explores histories of Israeli settlements on Palestinian lands and imaginative resistant strategies of Palestinians. Sansour is a prolific artist whose output has been widely exhibited, written about, and recognized internationally. My discussion here does not offer a comprehensive survey of Sansour's work, aspects of which have been treated elsewhere.[5] Instead, I bring focused attention to one part of the trilogy, *In the Future They Ate from the Finest Porcelain*, and in particular to the film's protagonist known simply as the "Narrative Terrorist." The Narrative Terrorist is a Palestinian resistance fighter who takes archeology as her domain of political intervention. The Narrative Terrorist aims to change the archeological record of Palestine by depositing porcelain earthenware, belonging to a fictional bygone civilization, into the earth in the hopes of alternative future histories.

My focus on the Narrative Terrorist is intentional. She is a figure with a traumatic relationship to airstrikes and bombardments that appear to her in the form of weaponized insects and climatic monsoons in recurrent dreams. Her psyche torments her with this convergence of war and weather, an environment of terror that haunts her intimate space of rest and sleep. I am drawn to how this figure makes sense of the fragmentary nature of her memory and narrates stories that are counter to official histories, precisely because of her experiences of living under the violence of ongoing occupation. I am also drawn to how she is envisioned by Sansour, how her story is told in the video through colors, images, sounds, and narrative devices.

Who is a narrative terrorist, and why would one be labeled in this way?

The protagonist of Sansour's video is such a figure. Her mission is to deposit fragments of porcelain and bones into the earth in order to change the archeological stratification of the occupied territories and to give rise to an alternative story for future archeologists to unearth. Throughout the video, we learn about the dangers of telling counter-settler-colonial stories. The Narrative Terrorist has a warrant for her arrest and is being addressed by an unseen interlocutor who oscillates between a psychologist and a lawyer trying to understand her mission.

Listening to the Narrative Terrorist's responses to her interlocutor, we find ourselves adjusting our perceived understanding of time and are urged to calibrate our imagination to the geological timescale of the Earth itself. When asked by her interlocutor how she intends to convince future archeologists that her buried bones and porcelain belong to multiple generations across time, the Narrative Terrorist explains that she manipulates carbon levels in each deposit in order to vary their material stratifications across time. "A buried object absorbs water and radiation at a steady rate," she tells her interlocutor, "ceramic dating simply measures the amounts. By saturating porcelain with high doses, we add centuries to its age."

Carbon dating is central to how archeologists date objects belonging to the past. Carbon dating measures the ratio between heavy to regular carbon atoms in living organisms.[6] As Samantha Frost explains it, "When an organism dies and its carbon composition is no longer in equilibrium with its environment (no eating, no equilibrium!), it will gradually have less and less heavy carbon than a similar living organism."[7] When living

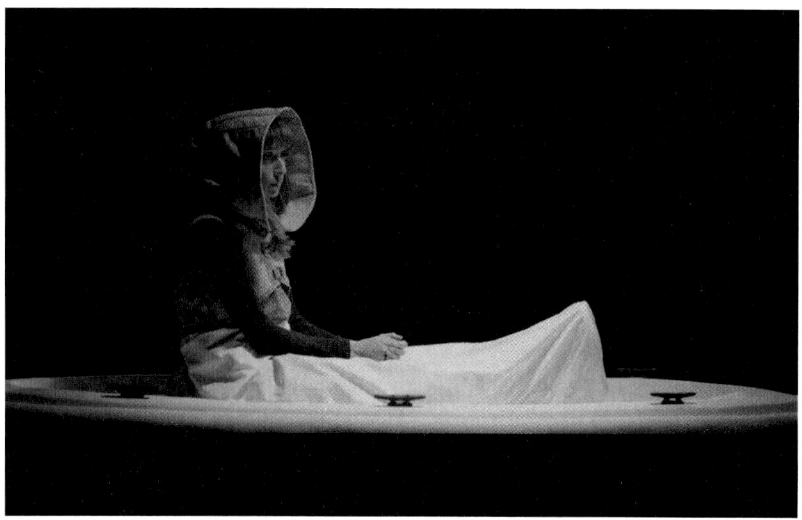

FIGURE 17.1 The narrative terrorist is reclined on her deathbed that at once resembles a spaceship waiting to propel her into another dimension. Still from Larissa Sansour and Søren Lind, *In the Future, They Ate from the Finest Porcelain*, 2016. Courtesy of the artists.

things die, the process of taking in carbon, metabolizing it, and then releasing it back into the atmosphere ends. Carbon dating measures the age of a dead organism by gauging the amount of time that has passed since its intake/outtake process has ended.

For the Narrative Terrorist in Sansour's video, alteration in carbon levels is hardly a definition of decay—or even death in the human sense of the word—but a mode of temporal transformation. She conceives of carbon fluctuations as time travel across geological strata. Throughout the video, we see the Narrative Terrorist reclined on her deathbed that at once resembles a spaceship waiting to propel her into another dimension (figure 17.1). In these scenes, it is the notion of life within the temporality of millennia that compels her to bury her bones alongside porcelain deposits. The future to which her bones give rise are mattered at an atomic level, a scale that rebuilds the earth from the ground up. In Sansour's video, it is not humans alone who make and unmake worlds. Rather, it is the material and atmospheric movements of the Earth itself that stand witness to the rise and fall of humans and the civilizational narratives they spin.

The temporality of carbon in Sansour's video offers a radical dissolution between the living and the nonliving and hence an ethical reimagining of biological selfhood. While the Narrative Terrorist in Sansour's video appears in the form of a human being, it is the future dissolution of her cellular structure into the earth that defines her as a living organism. It is indeed heavy carbon (carbon 14) and its rate of disintegration that weighs in on what counts as a living organism.

What Sansour's video offers us is a transformation of a terrorist into terra. She sits on her spaceship awaiting her internment into the ground. Her bones are to become absorbed by carbon in order to present a different selfhood: Not a terrorist but a Terran, a body that is entangled with the Earth itself. Carbon has had a coveted place in scientific narratives of life-forms on our planet. "Carbon defines life on Earth," writes John F. Marra in his book *Hot Carbon*: "All life is based on carbon."[8] Carbon is found in all Terrans because of its chemical versatility. We know carbon in gas form every time we exhale it as CO_2. We feel carbon in solid form when we touch a tree, work with charcoal, press an insect's exoskeleton, or clip our nails. We smell carbon in liquid form at the gas station and in our bottles of olive oil, as both oils are formed from methane molecules CH_4.[9] Carbon can exist in complex forms, in three-dimensional molecular chains of our DNA intricately housing metals, such as iron in our blood, that transfer energy across our bodies.[10]

Carbon has also narrated our geopolitics. In his well-known book *Carbon Democracy*, for instance, Timothy Mitchell has argued for carbon as the enabler of democratic politics. "What if democracies are," Mitchell asks, "carbon-based? What if they are tied in specific ways to the history of carbon-fuels?"[11] For Mitchell, the shift from renewable energies to the use of coal and fossil fuels as predominant generators of energy resulted in democratic governance in carbon-consuming countries in the Global North while disrupting labor organizing and egalitarian social relations in regions where fossil fuels are mined and extracted. It is petroleum's liquid form, in Mitchell's analysis, that has allowed for its ease of transportation across pipelines from one region to another, geographically separating and dispossessing oil-producing regions.[12] Oil's liquidity, in Mitchell's assessment, is an actor in colonial and imperial relations that has curbed democratic politics in oil-producing countries in West Asia, including Iran, Iraq, and Kuwait.[13]

In Sansour's video, carbon narrates the geopolitical texture of the future. Considering the centrality of carbon in narrating myths of nationalist and colonialist belonging, we can ask: Is carbon the future archeologist imagined in Sansour's video? Is it carbon itself that stands witness, in the future, to the dissolution of settler colonialism in Palestine? The age of the Terracene does not hold humans as sole inhabitants of the future. It is uncertain whether or not humans, in any genre, will proceed into the future. If they do, it remains unclear whether they will continue to pursue cultural endeavors such as archeology, historiography, or statehood. If the question of human existence on the planet is speculative, so are the occupations and preoccupations of future humans with regard to land and colonial settlement. In Sansour's video, today's "terrorists" are tomorrow's Terrans, open to writing other narratives.

While carbon presents future potentiality for the Narrative Terrorist, Sansour's video is also attentive to the military and climatic catastrophes that settler colonialism has enacted on Palestinian lands. Here is a glimpse into the landscapes of the Terracene as presented in Sansour's video:

Weaponized Insects

A layer of yellow-brown dust fills the screen in the opening shot of Sansour's video. Momentarily the dust begins to settle, revealing a series of metallic insect-machines lifting off the ground (figure 17.2). These insect-machines resemble military aircraft, combat planes with corrugated roofs that curve like spines. Their faces are glass windshields glistening gold in the hazy dust of the surrounding desert. One by one, the insect-machines push off their spindly legs, directing their gaze in our direction. As quickly as they had appeared, the insect-machines now begin to disappear overhead, leaving the screen filled with dust. Emerging out of this golden haze is a voice: "Sometimes I dream of porcelain falling from the sky, like ceramic rain," she begins to narrate in Arabic.[14] "At first it's only a few pieces falling slowly like autumn leaves. I'm in it silently enjoying it. But then the volume increases, and it's a porcelain monsoon, like a biblical plague." In scenes later in the video, we see this dream visualized on the screen as insect-machines drop metallic capsules, filled with shards of porcelain, onto the landscape below. The capsules descend, one by one, onto the desert plane and then pop open to release porcelain plates that fall like rain, first in a slow trickle and then in a heavy downpour. The narrative voice in Sansour's video belongs to the Narrative Terrorist herself. In scenes of bombardment, we see the Narrative Terrorist holding her head in her arms, bowing down onto the ground in order to shield herself from

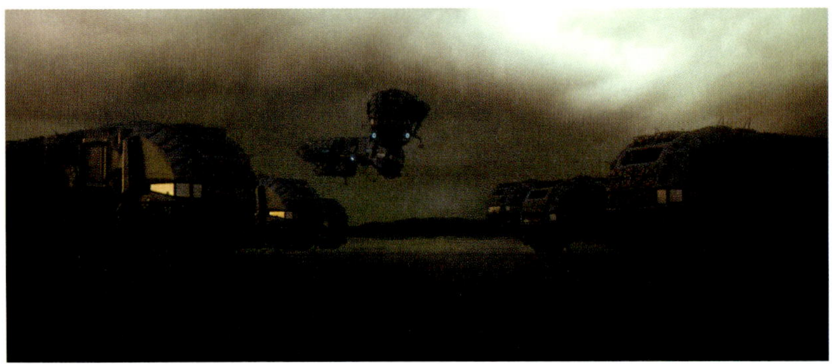

FIGURE 17.2 These insect machines resemble military aircraft, combat planes with corrugated roofs that curve like spines. Their faces are glass windshields glistening gold in the hazy dust of the surrounding desert. Still from Larissa Sansour and Søren Lind, *In the Future, They Ate from the Finest Porcelain*, 2016. Courtesy of the artists.

the sudden monsoon (figure 17.3). In such scenes, we witness a visual, as well as narrative, overlay of war and weather as bombs turn into monsoons delivered by swarms of militarized insects.

The visual morphing of insects and fighter jets in Sansour's video alludes to contemporary practices of entomological warfare. The use of insects has a long military history but has found new expressions within contemporary technoscientific developments. Starting in 2003, the US military began to invest in new industries and scientific research specializing in entomological warfare in order to develop techniques designed specifically for the war on terror.[15] These included methods such as "swarming" and the use of drones modeled on detailed algorithms after ants, bees, and beetles.[16] As the entomologist Jeffrey Lockwood writes in his study of insect weaponization in the military, "Today, scientists are designing insect-machine hybrids—tiny cyborgs to infiltrate enemy positions, gather military intelligence, and assassinate key individuals."[17] These are bugs whose anatomical, navigational, and sensory capacities are mechanized and mobilized for military combat within war zones. In 2008 for instance, the US Defense Advanced Research Projects Agency (DARPA) funded research to control and develop muscular structures of insects with GPS technology so that they could be remotely navigated to targeted sites.[18] Known as Hybrid Insect Micro-Electro-Mechanical Systems (HI-HEMS), these insect cyborgs receive implants in early stages of their metamorphosis that fuse with their

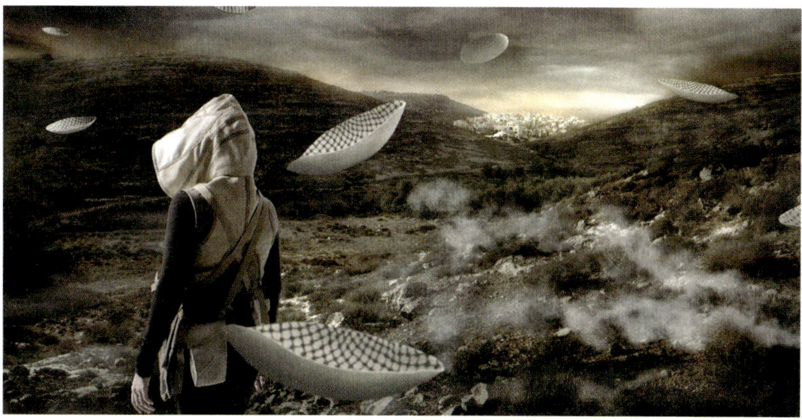

bodies as they grow.[19] They are hence bred and physiologically mobilized for warfare and aerial surveillance.

Employment of insects for warfare is premised on the devaluation of insect life. Insects appear alongside other nonhuman animals, such as dogs, to carry out military tasks that include the detection of landmines.[20] Insects are deployed on the front lines, the first to be exposed to harmful chemicals that their bodies cannot withstand. Current directions of research and development in the military utilize insects as laborers for human ends, instrumentalizing their anatomy, sensory capabilities, and communicational skills for warfare. Not only is this a coercive extraction of insect labor, but the incorporation of insect populations into the military leads to their biopolitical management, which has adverse effects on biodiversity. As Renisa Mawani has argued, the protection of one population of insects for industrial use (such as bees) can mean the annihilation of other insects (such as bedbugs) within urban centers.[21] Exploitation of feral insects is hence tied to new forms of control and governance that exceed the management of insect colonies alone. "This is the crux of biopolitics," Mawani writes, "the liveliness of some depends on the death of others."[22]

Killing insects in large populations had already been underway in the last century when chemists, entomologists, and military researchers developed chemicals that could kill multiple species at once. Development of novel explosives during World War II, for instance, produced new chemicals that were marketed and manufactured as pesticides.[23] Such models for mass killings of multiple species initiated by modern warfare is not only premised upon the devaluation of nonhuman lives but the animalization of enemy populations. This is acutely demonstrated today as insect cyborgs are conceptualized for military combat. The war on terror not only harnesses insects to advance new methods of movement, communication, and surveillance, but it does so based on the assumption that the enemy is acting like insects.

Tactics such as "swarming," for instance, were formulated to emulate and predict an enemy who is perceived to be "without 'front lines,' without a 'definable territory,' without a singular ideologically definable group, and without a 'nation state.'"[24] It was this definition of the terrorist as a dispersed network that "will not fight by rules of ethical warfare" that necessitated the conceptualization of the battlefield after insect intelligence.[25] Swarming, according to Eyal Weizman, is currently favored by the Israeli army because it aims to combat the "diffused nature of Palestinian resistance."[26] Unlike previous maneuvering tactics, swarming is a decentralized military technique that is in constant long-distance communication and is designed to attack from several directions simultaneously.[27] Entomological combat is thus an appropriation of one life form to kill another. It treats insects as disposable life as well as prototypes for killing others.[28] Here insects and terrorists merge to create a multispecies assemblage of killable bodies.

Sansour's video is apt at conveying the intersection of devalued multispecies lives through visual, sonic, and narrative form. As noted, the video begins with a row of insect cyborgs lifting off the ground to deliver bombs inserted into their mechanical bodies. The video brings a great deal of attention to the meticulous design of insect cyborgs. In one scene, a darkened chamber within the body of an insect evocatively comes into view, revealing rows of assembled bombshells rotating on a revolver. The video conveys these mechanized actions sonically through cold sounds of hinged metal that snaps open to release bomb capsules onto the desert landscape below. Caught in a swarm of cyborg insects is none other than the video's narrator, the Narrative Terrorist, who tells of a recurrent dream in which she is caught in a trickling rain thick with porcelain particles. The light rain inevitably turns into a heavy monsoon pounding her body with porcelain objects. As she cowers onto the ground under the torrent, she becomes both target and witness to the destruction and extinction of lifeworlds around her (figure 17.3).

War's Ecology

The ecology of war, so aptly conveyed in Sansour's video, raises broader questions about biopolitical managements of multispecies lifeworlds on militarized, settler-colonial lands such as Palestine. The notion of biopower was famously theorized by Michel Foucault in his 1976 lectures, where he described a new form of state power emerging in the nineteenth century that was concerned with the livelihood of populations. Foucault coined the term *biopower* to name governmental projects that monitored birth and mortality rates, constructed large-scale plans for identifying and eradicating endemic disease, managed health risks in ailing and elderly populations, and managed infrastructural efforts designed to guard urban and rural spaces against erosion and deterioration.[29] What distinguishes biopower from other forms of power for Foucault is that it brings biological matter under state control. Biopower, he notes, "is applied not to man-as-body but to the living man, to man-as-living-being; ultimately, if you like, to man-as-species."[30] Biopower's sphere of influence is thus not simply the social life of humans but humans as biological species, who are environmentally entangled with complex networks of other species. Biopower guards the human against biological and climatic dangers by governing what poses a threat to human populations' well-being. It is no surprise that Foucault's examples of biopower revolve around biological and ecological disruptions of human social life. Concerned with controlling swamps, floods, and epidemics, biopower's sphere of administration is, in Foucault's words, "the geographical, climatic, or hydrographic environment," the very multispecies habitat of living organisms.[31]

Biopower thus describes social organizations that make man-as-species live while killing all that threatens it. In Foucault's text, the threat to man-as-species is figured as ecologies of climatic disruption (swamps) and endemic disease plaguing human populations. Man-as-species is here pitched against climatic and microbial organisms that become an assemblage of killable life forms. This is precisely why what counts as *bio* in biopower is a selective rendering of life that not only excludes a whole range of biological organisms (such as insects and viruses) but also humans who come to be known as terrorists. As I have elaborated throughout this book, ailing and racialized bodies subject to mass killings are the ecologies of terrorism. Terrorists are categorically excluded from man-as-species (the Anthropos), but are ecological threats that do not receive biopolitical protection. Under the war on terror, the terrorist, the monsoon, the flood, and the virus are combined. "To be the Virus," writes Povinelli, "is to be subject to intense abjection and attacks, and to live in the vicinity of the Virus is to dwell in an existential crisis."[32] This "existential crisis" is a crisis of what counts as existence and the fraught nature of who counts as the biological *bio* to be protected by biopower.

Geographies and ecologies of terror are hence demarcated and bordered off from biopolitical protection. "This is the figure of today's threat," writes Brian Massumi, "the suddenly irrupting, locally self-organizing, systematically self-amplifying threat of large-scale disruption."[33] The threatening enemy of man-as-species, according to this definition, is unpredictable. It can show up, like a monsoon or a hurricane, anywhere at any time to cause enormous damage. When not actively causing disturbances, the enemy subsides into the background but remains active, still threatening on the horizon. The image of today's enemy is environmental. "Its continual micro-flapping in the background," Massumi writes, "makes it indistinguishable from the general environment, now one with a restless climate of agitation."[34] The terrorist is not simply an epidemic virus but an environment in flux, churning in a state of perpetual unrest.

This image of threat as dormant, as that which can erupt at any moment, leads to a form of governance that is future-oriented. We see biopower at work when we read weather forecasts, medical statistics, and insurance pamphlets narrating catastrophic scenarios looming on the horizon. We are engrossed in biopolitics when we tune into knowledge-systems that not only describe the present state of affairs but attempt to manage the future before it even arrives. Choreographed by what Kodow Eshun has termed "the Futures Industry," biopolitics generates economic predictions, medical and educational reports, risk assessments, and forecasts about life expectancy and natural resources.[35] While Foucault primarily theorized biopower in relation to "security mechanisms" designed "to optimize a state of life," it is clear that enhancement of life is not its main effect in large parts of the globe.[36] A mere look at current news headlines, for instance, brings us face to face with predictions for years of instability, risk, and vulnerability for the majority of countries in West Asia and Africa. A short sampling of recent headlines on West Asia reads: "The Middle-East's Chaotic Future" (*Washington Post*, 2015); "Here's Why the Middle East Will Be 'On Fire' for the Foreseeable Future" (*Business Insider*, 2014); "Syria's Future: A Black Hole of Instability" (*New York Times*, 2016); "Future of Israel/Palestine More Uncertain than Ever,' Warns Senior UN Official" (*United Nations News Centre*, 2016) "A Year of ISIL: 'There Is no Future for

Iraq'" (*Aljazeera*, 2015); "Trump's Victory Injects Uncertainty into a Chaotic Middle East" (*Time*, 2016); "New Conflicts Are Already Shaping an Already Volatile Middle East" (*Economist*, 2021).

These headlines are not mere descriptions but active mattering of the globe into distinct geographies of terror. These are regions that are not simply at risk but risky: a risk that is itinerant, a risk that is viral. The Futures Industry gives us tales of breeding grounds for terror that must be thwarted before migrating to other sites. A country such as Pakistan, for instance, has been formulated, in Junaid Rana's words, "as a feeder state that produces terrorism to be exported abroad and that stands at the front lines of the War on Terror."[37]

A key concept in contemporary governance of such threats is preemption. "Preemption," Massumi writes, "is a time concept" which implies "acting on the time before: the time of threat before it has emerged as a clear and present danger."[38] Massumi insists on the temporal nature of contemporary governance in order to adjust our understanding of biopower from one that describes power over life (bio) to one that has a hold on the time *before* life has had the opportunity to emerge. Preemption attempts to control the potential for future existence. In Massumi's words, this is power that enforces itself in "pores of the world where life is just stirring, on the verge of being what will become, but as yet barely there."[39] This is exemplified by the power of the US military that preemptively marched into Iraq in 2003 to halt the development of what George W. Bush called "weapons of mass destruction," which the soldiers never found but they themselves became for the Iraqi people. Preemption is future-oriented: a future that it seeks to preemptively act upon so as to control its very becoming.

Living in geographies of terror is to live as part of a threatening environment of emergence. The protagonist in Sansour's video gives voice to the dystopia that surrounds her past, present, and possible futures. In a poignant moment in the video, the Narrative Terrorist remarks that she lives with a profound sense of loss because everything around her dies and disappears. "This place was always a barely functioning dystopia," she declares, "it all disappears little by little." Her interlocutor in the video concurs, "The apocalypse never is that single cataclysmic event. It sneaks up on you." To which the Narrative Terrorist responds, "Ever since I can remember, it was a time of disappearance. The bereavement is both material and aesthetic. Smells, sounds, views, the very sense of motion. All gone."

I quote this dialogue at length because it speaks to a distinct difference between the experience of war in war zones and the ways that threat is imagined and defined by the war on terror. Unlike the sudden, eruptive and apocalyptic notions of threat promoted by the military-industrial-complex, those living in war zones experience threat on an ongoing basis. Violence in war zones is not exceptionalized with singular markers, such as 9/11, but is ceaseless and uninterrupted. Apocalyptic visions, as Sansour's protagonists point out, sensationalize threat as sudden cataclysmic eruptions in need of biopolitical control. In contrast, the Narrative Terrorist describes a prolonged, almost quotidian, experience of everyday violence. "Ever since I remember," she notes in the dialogue, "it was a time of disappearance." Loss, in this statement, is not a singular event but as old as one can remember. It is an experience traversing generations.

The Narrative Terrorist's prolonged experience of extinction is reminiscent of what Rob Nixon calls "slow violence."[40] In contrast to the spectacle of outbreaks, slow violence is a less visible experiences of loss. "Slow violence," in Nixon's words, is "violence that occurs gradually and out of sight, a violence of delayed destruction that is dispersed across time and space, an attritional violence that is typically not viewed as violence at all."[41] Slow violence can name the aftermath of an explosion, for instance, whose chemical residue may appear in living organisms over generations. These are forms of violence that may not appear today but have psycho-somatic effects in living beings beyond our perspectives and far into the future. Slow violence names complex networks of micro- and macroaggressions taking environmental, patriarchal, racist, ableist, and economic forms with long-term effects. These are violences experienced in cumulative forms that chip away at lifeworlds "little by little" over time. The Narrative Terrorist's aesthetic description of bereavement as a loss of familiar sensations of sounds, smells, and movements conveys a prolonged ecology of extinction, one that coexists with more visible forms of aggression to create total environments of depletion.

It is precisely such wastelands that compelled Achille Mbembe to offer an addendum—or perhaps a corrective—to Foucault's concept of biopower. While Foucault's biopower described optimization of life through insurance plans, social security, and modern medicine, it said little about economic sanctions and military expenditures meant to tear down infrastructures and destroy social and ecological networks. In his essay "Necropolitics," Mbembe asks: "Is the notion of biopower sufficient to account for the contemporary ways in which the political, under the guise of war, of resistance, or of the fight against terror, makes the murder of the enemy its primary and absolute objective?"[42] In other words, while biopower is in the business of "optimizing" life for some, it does not describe the concurrent injuring and impairment of others. "I have put forward the notion of necropolitics and necropower," Mbembe writes, "for the various ways in which, in our contemporary world, weapons are deployed in the interest of maximum destruction of persons and the creation of *death-worlds*."[43] In Mbembe's formulation, the "life-worlds" of biopolitics coexist with the "death-worlds" of necropolitics, yet their boundaries are strictly guarded and policed on a global scale.

Mbembe rests his conceptualization of necropolitics on historical and contemporary instances of death-worlds in plantation slavery, apartheid South Africa, and Palestinian territories of Gaza and the West Bank. In each case, he describes specific workings of necropolitics on grounds that aim to destroy social and environmental ecosystems. His evocative detailing of military tactics in Palestine bear close resemblance to those depicted in Sansour's video. Mbembe describes territorial fragmentation of Palestine into isolated lands that are bulldozed, "demolishing houses and cities; uprooting olive trees; riddling water tanks with bullets," which are then policed and surveilled from above by helicopters.[44] Such leveling of Palestinians into the ground mirrors Sansour's dream of a military monsoon that not only kills individuals but destroys entire habitats surveilled from above.

Life in militarized wastelands are demoralizing because they are expected to remain unchanged for generations. The narrative arc of the Futures Industry feeds us dispiriting statistics, convincing us of our "predatory futures" and insisting that at least "the next 50 years will be hostile."[45] These predictions are unnerving because, as Eshun notes, "they command us to bury our heads in our hands, to groan with sadness."[46] Rather than the grinning faces of biopolitical administrators selling insurance packages, necropolitics faces us in despair. It is no surprise that artists attempt to intervene in this futurist vision: a vision that urges us to bow our heads in distress and acquiesce to its predatory force.

If we agree that the knowledges generated by the Futures Industry are not mere observations but active mattering of a region in turmoil, then how stories are narrated matter immensely. To tell a story against dystopic algorithms is to be a narrative terrorist. It is narrative terrorism to imagine life where the Futures Industry only sees damage and decay. It is not short of narrative terrorism to claim a home that is actively managed for your exile. More radically, it is narrative terrorism that wrests these regions from the human scale of knowledge-production altogether—"the next 50 years"—throwing them into a temporality that does not center the human but thinks with the timescale of alternate geoforms.

Crude Aesthetics

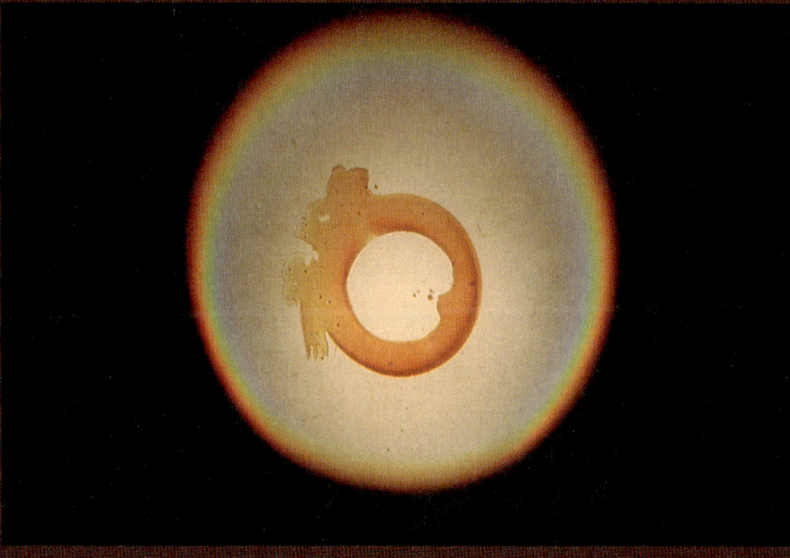

18

Texas Crude

I arrived at her studio on a hot summer day. Los Angeles in August is often full of smoke, with wildfires burning in canyons and rugged hillsides where thick brush erupts in a blaze too large for firefighters to contain in the dry arid heat. The layer of smoke that hung in the air, heavy with warning and anticipation, was the perfect setting for our conversation about oil. I was meeting Gelare Khoshgozaran in her Los Angeles studio to talk about her recent work with petroleum. Like myself, she had been researching political histories of oil extraction and was examining the role of art and visual culture in presenting such histories. We both had an interest in the fraught imperial legacies of petroleum industries in Iran, one of the earliest and largest oil-producing economies.

What Khoshgozaran had to tell me that day was an unexpected story about two gallons of crude oil that had refused to become art. As she described it, she had decided to experiment with crude oil as a visual medium and had ordered two gallons from a company in Texas called Texas Raw Crude (figures 18.1 and 18.2). When the package arrived in her studio, with a hefty bill of $150 USD, it became immediately apparent that crude oil was no mere inert material that could be put to use as an artistic medium. Instead, the package had arrived with a pungent smell that had already filled the room with its presence. This was a material with its own aesthetics that impinged itself strongly upon the nose.

Khoshgozaran was initially optimistic. She imagined that the smell would soon dissipate. It was perhaps the tight packaging, and the long distance the shipment had traveled, that had created such a pungent smell. The odor must have been trapped in the box, she thought, and would soon disperse if she left the package outside in open air. "What did it smell like?" I asked. Without hesitation she exclaimed, "Like a million dead bodies!"

What was the source of this putrid smell? What is in crude oil?

The package had some answers to these questions. Texas Crude had included paperwork with clues about the crude oil's chemical makeup. The company had sent along an analytical laboratory report summarizing what the lab had found in the sample shipment. In numerical language, the report explained that crude oil was highly combustible. It set its "flash point" at 122° F and its "fire point" at 130° F. This meant that the oil in her studio would ignite at 122° F and would keep on burning if the temperatures shot up to 130° F. Going by these numbers in the report, one could safely assume that the package in the artist's studio was at least not flammable. East Los Angeles is known to have temperatures as high as 112° F in the summer months, but not high enough to spontaneously ignite these two gallons of crude oil.

But the smell! That was another story altogether. The laboratory report had something to say about the smell too. The report showed that the crude oil they tested included hydrogen sulfide. Numerically it was gauged at "<1.0 ppm." What does this mean? Hydrogen sulfide (H_2S) is a colorless gas. It is released when plants and animals begin to decay. This is why hydrogen sulfide is often found at mining and fossil fuel extraction and refinement sites.[1] When we open the earth and dig below we find organisms decomposing into pure muck, into layers of oozing matter that had once faced the sun above in the light of the living. But down below, in the absence of oxygen, flesh becomes matter, and this process of decomposition produces the invisible gas we know as hydrogen sulfide.

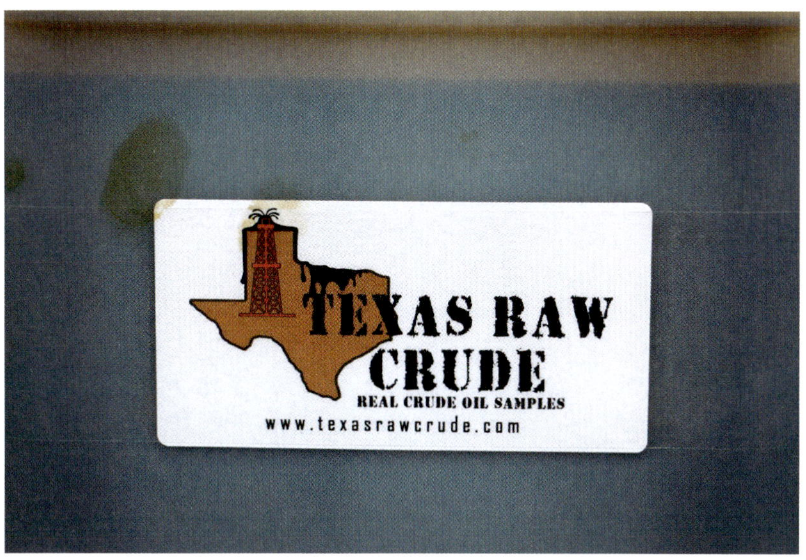

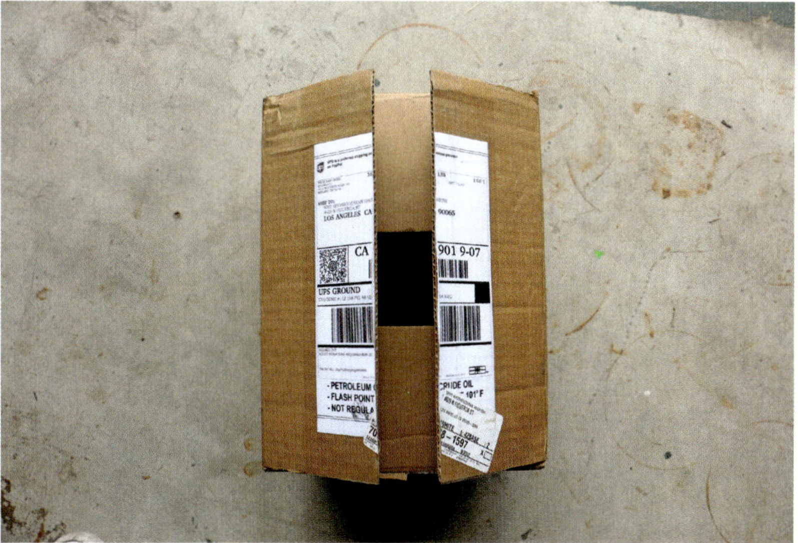

FIGURES 18.1 AND 18.2 The package had arrived with a pungent smell that had already filled the room with its presence. Gelare Khoshgozaran, ephemera from *Crude*, 2018. Courtesy of Gelare Khoshgozaran.

Not being able to see hydrogen sulfide is not a problem. It does not indicate any impairments in our vision or nervous system. Troubles begin when we lose our ability to smell it. The medical consultant Tee Guidotti, while working at a petroleum extraction site, reports that oil-field workers are almost glad to smell the putrid, "rotten egg" smell of hydrogen sulfide. This is because, they say, "you're not really in trouble until you can't smell it anymore."[2] The issue is that at higher levels, hydrogen sulfide paralyzes the olfactory system, inhibiting our ability to smell.[3] Such a scenario is a warning for worse conditions to follow, including loss of breath, amnesia, loss of consciousness, and even death within four to eight hours.[4]

While an olfactory collapse results from high exposure, hydrogen sulfide is offensive to the nose at fairly low levels. If you can smell it, it means that it is present in some amount. Its olfactory threshold—the level at which you can smell the substance—is set at 0.01 ppm. This is a small fraction of what showed up in the laboratory report shipped to the artist's studio. Her lab report found close to 1 ppm. At this level, hydrogen sulfide is much more pungent and very toxic. At numbers ranging between 1–5 ppm, hydrogen sulfide is found to have a dizzying odor and can lead to "nausea, tearing of the eyes, headaches, or loss of sleep with prolonged exposure."[5]

It is no surprise then that the artist was unable to keep the package in her small studio and had resolved to leaving it outside. But the air over Los Angeles, choked with smoke and smog, was no match for the rotten smell that stuck to it like thick yolk. As the days went by, the artist found the foul odor to be claiming an increasingly larger radius around her studio. Still unwilling to give up, she decided to put the package in a refrigerator. Perhaps there was a way to freeze the smell out of her crude oil. This did not work either. It was as if the substance was rebelling against her very senses. How could she work with a material such as this one? What is there to do with a material that came with its own aesthetics, its own sensibility? How could she make art with a substance impacting her olfactory system in such a way that overwhelmed all other senses? What could she bring to a material that refused a formal transformation? Could the crude oil in her studio ever go from putrid to harmonious? From nausea to pleasure? After over six months of struggle, the artist gave up and parted with the substance altogether. She found a way to dispose of it via hazardous waste. A trace of the crude oil, however, remains visually as part of a short experimental video the artist made titled *Crude*, where a smear of oil interacts with projected light (figure 18.3).

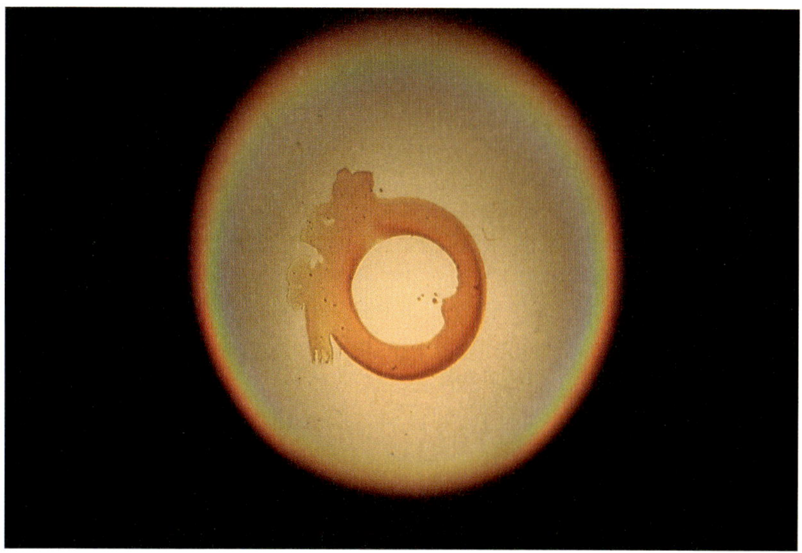

FIGURE 18.3 A smear of oil interacts with projected light. Gelare Khoshgozaran, still from *Crude*, 2018. Courtesy of Gelare Khoshgozaran.

What can we make of such an episode? Khoshgozaran's experience with the pungency of crude oil says much about oil's aesthetic materiality. Crude oil is a substance—indeed a million dead organisms compressed into gelatinous form over time—that confronts us with its toxic force. This is a substance that refuses our approach. In our presence, it issues a warning telling us to keep away. Do not touch me or you will burn! Do not smell me or you will collapse! Crude oil expresses this sentiment with a pungent smell that threatens to knock us out. In the presence of crude oil, we are caught in an aesthetic battle. It is our senses against it. It can shut us down by cracking the olfactory, by disrupting our proprioception, our sense of balance and consciousness. It can fill our lungs until they burst.

Toxicity is not often described as an aesthetic experience. We should ponder this oversight. As noted earlier in this book, the term *aesthetics* comes from the Greek word *Aisthitikos*, which means "perceptive by feeling."[6] It refers to our capacity for sensory experience. When the external organs on the surface of our bodies—our nose, eyes, ears, mouth, and the sensitive tissues of our skin—mediate the boundaries between our bodies and the outside world, we are in the realm of aesthetics. The "original field of aesthetics," as Susan Buck-Morss describes it, "is not art but reality."[7] In its Greek sense, aesthetics does not venerate objects of perception. It simply refers to our capacity to perceive. The hierarchal classification of our senses comes later with Enlightenment philosophers, such as Immanuel Kant, who privileged those sense perceptions that built the largest distance between us and the outside world. In Kant's schema, senses such as hearing and sight were "objective" because they "require[d] the mediation of light or air" between the subject and the perceived object.[8] When we see and hear things, our bodies do not come into direct contact with what we perceive. Sight distances us from what we see. It works through the mediation of light. Hearing distances us from sound, needing air particles to flow through.

In contrast, smell and taste fall to the bottom of the aesthetic hierarchy because, as Jacques Derrida describes it, "the sensible gets mixed in, with saliva for example, and penetrates the organ without preserving its objective subsistence."[9] Licking and sniffing take the outside in and are classified as base acts accumulated at the bottom of the aesthetic hierarchy. This explains why visual arts and music remain at the apex of sensory perception while proximal senses of touch, taste, and smell are associated with sensuality, sexuality, and other instincts relegated to the lower orders of aesthetic perception.[10] Proximal senses bring us into direct contact with people and things. Proximal senses are not "objective" but sites of entanglements and contamination.

We might say that toxins revel in our base senses. They mix with our fluids, with mucus, with saliva, and slide into the intimate organs of our bodies. Toxicity is a good place to explore aesthetics because it brings the distancing mechanism of our sense organs into crisis. When we inhale toxins, our sense organs become enmeshed with the outside world. In the presence of a colorless gas, such as hydrogen sulfide, we cannot rely on the security of our "objective" sense of vision. Hydrogen sulfide slips across our eyes and down into our gaping nasal and buccal cavities. Once inside, the colorless gas becomes a part of our moist internal organs traveling down the hollow respiratory and alimentary canals. When we host toxins, we begin to question where the inside begins and the outside ends. We are, after all, anatomically crossed with open tracts that manage the passage of liquids and gas. Our digestive and respiratory systems are the most exterior spaces of our bodies that are paradoxically held on the interior of our bodies. When toxins enter, we are reminded of the complex passageways of our anatomy that flip us inside out.

Intoxication is an aesthetic experience where our sense organs become bound with toxins. Intoxication makes it difficult to designate a separation between the body and the toxin. They meld and act together. This is what Mel Y. Chen has called our "toxic sensorium," a sensory apparatus that binds our bodies with objects balancing on a felt orientation toward the world.[11] "It is never a simple matter to discuss toxicity," Chen writes, "to objectify it."[12] With toxicity, objectivity becomes a farce, a slippery fiction that is difficult to uphold. Toxicity engages our proximal senses. In the presence of toxins, such as crude oil, we perceive through contact. Our skin becomes enflamed, our eyes water, our senses become overwhelmed. Engaging our toxic sensorium means a move beyond separating ourselves from the objects we encounter and acknowledging that toxins work through and within the porous boundaries of our bodies.

This final part of the book takes up the challenge of engaging toxicity as an aesthetic perception. Can toxic materials such as oil teach us something about how we sense ourselves in the world? In the course of researching and writing this book, I have often wondered about traces of petrochemicals in my body. What would a lab find in my bloodstream, in my cellular structure? What is my toxic physiology? What kinds of contaminants do I carry as someone who grew up in the polluted city of Tehran and who has lived in parts of the world that sometimes have more cars than people? The Canadian poet Adam Dickinson took the steps I only ever speculated about by sending samples of his blood, urine, feces, and sweat to a lab for testing. What he finds is the chemical trace of his historical and geographical place. "I wear uranium from well water in the Canadian Shield and from the nuclear testing that marks me as a child of the Cold War," he writes, "I house bacterial colonies that have become empires of the Western diet, fueled by sugar, salt and fat."[13] Dickinson's work tempts me to send my own fluids to the lab but before I do, I read these lines in Dickinson's book, "What is inscribed in me is in you too."[14]

We are the physiological traces of our place and time. We are hosts to multiple microbes and organisms whose interactions with our bodies leave us questioning where our autonomy or separations from them begin and end. We are composite, contaminated beings mired within multiple bodies, histories, generations, and geographies. Contamination is what makes life possible. Anna Lowenhaupt Tsing has powerfully noted that "everyone carries a history of contamination: purity is not an option."[15] For Tsing, to be contaminated is to be transformed by our encounters.[16] Contamination is not simply about toxicity but about how we engage the world and others within it. This is the sense in which Kathleen Stewart also uses the term *contaminated* when she asks for a "contaminated theory" rather than an objective one. Contaminated theorizing "disrupts the distance between observing subject and the 'real' world of objects," Stewart writes. "It mixes with its object and includes itself as an object of its own analysis."[17]

Contaminated theorizing requires the theorist's intimate participation. It is akin to how Khoshgozaran engages with crude oil, where it is the material itself that directs our aesthetic relation to it. Unlike extractivist demands that crude becomes refined—cleansed of its impurities for use as fossil fuel—Khoshgozaran's practice ruminates on crude aesthetics. This is an aesthetic approach that refuses human mastery over subterranean fossils, engaging instead with oil's pungent and toxic materiality. It is difficult to conclusively decide why Khoshgozaran and I—alongside a handful of other Iranian artists and scholars today—share an interest in crude oil. It is perhaps due to our contaminated histories, our entanglements with oil in physical, psychological, historical, and political ways. We suspect that oil has something to say about our place in the world, about our histories as imperial subjects, about the ongoing wars that have shaped our geopolitical belongings. It is clear to us that the story of crude oil is the story of our aesthetic sensibilities.

19

A Fire!

In 1958, the Iranian documentary filmmaker Ebrahim Golestan was commissioned by the National Iranian Oil Company (NIOC) to capture an incident at an oil well in the southwest of Iran. An oil well had erupted into a blaze of fire, and the film crew was tasked with capturing the efforts of the oil company to subside its flames. In this film, titled *A Fire!*, we arrive at a petroleum drilling site in the city of Ahwaz, located in the southwest of Iran, to watch the consequences of the eruption and the company's methods of containment. This was not the first time that Golestan had been asked to make a film for the oil company. A year earlier, he had traveled to the southwest of Iran to film an educational piece about the company's oil discoveries in the region, a piece that had established him as a documentary filmmaker.[1] This time, in 1958, he had set out to film the company's efforts to contain one of the biggest fire disasters at an oil well that took seventy days to complete.

As those who have watched Golestan's documentary have assessed, this thirty-minute short is more than a simple documentary. At the time of its completion in 1961, it was screened and lauded at the Venice Film Festival and praised by the art community at home.[2] A local film critic praised *A Fire!* for having saved Iranian cinema, crediting in particular the film's superb editing. "Considering its stunning editing," the critic wrote, "it elevates the film from merely an educational piece about fires in oil wells."[3] The filmmaker and the editor, he continued, "have created a pure work of art out of the blazes of fire."[4]

A Fire! was edited by the well-known feminist poet Forough Farrokhzad who would go on, in the following year, to make her signature film *The House Is Black* (1962), a film praised for inaugurating Iranian new wave cinema.[5] What her style of filmmaking introduced to Iranian cinema, as Sara Saljoughi has argued, is a fluid overlay of fact and fiction.[6] More specifically, her work treats cinematic image as poetic language. As a poet, not only did her cinematic output include poetic voice-overs but created a specifically poetic cinematic language. Her films are provocative for how poetry, in her hands, becomes the language "through which cinema is politicized."[7] In other words, her cinematic style did not merely add poetry to cinema but mobilized cinema for political work.

Given her role as the editor of *A Fire!*, we must look to the film's editing to understand its political intervention. We must look to the sequential flow of images, to the abrupt cuts and jarring juxtapositions. We must look to the alignment of color and sound for clues to its political poetics. What are the petropolitics of this film and how are they conveyed in cinematic language? What contaminated histories does this documentary film tell? In order to answer these questions, I want to first provide a summary of the film with a focus on the alignment of images and sound through the editing process and then take a brief detour into the historical context in which the film was produced. I will then return to the politics of oil's aesthetics of dissent.

A Fire! opens with an explanatory remark about the events that had brought the film crew to the scene. "In the Spring of 1958," the film begins, "an oil well was being drilled at a place near Ahwaz in Iran. The drilling bit had passed through the gas-filled layers and was penetrating the oil bearing rocks." A bright yellow sign spelling "Danger" in both Farsi and English fills the screen like a portent of the events to follow. The film then cuts to a sheep grazing on a hillside. The sheep skips around in a circular motion before joining its flock across the ridged landscape. A group of children chase one another among mud huts in the neighboring area. "Suddenly, a spark flew," announces the film's English-speaking narrator in a British accent. The film is now orange with flames rolling with the noisy rush of a waterfall across the screen. "Soon after," the narrator begins in a calm voice, "the fire became a part of the landscape." Black smoke rises from the flames and stretches for miles across the pastures below. The camera pans over the landscape to follow the billowing smoke poised over the horizon. "Sheep are accustomed to it," the voice-over continues, "but men sought ways to kill it."

This initial juxtaposition of the fire with grazing animals and roaming children in every scene sets the tone for the political language of editing exhibited in the remainder of the documentary. The camera now begins to film a crew of men from the oil company, in their hard hats and thick gloves, building devices to battle the flames. "The fire was made up of gases which shot up into the air from the well and instantly burst into flames," explains the narrator: "It was decided to smother the jet of gas right at the source." Men carry heavy bags of cement, pouring heaps of its powdered content around the walls of the well. They build metal pipes to direct water from the Karun River to soak the landscape surrounding the fire. They build metallic shields to facilitate their approach toward the flames.

"The operations were led by a man tempered by many fires," the narrator explains, his name is Myron Kinley. Born in the United States, Kinley had devised a method of extinguishing fires at oil wells using dynamite. As the narrator explains, "The fire was to be killed with the mighty puff of an explosion." Kinley's "puff method" used dynamite to separate the flame from its source. Similar in principle, but vastly different in proportion, to blowing out a candle. Explosives, such as dynamite, are used to send shockwaves to the site of the fire so as to separate the burning flames from their endless supply of fuel pouring out of the ground. The men were fighting fire with fire.

As the night falls, columns of smoke blend into the dark sky, offsetting the deep glow of orange-red flames. "And when darkness came and the searing heat of the desert gave way to the crawling cool of the desert night," the narrator recites, "the duel was on." The men in their metallic armor continue to build a large claw. They fasten a hook at the edge of a crane to clear the burnt wreckage at the well and to deliver the dynamite. "The long arm" says the narrator, "carries forward the gift of death." We hear the collective voices of men pushing the instrument forward. These scenes retain the voices of Farsi speakers, the men working at the front lines of the fire. They work with the chant of "Ya, Ali! Ya, Ali!," summoning their Shi'i imam Ali for strength. The camera looks up to the sky, capturing the moon shining in its dull, fulvous light.

"Little was gained," the narrator utters in dismay: "Night passed and dawn came and harvest time came to the neighboring fields." At the heart of the documentary are scenes of harvest with fire and smoke billowing on the horizon. The loud rush of enflamed gas and the clanking of the instruments now give way to a melancholic song in the local dialect. The camera now sits low, kneeling down with the men and women hunched over their crops in the adjacent fields. It follows them at their feet as they step into yellow fields, picking grains that brush up against their knees (figures 19.1–19.3). Men with twists of turban shielding their heads from the heat and women with long veils blowing in the light breeze bend over at their hips to cut clusters of grain with sickles in their hands. The yellow fields stretch below their feet to join the flames on the horizon, rolling up like fluffs of clouds into the sky. The camera follows the men and women close as they pick up sheaves of wheat in large bundles. Columns of black smoke paint the sky as a woman rolls a bucket down a well to collect water. The locals gather together around an outstretched cloth laid out onto the ground to share food. They break bread to dip into separate pots holding rice, yogurt, and various kinds of stew. They drink water out of warped tin cans. They squat on the ground stirring sugar cubes into their tea cups. They rub their eyes and gaze at the orange glare rising up in the horizon.

It is difficult to watch oil workers captured by Golestan's camera in direct contact with natural gas without imagining the impact of the flames and soot on their lungs, their skin, their eyes. It is hard not to wonder about their toxic sensorium, their felt orientation to the fire and its contaminated trace within their bodies for years to come. When I think back to the effects of small amounts of hydrogen sulfide found in the crude oil in Khoshgozaran's studio, I am amazed at the proximity of these oil workers to the scene of fire captured on film. It is even more difficult to watch scenes of food consumption and mothers rocking their children to sleep without wondering about the physical trace of oil and gas in their bodies at the cellular level. It is impossible to watch segments of harvest in the film without considering the ingestive histories of petrochemicals at the national level. How contaminated is the soil and the water wells adjacent to these oil wells? I cannot watch the film without pondering about the

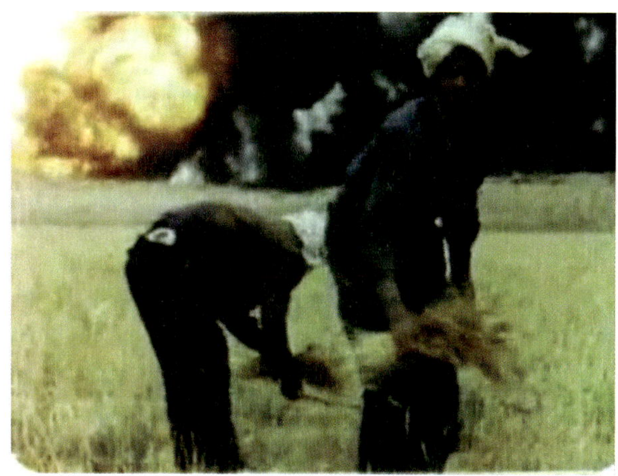

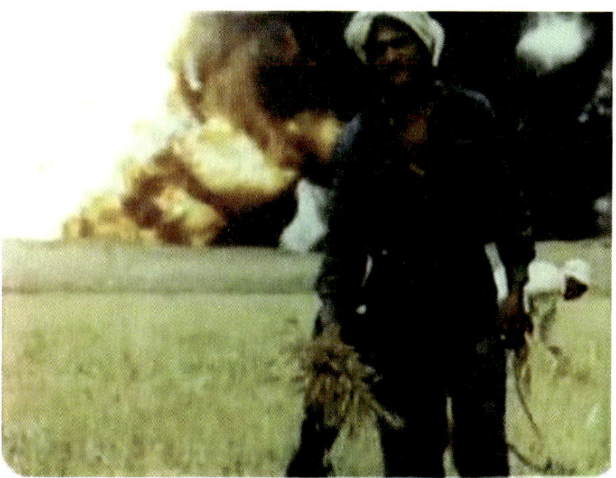

FIGURES 19.1–19.3 Men with twists of turban shielding their heads from the heat and women with long veils blowing in the light breeze bend over at their hips to cut clusters of grain with sickles in their hands. Stills from *A Fire!* dir. *Ebrahim Golestan*, 1958.

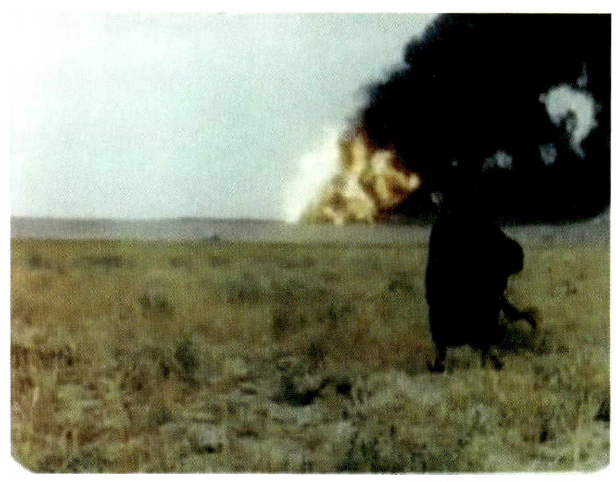

circulation of that year's harvest among locals and beyond. It is the film's editing, its juxtaposition of the blazing fire with scenes of harvest, that gives us pause to think about the overlap between oil, food, and contaminated histories.

"And still the fire was raging," announces the narrator: "The inhabitants of the nearby village had to be moved away. If the flames were put out, the place would be smothered in gas from the wild well." A few men set up a handful of white tents in a desert landscape. How far away is this new location that the villagers have been moved to? The film does not specify. Yet, we can see that the landscape remains the same as a yellow column of flame continues to be visible above the ridge of their tents. The sun glares as trucks pull up with the villagers' belongings. Children jump out of wagons carrying odds and ends. Women transport their belongings wrapped in large cloths above their heads. The film now transitions more rapidly between the oil crew delivering explosives to the fire and displaced villagers settling into their tents. The voice of a woman's soothing lullaby permeates these scenes as she rocks her children to sleep. A few miles away, explosives blast while children cry. A rapid sequence of explosive eruptions follows, each rocking the Earth in tandem with a mother's arm swinging her baby's crib. "There were many explosions," the narrator explains, "but after each the dead flames would leap back to life prompted by some persisting heat or vagrant spark."

After the last explosion, the flames subside, allowing the camera to see a tall pillar of natural gas shooting out of the earth. The crew begin to install an industrial valve to contain the gas rising above them like two white horns. When the valve is finally shut, seventy days had passed. "The remains of the fire, the broken poles, the twisted pipes and the mangled hooks," the narrator concludes, "the remnants of the scorching smoke and the salty desert dust, of days of sleepless eyes and nights of vigil and hope, of gasping and gazing, they all had to be cleared from the well site." The fire had been extinguished. The documentary ends with a final quote: "The fire was put out and the well now shut . . . and the effort continued to drill another well but that is another story. We call this picture *A Fire!*"

As my description of the film attests, the narrative plot is the oil company's ultimate suppression of an eruption at an oil well and their triumphant harnessing of natural gas through a large valve drilled into the earth. Intermittently, however, the camera tends to roam away to film the inhabitants of the surrounding area. In these scenes, the voices of oil workers muffled by the sounds of their machinery and extinguishers are interrupted by songs hummed by the men and women bent over their crops. In these scenes, we see farmers harvesting their fields against the backdrop of roaring flames looming large on the horizon. We watch them eating food and resting and rocking their children to sleep. Such scenes of local inhabitants, with their songs and voices scattered throughout the film, are unusual for educational documentaries made by oil companies. In my reading of the film, these scenes attest to the political poetics of its editor who juxtaposed the victorious narrative of conquering the harrowing forces of nature with living conditions in the vicinity of petroleum extraction sites.

To grasp the political significance of this film in more detail, it is important to examine the context in which it was made. When *A Fire!* was commissioned in 1958 by NIOC, the company had only just acquired its new "national" title. A mere four years earlier, the company had been known as the Anglo-Iranian Oil Company, one that had operated in Iran since oil was first struck by the British investor William Knox D'Arcy in the southwest region of the country in 1908.[8] Since its inception, D'Arcy's oil concession in the region was fraught with controversy. The contract had raised legal and ethical questions surrounding who could legitimately own fossil fuels trapped in lime-shale formations underground.[9] Who owned the land above the carbon-rich rocks? Who worked the land? Who built the infrastructures of oil extraction, and who was trained to acquire the skills necessary to do so? Who received the profits? Who lived in company housing and who was evacuated? These were questions that fueled disputes and labor strikes throughout the company's operations in Iran. The lack of resolution for such issues led to public demands for the nationalization of Iranian oil.

In 1951, massive public support for the newly elected prime minister, Mohammad Mosaddegh, enabled the approval of a bill to nationalize the Iranian oil industry.[10] The British company immediately retaliated by summoning international support to boycott Iranian oil and to place sanctions on the Iranian government. Financial blockage was an effective form of controlling access to the fields that were entirely shut down by June 1951.[11] Despite the boycotts, Mosaddegh's government continued to negotiate for Iran's sovereign rights over its natural resources and the revision of the terms of the concession. Before much success, however, his government was overthrown in 1953 in a coup orchestrated by the United States government and the CIA known as "Operation Ajax," followed by the installment of a government in Iran sympathetic to Anglo-American needs.[12] To ease anti-imperial sentiments in the Iranian public, the company was renamed National Iranian Oil Company. While NIOC nominally split with British Petroleum (BP), it continued to serve its interests on the international market.[13] The 1953 coup, as Katayoun Shafiee explains it, "effectively closed off the political possibility of more democratic forms of oil production as originally demanded by oil workers."[14]

A Fire! is made in the aftermath of this failed effort at nationalization and it is, in my reading, a reminder of the continuation of the company's failure to address local conditions of life in Iranian oil towns. Oil fields in the 1950s were sites of ongoing political struggle with massive protests spreading across the country.[15] At issue were jobs, education, and living conditions. One of the pressing issues was demands for the employment of Iranian workers in higher positions within the oil industry. Despite the fact that many Iranians migrated to extraction sites from all over the country, they were predominantly employed as unskilled laborers.[16] The top managerial positions as well as the well-paying technical jobs requiring higher skill sets were taken by British employees living in the country and a smaller number of elite Iranians. The company's employment model since its inception had provided training along racial lines, ensuring lower status for local and migrant South Asian workers employed in the company.[17] "From the start," Shafiee writes, "the company chose to organize and manage oil operations by fixing the skill set of the managerial and technical elite and the labor power to race, in locations of housing and work."[18]

Racial segregation was thus not limited to the workplace but influenced the infrastructural and urban development in southwestern oil towns in Iran. Towns built by the Anglo-Iranian Oil Company had many features of colonial cities. They were demographically segregated into bungalows for British workers while a large number of Iranians, Arabs, and South Asian migrant laborers lived in separate areas consisting of mud huts and structures built out of "sticks or bamboo and covered with palm leaves."[19] Class and racial barriers were features of the urban infrastructure that were flagged by access to social and cultural facilities. British staff had amenities such as cinemas, bus transportation, drinking water fountains (racially marked "not for Iranians"), and sports clubs.[20] In the aftermath of the explosion documented in *A Fire!*, for example, the British engineer at the site, Bryce Cameron, writes that the company residents in the area had "all the amenities of company oilfield life but lacked a swimming pool. Now, after the construction of the emergency pipeline to bring water from the far away

Karun River to fight the fire," he continues, the "club had all the water it needed. . . . At long last the residents had their pool!"[21]

In contrast, local and migrant laborers—most of whom arrived from the Persian Gulf region and India—lacked basic facilities. Inspectors traveling to southwest Iran spoke of deplorable living conditions for workers. They noted lack of basic facilities such as clean drinking water and were puzzled when they were shown company identification cards by individual laborers living in slums.[22] Housing consisted of sections titled Chadorabad (cloth and tent housing), Halabiabad (housing made out of tin), and Haseerabad (housing constructed from paper and straw).[23] Company amenities were off-limits to laborers, and

> they shared life amid networks of giant pipes, beneath cavernous holding tanks, and in the shadow of towering smokestacks from which plumes of flame leapt up day and night. The air was heavy with sulfur fumes, a constant reminder of the vast wealth that was pouring from Iranian soil into Anglo-Persian's coffers.[24]

A Fire! was made amid this everyday life of colonial urbanism, racial segregation, and social unrest. How did cinema enter into this context? How did it function under the newly minted NIOC, which had inherited the legacy of its imperial predecessor? Prior to nationalization, cinema had occupied a distinct role within the Anglo-Iranian Oil Company. It was used as a promotional tool for bolstering the company's image internationally.[25] Films transformed daily activities of the oil company into spectacles of modernity through sublime renderings of machinery and infrastructures needed for the extraction of oil and natural gas. "Modernity was constructed," Mona Damluji writes, "in terms of industrial technologies of oil that conquered and controlled inhospitable and barren Persian desert landscapes."[26] Early silent-era films presented spectacular displays of the industry's technological skill, from extraction and refinement methods to transportation through pipelines and tankers to domestic and military consumers in England.[27] Iran was a mere backdrop to the oil company's activities, and when Iranians began to appear in later films of the 1940s, it was to amplify their adoption of Western-style modernity.[28] Oil films presented petroleum as the necessary fuel of domestic and military advancement in England and the only route toward modernity in Iran. Such an image, Damluji writes, "renders invisible the material and social conditions of Iran's working class that resulted from the development of the oil industry."[29] Oil films of the Anglo-Iranian Oil Company, in other words, forgot the bodies that made modernity possible. They glossed over social unrest facing the industry and active protests spreading in its midst.

The oil industry's nationalization did not tamper its cinematic mission. Shortly after nationalization, the oil company began to establish a film department, providing equipment and accessories to invited Iranian filmmakers, such as Golestan, to make films for the industry.[30] Regarded as the first documentaries of Iranian cinema, these films show extraction and refinery sites in the southwest region and the affairs of British workers in Iran.[31] As Hamid Naficy has argued, the National Iranian Oil Company employed film to depict "Iran's progress and modernization, highlighting the role of the Shah and the NIOC in that direction."[32] The oil company had thus joined the overall mission of the sympathetic Anglo-American government of Mohammad Reza Shah, to promote the significance of oil in Iran's path toward Western-style modernity.[33]

I read Golestan's *A Fire!* against the grain of this modernizing impulse within the history of documentary filmmaking in Iran. Made as the last film before his resignation from the company,[34] the film's depiction of rural poverty is a pointed departure from earlier oil films that disregarded the local context.[35] Instead, *A Fire!* produces visual continuity between events at petroleum extraction sites and those living in close vicinity in order to mobilize a critique of the industry's exclusive vision of modernization and neglect of the local communities. This turn toward rural and village life as a critique of Western-style modernization is indicative of wider literary trends of the time. Poetry, novels, prose, and essays written in the 1950s and 1960s are preoccupied with presenting marginalized segments of society as politicized literary subjects.[36] The village, according to Fatemeh Shams, is politicized "by leftist intellectuals" in this period, "to protest against modernization," and to offer "literary critique of the state's autocratic modernization policies."[37] Accordingly, scenes of rural life in *A Fire!* voice a critique of industrialized modernity in Iran.

As I watch the film, I find the most exceptional aesthetic element in *A Fire!* to be its ability to present the fire itself as an agent of dissent within the social and political context of Iran's oil industry. Instead of a colonialist narrative of capture, this film mobilizes the explosive fire at the rig to speak for the widespread social unrest looming on the horizon. Oil, in this film, is on fire. How can it not be read as a forceful display of dissent? Golestan's camera captures the material force of oil and gas that is directly at odds with the oil company's desire to direct a smooth flow into pipelines. At a moment when oil workers' demands for nationalization were fueling widespread anti-imperial sentiments in the country, the fire at the oil well was joining the population in its political demonstrations. Commentators at the time interpreted the fire that broke out at the well in many ways. Some understood it to be sabotage. Others blamed its outbreak on incompetence and a lack of skills and professional knowledge. The British engineer, Bryce Cameron, working in the country during the fire's outbreak at the well describes the scene as follows:

> Suddenly and without warning to the crew working on the derrick floor, the gas in the reservoir, at a pressure of 2,500 pounds to the square inch, shot up with a scream and immediately caught fire. All the men jumped for their lives and thank goodness no one was injured. This was the first blow-out and fire in the Company's fifty-year history so it came as a shock to many, but to the mobs in the streets of Tehran, it appeared that the British were not going to gracefully hand over the oilfields but instead were bent on sabotage.[38]

As Cameron's description here suggests, the fire itself was never perceived as apolitical, but rather as a politicized agent participating in everyday social events. In his description, Iranian protestors at the capital in Tehran viewed the fire as arson. They suspected that the fire was orchestrated sabotage by British managerial staff in the face of demands for the industry's nationalization.

The British media had its own narrative spin on the events. The fire, as Cameron points out, had coincided with protests in Tehran. Newsreels from the period show that these protests were organized outside the British embassy coinciding with the arrival of Averell Harriman from the United States on a diplomatic mission to mediate the dispute between Iran's government and the Anglo-Iranian Oil Company.[39] British commentators of the event highlighted the rarity of such fires, emphasizing, as does Cameron, that it was the first of its kind in the company's history of operations in Iran. Why would a fire break out now, just as the British were exiting the scene? As if to respond, the media emphasized the lack of local expertise to handle fires of this scale. Showing footage of the fire juxtaposed with Harriman's negotiations with the Shah, one newsreel praised the crew's leader, Myron Kinley, for extinguishing the fire, emphasizing that "they are experts and experts are what Persia would lack as Mr. Harriman points out to premier Mosaddegh."[40]

The display of American expertise, and the lack of such skills among Iranians asking for nationalization of their oil industry, was a not so subtle argument against British departure from the oil fields. References to Iran's lack of expertise was echoed in other media segments, such as a documentary film tiled *Rig 20*, produced by BP, concerning the same fire in Iran.[41] In a narrative voice, similar to the voice-over narrating the events in *A Fire!*, this fourteen-minute short film emphasized the singularity of the fire in the company's operations in Iran and the lack of local expertise to tackle its force. When explaining the extent of a fire so large that "within 40 miles of its raging furnace it was impossible to speak," the narrator explains that "with no experience of fighting fires of this scale, the work of extinguishing this terrific conflagration was beyond the resources of those in the oil field." Such references were not only infantilizing commentaries about a nation's struggle for autonomy but forgetful of the Anglo-Iranian Oil Company's history of racialized education that created such knowledge disparities.

A Fire! was produced in the aftermath of what is considered a failed nationalization of the oil industry and could be read as weighing in on its political place within these debates. In its juxtaposition of the fire with harvest time coming to the adjacent fields, the film conveys a steady voice of dissent throughout the film. Despite scenes of the company's battle with the flames and its ultimate display of mastery over nature in a colonial and masculinist performance, the film also documents scenes of physiological entanglement between humans and petrochemicals. The film's masterful editing turns a colonial plot—beginning with geological dissent and ending with the heroic harnessing of natural energy—into a history of embodied struggle with modernity, industrialization, and toxicity. This is a film that speaks to contaminated histories at petroleum extraction sites and which imbricates oil's aesthetics of dissent with a sociopolitical national history.

Petrorefusal

How does oil enter critiques of colonial industrialization? My discussion thus far has laid out the sociopolitical context of Golestan's *A Fire!* Yet the question still remains: What can we make of the aesthetics of petroleum within this film? How does the materiality of oil amplify our sense of the political upheaval that the film attempts to depict? What can we make of the aesthetic presence of oil and gas that ignites each frame? It is, after all, petroleum itself that brings all the various actors—the filmmakers and the oil crew—to the scene. How can we read this film from the perspective of this nonhuman agent? Can nonhuman actors, such as crude oil, tell stories of their own? Political ones at that!

Questions about agential sensibility of nonhuman materials are difficult to ask. We can fathom what we sense when we encounter materials, such as crude oil, in their toxicity. But it is a challenge to consider what oil itself senses. Aesthetic theory has a long tradition of placing the human at the center of thought with little to no consideration for sentient and perceptive agents outside of the human body. As Katherine Hayles has provocatively asked, "What would it mean, then, to imagine an aesthetics in which the human is decentered and inanimate objects, incapable of sense perception as we understand them, are included in aesthetic experience?"[42] What would happen, in other words, if we thought aesthetics through the materiality of a substance such as crude oil? Can crude oil, as a sentient, living matter, enable aesthetic knowledge in such a way that breaks down the boundaries between the human and the nonhuman?

To contemplate this possibility, I want to return to the episode at Khoshgozaran's studio: the two gallons of oil that refused to become art. When Khoshgozaran ordered her package of Texas crude oil, she did not consider this material's capacity for refusal. Its pungent smell and toxicity brought a crude aesthetic sensibility that refused to become refined into an art object. Such episodes of petroleum refusal, I would suggest, are not new but form the very basis of our knowledge and interaction with crude oil for at least a century. Oil refuses our approach. Every time a drill bores into oil-bearing rocks, it has to navigate the highly flammable layers of oil and gas that can spark under the pressure of the drill and break into a blaze of fire. Extractive practices of the last hundred years have everywhere born witness to petroleum's aesthetics of dissent, to those numerous accounts of oil's refusal to find a smooth flow out of the earth and into a pipeline.

I call crude oil's refusal to become fuel *petrorefusal*. We see petrorefusal in films such as *A Fire!*, where flames scorching the film present an aesthetics of dissent, a performance of refusal to the men's approach, and an affront to further drilling into the Earth's geological layers sedimented into oil and gas over time. Petrorefusal shapes the foundation of how we come to know oil. Dissent happens to be not too far from aesthetics in that it also participates in the discourse of the senses. The word *dissent* derives from the Latin verb *dissentire*, meaning "differ in sentiment." To dissent is to know differently in accordance with our sensibility. To dissent is to sense differently so as to form a different sentiment. This brings dissent into the realm of aesthetics—which is the realm of the intelligible and the sensible. To dissent is to reactivate aesthetics in order to sense otherwise, to know otherwise. At extractive sites, crude oil has a sentience that differs from our own. When prodded and provoked to follow a straight path out of the well's shaft, it proposes a different sentiment. When it catches a spark and erupts into flames, oil issues an aesthetics of dissent in fire, one that is at odds with our desire to capture its energy as fuel.

In *A Fire!* petroleum-generated fire joined Iranian oil workers in their protest against the Anglo-Iranian Oil Company. It is no surprise that the explosion at an oil derrick became a media metaphor for the workers' sentiments against the imperial oil industry in Iran. Fire conveys the passions of the masses and the inability of governments to contain their unregulated spread where mass strikes appear to spread like wildfires.[43] "It is no coincidence that the idea of curfew to regulate the movements of urban bodies," write Nigel Clark and Kathryn Yusoff, "derives from *couvre feu*—the covering or extinguishing of fire."[44]

While fire can have metaphoric relations to mass movements, it is also important to move beyond the metaphor and to see fire as an active agent in protests where participants are asking for—and enacting—changing relations to ancestral fossils that are today regarded as fuels by petrochemical industries. In such instances, fires join human protestors to enable alternate futures. Fire is deconstructive. It burns so as to build anew. It has the ability to enact futures that are unlike what we find in the present.

20

The Devil's Excrement

Years ago I learned that the Venezuelan oil minister and founder of International Organization of Petroleum-Exporting Countries (OPEC), Juan Pablo Pérez Alfonzo, referred to oil as the "devil's excrement." What an expressive idea! I visualized the devil as an energetic presence, a gust of wind, a tornado picking up dust from the ground, throwing mud at trees that fall into the ocean. I envisioned the devil as invisible but heavy, a thick wind that registers itself on the body as resistance, pushing back and impeding movement. Alfonzo's phrase conjured for me a swirling energy, a cyclone (like Pazuzu), crushing objects together and laying them to waste. The excrement was the trail that the devil left behind as it moved through cities and forests churning matter together indiscriminately. This, after all, is how oil is produced. A process with a temporality that began millennia before us and into millennia after us, exceeding our imagination and embodied experiences of being. Much like excrement—which is formed in its formlessness out of red beets, golden raisins, and cream of broccoli soup—oil is processed life awaiting its resurrection into new forms.

The tellurian process of petroleum production within marine sediments and the Earth's crust is not inherently evil. It is merely the cyclical process of life and death facilitated by microorganisms that work to break down animal and vegetable matter back into the earthly elements they came from. Geologists agree that "oil was formed from organic matter" and that "microorganisms must have contributed to the process of [its] formation."[1] Bacteria and fungi metabolize organic matter, dissolving cellular structures that led to petroleum production. This metabolic process, I believe, is what connects the digestive mechanism of the earth with that of humanimal bodies. And it is indeed such parallelisms that push Alfonzo's invocation of "excrement" from a metaphorical mode of imagining petroleum to a plausibly material one. Petroleum is the toxic byproduct of the dissolution of organic matter just as excrement is the waste product after food is broken down by the microbiomes residing within our alimentary canals.

Yet, it is the "devil" that adds an additional affective charge to the tellurian excrement that Alfonzo was contending with. His phrase amplifies his distaste for base matter to one where excrement is extra revolting because it belongs to the devil. When Alfonzo coined the term, he was not thinking about the arcane process of petroleum production over the course of millennia. His declaration was informed by the political effects of oil extraction and the social structures of its industrialization within modern nation-states. Alfonzo's term had a terrorizing affect and a temporality that was not the deep timescale of petroleum production. Memorialized in his 1975 book *Hundiéndonos en el excremento del diablo* (Sinking in the devil's excrement), the "devil's excrement" was meant to express the unwanted effects of the oil economy for oil-producing states. Alfonzo's concern was the unexpected turn with which oil becomes a curse for those who get too close: those who live above bedrocks in which petroleum is found, those who extract it, those who refine it, and those who sell it. The "devil's excrement" is diabolic. It was coined to describe the way that petroleum's monetary benefits unpredictably sink oil-producing state economies.[2]

The devil in Alfonzo's description is a curse. It is a lurking figure, descending upon us to be contrary, to turn wealth into mud and petrodollars back into the paper pulp they came from. The devil is there to terrorize and to impede oil-producing countries' progressive aspirations. When I first heard the phrase "devil's excrement," I felt its energetic presence. It was as though I had met it before. It was as though it had been an (un)known actor in the drama of my life and the sociopolitical histories I had inherited. The devil was there in the middle-class aspirations of my parents' generation, who believed in the promise of development for modern Iran. Oil had led Iran's path toward social change in the first half of the twentieth century and had set the tone for the production of an economy that relied heavily on this one natural resource. Like many oil-producing countries, such as Alfonzo's Venezuela, the devil was at work in Iran's petroleum-dependent economy, which proved unable to successfully utilize oil revenues into a harmonious social order.

Our imagination comes in handy when complex power structures operating within social economies are difficult to understand and even more difficult to explain. How else can one explain the wide gap that exists between the promise of modernity that came from industrialization and the lived experiences of dispossession? Sociologists go to work with charts and graphs, measuring the price of oil against what petroleum-exporting states spend on their local infrastructures. They point to deficits and the state's failures to deploy revenues earned from selling off natural resources effectively. In the context of Iran, the political scientist Hossein Mahdavy proposed the concept of the "Rentier State" to explain the Iranian state's disregard for the local economy. "Rentier States," Mahdavy writes, "are defined here as those countries that receive on a regular basis substantial amounts of external rent."[3] "What is more important perhaps," he continues, "is to recognize that however one looks at them, the oil revenues received by the governments of the oil exporting countries have very little to do with the production processes of their domestic economies."[4]

The devil here is the one who pays the rent and collects the rent and it does not hesitate to come and greet us through the pie charts and numerical graphs. The devil comes to haunt us in its ethereal form. The devil's morphology might not be recognizable, it may not appear with humanimal attributes, with horns twisting out of its cranial crown. It may not be theriomorphic with a tail tucked into its pelvic cavity. Yet the devil is there. It is there as a gaseous, atmospheric presence that hisses between the lines of the social scientists' graphs and abstract shapes. People living in these countries know the devil and can point it out when they see it. While oil culture scholars have cautioned and deterred us from using terms such as "resource curse" for its deterministic and essentialist capacities, we cannot argue with the devil.[5]

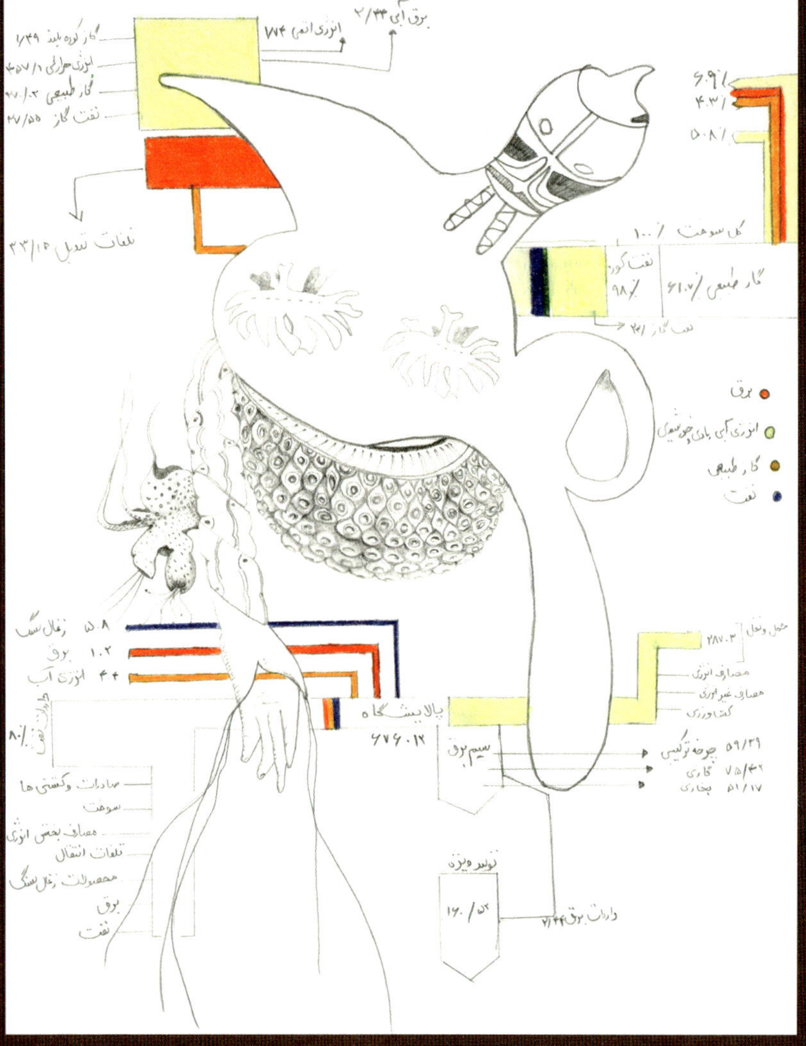

FIGURE 20.1 The devil is the one who pays the rent and collects the rent and it does not hesitate to come and greet us through pie charts and numerical graphs. Salar Mameni, *Untitled*, 2020.

I began my creative practice as a visual artist. Writing, in comparison to drawing, has always felt like an endurance performance. Writing a book requires countless hours of research, reading, thinking, theorizing, drafting, diverging, and actual writing and editing. Engaging in this performance demands a great deal of faith in ongoing personal and institutional support, intellectual and financial resources. More importantly, it requires a sustained belief in futurity: faith that futures will continue to arrive despite land appropriation and climate catastrophes as a result of war and centuries of settler-colonial, militarized extractive practices across the globe. I am grateful to the creative practices of artists who held futures in sight for me as I wrote: Gelare Khoshgozaran, Morehshin Allahyari, Fatima Al-Qadiri, Larissa Sansour, Diana Al-Hadid, Alia Ali, and Abbas Akhavan.

Thank you for the keen insights you bring to your aesthetic and political practices and for making this book possible.

The writing of this book began in earnest in 2016 during my postdoctoral fellowship in the Feminist Studies Department at the University of California, Santa Cruz. I am grateful to the UC Office of the President for the fellowship and for the support of the feminist studies community at Santa Cruz: Anjali Arondekar, Gina Dent, Karen Barad, Donna Haraway, Nick Mitchell, Neda Atanasoski, and Neel Ahuja. Thank you Neel for your very early enthusiasm when this book was just a simple idea. Thank you Derek Conrad Murray and T. J. Demos in the Department of History of Art and Visual Culture for your ongoing support over the years, and Mayanthi Fernando for bringing me back to UCSC to speak about this book in its early stages at the Center for Cultural Studies. Thank you Cleo Wölfle Hazard and July Hazard for the camaraderie during the postdoc year.

The book's theoretical scaffolding has benefitted from the intellectual rigor of many dedicated readers. Thank you Roshanak Kheshti, Sora Han, Laura Harris, Iván Ramos, Amy Cimini, Mairead Sullivan, Bernadine Hernández, Viviana MacManus, and Ren Heintz for the writing groups at various stages of this project. Thank you for listening to ideas that have found a home in this book in conference rooms and other corridors of academia: Ronak Kapadia, Sampada Aranke, Peter Simensky, Joo Ok Kim, Chris Perreira, Yumi Pak, Jasmine Syedullah, Manijeh Moradian, Ashvin Kini, Josen Diaz, Thea Quiray Tagle, Salvador Zárate, Davorn Sisavath, Rujeko Hockley, Rayyane Tabet, Christopher Kardambikis, Laurie Palmer, Emily Eliza Scott, and Heather Davis. My gratitude goes to the Visual Arts Department at UC San Diego for inviting me back to discuss this book with the community that saw me through the PhD years. I continue to learn from Mariana Botey Wardwell, Grant Kester, Norman Bryson, and the late Lesley Stern. I am grateful to Janelle Matthews: you are one of the most astute listeners I know.

For its completion, the book is indebted to the time and dedication of anonymous readers whose nuanced balance of praise and constructive criticism moved this book from a draft to a readable book of ideas. My appreciation goes to Courtney Berger at Duke University Press for being engaged and present at every stage, from initial acquisition to the polished finish. I am grateful to the series editors Mel Y. Chen and Jasbir K. Puar whose own intellectual journeys have been a model for me. The completion of this book would not have been possible without the support of my colleagues at UC Berkeley and, in particular, within my home department of Ethnic Studies: Juana María Rodríguez, Keith Feldman, Christian Paiz, Laura Pérez, Raúl Coronado, Shari Huhndorf, Beth Piatote, Thomas Biolsi, Peter Nelson, Carolyn Chen, Catherine Ceniza Choy, Lok Siu, and Khatharya Um. I am grateful to Dean Raka Ray and the Department of Ethnic Studies for the financial support that went into the final drafting, indexing, and color printing of this book and to Sandra Richmond, Jeannie Imazumi, and Uilani Hunt for ongoing assistance in administrative navigation.

Former colleagues in the School of Critical Studies at California Institute of the Arts have posed some of the important questions that sit at the heart of this book. I thank you for your curiosity and rigor. I am endlessly grateful to students in my graduate and undergraduate courses at both CalArts and UC Berkeley who have taken cross-disciplinary journeys across art history, Middle Eastern studies, feminist philosophy, queer and trans of color theories, petro-cultures, and environmental studies with me. It is to you that I owe some of the fine-grained reading and thinking appearing throughout the book.

Building these networks of support required land and resources. California, where this book was written is located on the ancestral, unceded territories of many Indigenous communities, among them the Chochenyo-speaking Ohlone people on whose ancestral lands, Huichin, I am currently a settler. I received my higher education at the University of California, a land-grant university benefitting from the nineteenth-century Morrill Act that granted Indigenous lands to the University of California for settlement and operational expenses. My educational institution and employer continues to benefit from settler-colonial acts of dispossession at the same time as it participates in the military-industrial complex that has caused mass-scale migrations globally, including my own.

As I write these words of acknowledgment, my own homeland is undergoing yet another wave of protests and mass uprisings led by women and ethnic minorities who oppose the Islamic Republic of Iran's police state. As they protest at home, I join my Iranian family, friends, and colleagues in the diaspora, who strive to participate in the fight for a day when activists, artists, and all who speak up against violent oppression are not imprisoned, tortured, and killed. Participation in this fight from the Western diaspora is complicated by who hears our voices and how. Currently, "amplifying the voices of Iranians" has become official state policy of countries such as the United States, which has a long historical record of arming nation-states and dissident groups across the globe. As thousands of Iranians march in the Western diaspora, I fear for the instrumentalization of our voices for further military intervention and proxy wars in the region. I was born amid an anti-imperial mass protest, whose unexpected outcome was the Islamic Republic's state formation in 1979 and the eight-year Iran-Iraq War that immediately ensued. This period was followed by the two Gulf Wars and the war on terror that have meant the proliferation of US military bases across the region, many of which are stationed along Iran's national borders. Protesting violence and oppression in Iran means opposing this entire machinery of war and the legacy of settler-colonial and imperial-state formations that benefit from an Iran in turmoil. For us in the Western diaspora, dismantling the police state has to begin with protest against the settler-colonial and imperial states that have time and again gone into war in our name.

I am forever indebted to my parents and siblings: you have supported me in the thick of war and revolution and have enabled all that I know about belonging and displacement across many and disparate diasporic enclaves through which we have survived. My love goes to Roshanak Kheshti for knowing me before I ever knew myself. Our fates are intertwined.

Creation Story

1 Hayashi, "Scientific or Narrative?," 4702. Hayashi provides a chart of the known copies of the manuscript, including their dates and current locations.

2 Hayashi, 4701–02; *jinns* are defined, by Merriam-Webster, as "one of a class of spirits that according to Muslim demonology inhabit the earth, assume various forms, and exercise supernatural power."

3 See Carboni, *The Wonders of Creation and the Singularities of Painting*; and Berlekamp, *Wonder, Image, and Cosmos in Medieval Islam*.

4 For a discussion of how Muslim cosmology incorporated a variety of Indigenous Arab cosmographic knowledge-systems, see Al-Abbasi, "The Arabs' Visions of the Upper Realm."

5 Hayashi, "Scientific or Narrative?," 4702.

6 Sariyannis, "*Aja'ib ve ghara'ib*," 454.

7   Prior, "Travels of Mount Qaf," 425–44.

8   Quoted in Sariyannis, *"Aja'ib ve ghara'ib,"* 455.

9   Bein, "The Istanbul Earthquake of 1984 and Science in Late Ottoman Empire," 911.

10   Crutzen and Stoermer, "The 'Anthropocene,'" 18.

11   See, for instance, the story of "The Mute Prince" with which Seshadri opens her book *HumAnimal.*

Chapter 1. Terror and the Anthropocene

An earlier version of this chapter appeared in essay form as Sara Mameni, "View from the Terracene," in *The Routledge Companion to Contemporary Art, Visual Culture, and Climate Change*, ed. T. J. Demos, Emily Eliza Scott, and Subhankar Banerjee (New York: Routledge, 2021), 100–107.

1   For a historical account of the concept of terrorism, see Collins, "Terrorism." For a discussion of Powell's comments on the "Terror-Industrial Complex," see Rana, "The Racial Infrastructure of the Terror-Industrial Complex."

2   Rana, *Terrifying Muslims*, 55.

3   Chakrabarty, "The Climate of History," 220.

4   Spivak, *An Aesthetic Education*, 373.

5   See George W. Bush, "President Bush Addresses the Nation," *Washington Post*, Sept. 20, 2001, https://www.washingtonpost.com/wp-srv/nation/specials /attacked/transcripts/bushaddress_092001.html.

6   Bush, "President Bush Addresses the Nation."

7   Scott, *Extravagant Abjection*, 98.

8   Said, *Orientalism*, 10.

9   Malm and Hornborg, "The Geology of Mankind?," 63–64.

10   Dyer, *White*, 2.

11   Chakrabarty, "The Climate of History," 217. See also Povinelli's epilogue to *Geontologies.*

12   Povinelli, *Geontologies*, 19.

13   Povinelli, "The Three Figures of Geontology," 61.

14   Povinelli, *Geontologies*, 19.

15   Raza Kolb, *Epidemic Empire*, 8.

16   Raza Kolb, 17.

17   Rana, *Terrifying Muslims*, 6.

18   Raza Kolb, *Epidemic Empire*, 17.

19   Puar, *Terrorist Assemblages*, xxiii.

20   Puar, 17.

21   Raza Kolb, *Epidemic Empire*, 16

22   Wald, *Contagious*, 158.

23 Wald, 157.

24 For discussions of the relation between immunity and defense, see Cohen, *A Body Worth Defending*; and Martin, *Flexible Bodies*.

25 Cohen, *A Body Worth Defending*, 3.

26 Crutzen and Stoermer, "The Anthropocene," 18.

27 Marzec, *Militarizing the Environment*, 8.

28 Belcher et al., "Hidden Carbon Costs of the 'Everywhere War,'" 66.

29 See Turney et al., "Global Peak in Atmospheric Radiocarbon," 1–9.

30 DeLoughrey, *Allegories of the Anthropocene*, 63.

31 Marzec, *Militarizing the Environment*, 11.

32 Marzec, 7.

33 Marzec, 10.

34 Ahuja, *Bioinsecurities*, 3.

35 Massumi, *Ontopower*, 27.

36 Massumi, 21 and 27.

37 Massumi, 11.

Chapter 2. Anti-Colonial Critique of the Anthropocene

1 Chakrabarty, "The Climate of History," 209.

2 Haraway, *Staying with the Trouble*, 49.

3 Crutzen et al., "The Anthropocene," 17–18. Regarding the time line for the Anthropocene, Crutzen and Stoermer write, "To assign a more specific date to the onset of the "anthropocene" seems somewhat arbitrary, but we propose the latter part of the 18th century, although we are aware that alternative proposals can be made" (17).

4 Crutzen et al., 614–21.

5 For *Capitolocene*, see Moore, *Capitalism in the Web of Life* and *The Capitolocene*. For *Eurocene*, see Grove, *Savage Ecology*, 5.

6 Todd, "Indigenizing the Anthropocene," 244.

7 See Davis and Todd, "On the Importance of a Date, or Decolonizing the Anthropocene," 761–80. For an analysis of Eurocene, see Grove, *Savage Ecology*, 5.

8 See McKittrick, *Sylvia Wynter*, 20.

9 McKittrick, 20.

10 Hua et al., "Atmospheric Radiocarbon for the Period 1950–2010," 2059–72. See also Marra, *Hot Carbon*, 66–67.

11 See for instance, Gusterson, *People of the Bomb*; Danielle Endres, "The Rhetoric of Nuclear Colonialism"; Anaïs and Walby, "Secrecy, Publicity, and the Bomb"; and Biswas, *Nuclear Desire*.

12 Mignolo and Walsh, *On Decoloniality*, 153.

13   For debates on the notion of the human in the Anthropocene, see Jackson, *Becoming Human*; Chakrabarty, "Postcolonial Studies and the Challenge of Climate Change"; and Caluya, "Fragments for a Postcolonial Critique of the Anthropocene."

14   McKittrick, *Sylvia Wynter*, 31.

15   McKittrick, 23.

16   For an in-depth exploration of the idea of "becoming human," see Jackson, *Becoming Human*.

17   Spivak, *Death of a Discipline*, 73.

18   Spivak, 73.

19   Spivak, 72.

20   DeLoughrey, *Allegories of the Anthropocene*, 66.

21   Cosgrove, *Apollo's Eye*, 15–16.

22   Spivak, *Death of a Discipline*, 72.

23   Spivak, 73.

Chapter 3. Provincializing the Anthropocene; *or*, Why Artists, Feminists, and Yemeni People Have Much to Say about the Cosmos

1   Zakariya, *A Final Story*, 39.

2   Zakariya, 39.

3   Prescod-Weinstein, *The Disordered Cosmos*, 131.

4   Prescod-Weinstein, 111.

5   Ahmed, *Queer Phenomenology*, 58.

6   Ahmed, 60.

7   Ahmed, 61.

8   Prescod-Weinstein, *The Disordered Cosmos*, 135.

9   This is a James Clifford and George E. Marcus quote in TallBear, *Native American DNA*, 14.

10   TallBear, 11.

11   Davies, *The Birth of the Anthropocene*, 45.

12   Zalasiewicz et al., "The New World of the Anthropocene," 2230.

13   Miller, "The Story of 'Scientist,'" 256.

14   Miller, 257.

15   Miller, 257.

16   Pinkus, *Fuel*, 49.

17   For an analysis of the relationship between industrial machinery and the Anthropocene, see Pasquinelli, "The Automaton of the Anthropocene," 311–26.

18   Daggett, *The Birth of Energy*, 15.

19   Chakrabarty, *Provincializing Europe*, 3.

20   Chakrabarty, 5.

21 Foucault, *The Order of Things*, 146.

22 Foucault, 145.

23 Quoted in Zakariya, *A Final Story*, 45.

24 Haraway, "Situated Knowledges," 581.

25 Crutzen, "We Live in the Anthropocene," 13.

26 Crutzen, 13.

27 Crutzen, 13.

28 Crutzen, 13.

29 Crutzen, 13.

30 Crutzen, 13.

31 Crutzen, 13.

32 See, for instance, Baggott, *The First War of Physics*; and Wilson, "Niels Bohr and the Young Scientists," 23–26.

33 Crutzen, "We Live in the Anthropocene," 13.

34 Crutzen and Schwägerl, "Living in the Anthropocene: Toward a New Global Ethos," *Yale Environment 360*, January 24, 2011, https://e360.yale.edu/features /living_in_the_anthropocene_toward_a_new_global_ethos.

35 Crutzen and Schwägerl.

36 Yusoff, *A Billion Black Anthropocenes or None*, 27.

37 Todd, "Indigenizing the Anthropocene," 244.

38 NASA, "Mars Pathfinder," Mars Exploration Program and the Jet Propulsion Laboratory for NASA's Science Mission Directorate, accessed Sept. 21, 2022, https://mars.nasa.gov/mars-exploration/missions/pathfinder/.

39 "3 Yemenis Sue NASA for Trespassing on Mars," CNN, July 24, 1997, http:// edition.cnn.com/TECH/9707/24/yemen.mars/.

40 "3 Yemenis Sue NASA for Trespassing on Mars." I want to Thank Alia Ali for bringing this case to my attention. I discuss Ali's video work inspired by this event in part 4.

41 Quoted in Pop, "The Men Who Sold the Moon," 197.

42 "3 Yemenis Sue NASA for Trespassing on Mars."

43 Pop, "The Men Who Sold the Moon," 198.

44 Pop, 196.

45 More information on the treaty can be found at "Treaty on Principles Governing the Activities of States in the Exploration and Use of Outer Space, including the Moon and Other Celestial Bodies," United Nations Office for Outer Space Affairs, accessed Sept. 21, 2022, https://www.unoosa.org/oosa/en /ourwork/spacelaw/treaties/introouterspacetreaty.html.

46 "3 Yemenis Sue NASA for Trespassing on Mars."

47 "3 Yemenis Sue NASA for Trespassing on Mars."

48 See, for instance, Burbach and Johnson-Freese, "The Outer Space Treaty and the Weaponization of Space"; and Altabef, "The Legal Man in the Moon."

49 Stauffer, "'You People Talk from Paper,'" 40. See "Treaty on Principles Governing the Activities of States in the Exploration and Use of Outer Space" for more information on the treaty.

50 Cruikshank, "Invention of Anthropology in British Columbia's Supreme Court," 26.

51 Povinelli, *The Cunning of Recognition*, 8.

52 "3 Yemenis Sue NASA for Trespassing on Mars."

53 Biagioli, *Gallileo's Instruments of Credit*, 3.

54 Dupré, "The Transnational Galileo," 468.

55 Dupré, 465.

56 Biagioli, *Gallileo's Instruments of Credit*, 3.

57 Biagioli, 3. See also Rutkin, "Celestial Offerings."

Chapter 4. The Anthropocene Is a Work of Art

1 Wark, "An Inhuman Fiction of Forces," 39.

2 Benjamin, "The Work of Art in the Age of Mechanical Production," 20.

3 Eiland and Jennings, *Walter Benjamin*, 674.

4 Benjamin, "The Work of Art," 19.

5 Benjamin, 20.

6 Quoted in Benjamin, 19.

7 Benjamin, 20.

8 Benjamin, 20.

9 Chow, *The Age of the World Target*, 30.

10 Chow, 27.

11 Chow, 28.

12 Chow, 29.

13 Virilio, *War and Cinema*, 81.

14 Virilio, 81.

15 Mavor, *Black and Blue*, 119.

16 Lippit, *Atomic Light*, 95.

17 Lippit, 94.

18 Lippit, 94

19 Lippit, 95.

20 Zalasiewicz et al., "When Did the Anthropocene Begin?" 196–203.

21 DeLoughrey, *Allegories of the Anthropocene*, 76.

Chapter 5. The Terracene

1 Cavarero, *Horrorism*, 4.

2 Cavarero, 4.

3   For further exploration of terror and territory, see Elden, *Terror and Territory*, Hindess, "Terrortory"; and Anidjar, "Terror Right."

4   Anidjar, 55. As a Farsi speaker, I recognize the Sanskrit root *tars* in the current Farsi word for fear, which further links terra and terror together from my own linguistic perspective.

5   Elden, *Terror and Territory*, xxix.

6   Elden, xxv.

7   Elden, xxv.

8   Salamanca, "Assembling the Fabric of Life," 66.

9   Pugliese, *Biopolitics of the More-Than-Human*, 5.

10 De la Cadena, *Earth Beings*, 25. Haraway also uses the word *Terran* to designate the Earth's inhabitants. See Haraway, *Staying with the Trouble*, 49.

11 De la Cadena uses the term *earth-beings* to translate the Spanish-Quechua word *tirakuna*: a composite of *tierra* (Spanish for earth) and *kuna* (a Quechua suffix). The word *tirakuna* describes "other-than human beings who participate in the lives of those who call themselves *runakuna*, people (usually monolingual Quechua speakers) who like Mariano and Nazario, also actively partake in modern institutions that cannot know, let alone recognize, tirakuna" (xxiii–xxiv).

12 Voyles, *Wastelanding*, 9.

13 Weizman, *Forensic Architecture*, 254.

14 Weizman, 254.

15 Morton, *Dark Ecology*, 13.

16 Morton, 14.

17 Morton, 14.

18 For a list of terms coined in reaction to the notion of the Anthropocene, see Mentz, *Break Up the Anthropocene*; in particular his chapter "The Neologismcene."

19 Mignolo and Walsh, *On Decoloniality*, 161.

20 Bureau of Linguistical Reality, accessed July 4, 2022, https://bureauof linguisticalreality.com/.

21 All words and definitions cited here are from the collective's website, https://bureauoflinguisticalreality.com/.

22 The collective's website includes the names of the authors of each phrase.

Chapter 6. Sensing the Terracene

1   See, for instance, Patrice Taddonio, "Inside a Sinking Dinghy Crossing the Mediterranean Sea," Frontline News, December 22, 2016, https://www .pbs.org/wgbh/frontline/article/inside-a-sinking-dinghy-crossing-the -mediterranean-sea/.

2   See, for instance, Slama Abdelaziz, "Our Terrifying Swim: Two Syrians' Jour-

ney through Dark Waters to Greece," CNN, September 14, 2015, https://www
.cnn.com/2015/09/14/europe/europe-refugee-crisis-swimming-to-freedom
/index.html, Last accessed July 6, 2021; and John Hall, "Syrian Refugee Ameer
Mehtr Swims for 7 Hours to Start New Life in Europe," Independent News,
December 21, 2015, https://www.independent.co.uk/news/world/europe
/syrian-refugee-ameer-mehtr-swims-7-hours-start-new-life-europe-a6781276
.html.

3   Kelley et al., "Climate Change in the Fertile Crescent," 3241–46.

4   Selby, "Climate Change and the Syrian Civil War," 260–74.

5   McClintock, "Monster, A Fugue in Fire and Ice," *e-flux*, June 1, 2020, https://
www.e-flux.com/architecture/oceans/331865/monster-a-fugue-in-fire-and
-ice/.

6   Freud, *Beyond the Pleasure Principle*, 23.

7   Buck-Morss, "Aesthetics and Anaesthetics," 8.

8   Battersby, *The Sublime,* 11.

9   Battersby, 11.

10   Buck-Morss, "Aesthetics and Anaesthetics," 3.

11   Battersby, *The Sublime*, 6.

12   For Kant, the world is imagined to be populated with those incapable of finer
taste: "The Indians . . . with their despotic sacrifice of wives in the very same
funeral pyre that consumes the corpse of the husband is a hideous excess";
"The Negros of Africa have by nature no feelings that rise above the trifling";
and "the Arab the noblest man in the Orient, yet of a feeling that degenerates
very much into the adventurous." See Kant, *Observations on the Feeling of the
Beautiful and Sublime*, 109–11.

13   Buck-Morss, "Aesthetics and Anaesthetics," 3.

14   Battersby, *The Sublime,* 7.

15   See Ferguson, "The Nuclear Sublime"; and Richard Klein, "Climate Change
through the Lens of Nuclear Criticism."

16   See Robbins, "The Sweatshop Sublime."

17   Baucom, *History 4° Celsius*, 60; See also Ray, "Terror and the Sublime in the
So-Called Anthropocene," 1–20.

18   Battersby, *The Sublime,* 1.

19   Battersby, 1.

20   Buck-Morss, "Aesthetics and Anaesthetics," 2.

21   Buck-Morss, 2.

22   Chuh, *The Difference Aesthetics Makes*, xi; Chuh, xii.

23   Chuh, 3.

24   Scarry, *The Body in Pain*, 165.

25   Scarry, 165.

26   Scarry, 165.

27 Chuh, *The Difference Aesthetics Makes*, xii.

28 Scarry, *The Body in Pain*, 165; Scarry, 285.

29 Scarry, 282.

30 Scarry, 282.

31 Scarry, 283.

32 Mills and Sterne, "Afterword II," 371.

33 Puar, *The Right to Maim*, 45.

34 Puar, 45–46.

35 Puar, 129.

36 Puar, 133.

37 Pugliese, *The Biopolitics of the More-Than-Human*," 7.

38 Puar, *The Right to Maim*, 136.

39 Raza, "Diana Al-Hadid," 55.

40 Raza, 54.

41 Aryn Baker and Majdal Anjar, "Syria's Looted Past: How Ancient Artifacts Are Being Traded for Guns," *Time*, September 12, 2012, https://world.time .com/2012/09/12/syrias-looted-past-how-ancient-artifacts-are-being-traded -for-guns/.

42 Baker and Anjar, "Syria's Looted Past."

43 Hansen, "Key Techniques in the Production of Metals," 140.

44 Hansen, 140.

45 Chen, *Animacies*, 167.

46 Chen, 167.

47 Pyatt et al., "An Imperial Legacy?," 771–78.

48 Bennett, *Vibrant Matter*, 55.

49 Bennett, 54.

50 Nixon, *Slow Violence*, 200–201.

51 Nixon, 232.

52 Siebers, *Disability Aesthetics*, 4.

53 Siebers, 4.

54 Falkenberg, "Phantom Limb," 17–18.

55 Falkenberg, 19.

56 Sobchack, "Living a 'Phantom Limb,'" 60.

57 Sobchack, 54.

58 Sobchack, 59.

59 Sobchack, 58.

60 Sobchack, 64.

61 Sobchack, 64.

62 Sobchack, 65, footnote 7.

63 Davidson, *Concerto for the Left Hand*, 153.

Chapter 7. Crude Aesthetics

1 Murty, "History of Crude Oil Refining," 1.

2 Murty, 1.

3 See, for example, the many uses of bitumen in Mesoamerica in Wendt and Cyphers, "How the Olmec Used Bitumen in Ancient Mesoamerica," 178.

4 See Sorkhabi's article for numerous examples of such practices, "Pre-modern History of Bitumen, Oil and Gas in Persia."

5 Barakat et al., "Organic Geochemistry Indicates Gebel El Zeit," 212.

6 Sorkhabi, "Pre-modern History of Bitumen, Oil and Gas in Persia," 153.

7 Gómez-Barris, *The Extractive Zone*, xvi.

8 Gómez-Barris, xvi.

9 Gómez-Barris, xvii.

10 Murty, "History of Crude Oil Refining,"2.

11 Murty, 3.

12 Henry, *The Early and Later History of Petroleum*, 5.

13 Henry, 11–12.

14 Wolfe, "Settler Colonialism and the Elimination of the Native," 388.

15 TallBear, "Beyond the Life/Non-Life Binary," 181.

16 LaDuke, *All Our Relations*, 2.

17 Liboiron, *Pollution Is Colonialism*, 8.

18 TallBear, "Beyond the Life/Non-Life Binary," 186.

19 TallBear, 186.

20 TallBear, 186.

21 Behdad, "Orientalist Desire, Desire of the Orient," 42.

22 Cited in Sorkhabi, "Pre-modern History of Bitumen, Oil and Gas in Persia," 157–58.

23 Clifford, *The Predicament of Culture*, 26.

24 Clifford, 26.

25 Clifford, 28.

26 Clifford, 27.

27 Clifford, 28.

28 Sorkhabi, "Pre-modern History of Bitumen, Oil and Gas in Persia," 173.

29 Cited in Sorkhabi, 173.

30 Spivak, *A Critique of Postcolonial Reason*, 26 and 30.

31 Spivak, 13.

32 Spivak, 13.

33 Spivak, 13.

34 Tompkins, "Crude Matter, Queer Form," 265.

35 Tompkins, 264.

36 Tompkins, 267–68.

Chapter 9. Listening to the Terracene

1   See "About," Fatima Al-Qadiri (website), accessed July 5, 2022, https://fatima alqadiri.com/music/fatima-al-qadiri/desert-strike/file/about-desert-strike/.

2   Myers, "The Video Game Aesthetic," 47.

3   Chow, "The Age of the World Target," 8.

4   See "About," Fatima Al-Qadiri (website).

5   "About," Fatima Al-Qadiri (website).

6   Goodman, *Sonic Warfare*, 7.

7   Goodman, 7.

8   Goodman, 7.

9   Cited in Kahn, *Noise, Water, Meat*, 62.

10   Kahn, 62.

11   Marinetti's "The Futurist Manifesto" was published in the French newspaper *Le Figaro* in 1909. See the original newspaper page and English translation at "The Futurist Manifesto by Filippo T. Marinetti—Full Text," Books on Trial, accessed July 5, 2022, https://www.booksontrial.com/the-full-text-of-the -futurist-manifesto/.

12   Benjamin, "The Work of Art," 20.

13   Paris, "The First Air Wars," 97.

14   Paris, 98–99.

15   Marinetti, "The Futurist Manifesto."

16   Kheshti, *Switched-on Bach*, 76.

17   See Fatima Al-Qadiri and Sophia Al-Maria. "Al Qadiri & Al-Maria on Gulf Futurism," *Dazed Digital*, November 2012, https://www.dazeddigital.com/music /article/15037/1/al-qadiri-al-maria-on-gulf-futurism.

18   Al-Qadiri and Al-Maria, "Al Qadiri & Al-Maria on Gulf Futurism."

19   Al-Qadiri and Al-Maria.

20   For a study of industrial development in the Gulf region and the infiltration of war and extractive economies, see Khalili, *Sinews of War and Trade*.

21   Al-Qadiri and Al-Maria, "Al Qadiri & Al-Maria on Gulf Futurism."

22   Eidsheim's *Sensing Sound*, 45.

23   Daughtry, *Listening to War*, 276.

24   Daughtry, 276.

25   Daughtry, 277.

26   Holly, *The Melancholy Art*, xvi.

27   Roads, *Microsound*, 7.

28   Roads, 39.

29   Barad, "Transmaterialities," 387.

30   Roads, *Microsound*, 7.

31   Vomar, "Listening to the Cold War," 80.

32 Vomar, 80.

33 Quoted in Kahn, *Earth Sound Earth Signal*, 135.

34 Kahn, 136.

35 Kahn, 136.

36 Eidsheim, *Sensing Sound*, 6.

37 Trower, *Senses of Vibration*, 4.

38 Trower, 2.

Chapter 12. Lamassu

1 See González et al., "Digitally Mediated Iconoclasm," 649–71.

2 Tuck and Yang, "Decolonization Is Not a Metaphor," 1.

3 The symposium was titled "Mobilization for Heritage: Iraq, Syria and other Countries in Conflict," see "#Unite4Heritage: United Nations University Joins UNESCO Campaign to Protect Heritage in Danger," UNESCO, accessed July 7, 2020, https://whc.unesco.org/en/news/1272.

4 This phrase is the organization's slogan. See "About Us," Rashid International, accessed July 7, 2022, https://rashid-international.org/#content.

5 See "About Us," Rashid International.

6 See CAA's February 22, 2015, statement signed by DeWitt Godfrey and Linda Downs, the then president and executive director of CAA. "CAA News Today," Collage Art Association of America, accessed July 7, 2022, https://www.college art.org/news/2015/02/26/caa-statement-on-mosul-museum-destruction/.

7 Dimock, *Through Other Continents*, 1.

8 Dimock, 1.

9 Crutzen and Stoermer, "The 'Anthropocene,'" 614–15.

10 Dimock, "Deep Time," 758.

11 Dimock, 759.

12 Tallbear, "Beyond the Life/Non-Life Binary," 198.

13 Danrey, "Winged Human-Headed Bulls of Nineveh," 133–39.

14 Danrey, 134.

15 Danrey, 135.

16 Danrey, 135.

17 Danrey, 135.

18 Danrey, 135.

19 I would like to thank Beth Piatote for suggesting a performative reading of Lamassu.

20 Morehshin Allahyari and Daniel Rourke, "The 3D Additivist Manifesto," Additivism.org, accessed July 7, 2022, https://additivism.org/manifesto.

21 Dimock, "Deep Time," 760.

22 Haraway, *Staying with the Trouble*, 49.

23 Taussig, *What Color Is the Sacred?*, 237.

24 LeMenager, *Living Oil*, 6.

25 Randy Martin cautions that war in these regions cannot be reduced to oil scarcity and a struggle over remaining oil supplies because such an argument makes fighting over resources appear inevitable. See Martin, *An Empire of Indifference*, 12. For another perspective that argues for the economic dependency on oil, see Beblawi and Luciani, *The Rentier State*.

26 Pyatt et al., "An Imperial Legacy?," 771–78.

27 According to a study by Pyatt and colleagues, the excavated copper and lead wadis in southern Jordan were active from the Bronze Age to the end of the Muslim expansion era. See Pyatt et al., 776.

28 Pyatt et al., 776.

29 Al-Damkhi, "Expected Scenarios of Environmental Threats," 393.

30 Al-Damkhi, 394.

31 LeMenager, *Living Oil*, 6.

32 Davis, "The Domestication of Plastic," 303.

33 Gretta Louw, "Your Shiny Plastic Future Is a Load of Crap: Morehshin Allahyari and Daniel Rourke's #Additivism," Hyperallergic: Sensitive to Art and Its Discontents, February 15, 2016, https://hyperallergic.com/275471/your-shiny-plastic-future-is-a-load-of-crap-morehshin-allahyari-and-daniel-rourkes-additivism/.

34 Louw.

35 Massumi, *Ontopower*, 228.

36 Ahuja, *Bioinsecurities*, 151–52.

37 Hayles, *How We Became Posthuman*, 1.

38 Hayles, 246.

39 Browne, *Dark Matters*, 109.

Chapter 13. Huma

1 Quote from the artist's website, Morehshin Allahyari, "She Who Sees the Unknown," accessed Sept. 28, 2022, http://shewhoseestheunknown.com.

2 Pandolfo, *Knot of the Soul*, 90.

3 See Pandolfo, 294–303.

4 Taneja, *Jinnealogy*, 10.

5 Taneja, 11.

6 Allahyari, "She Who Sees the Unknown."

7 Gómez-Barris, *Extractive Zones*, 41.

8 Muñoz, *Cruising Utopia*, 1.

9 Muñoz, 1.

10 Gómez-Barris, *Extractive Zones*, 49.

Chapter 14. Homa

1 Muñoz, *Cruising Utopia*, 1.

2 I borrow the term *carbon-privileged* from Ahuja, "Intimate Atmospheres," 375.

Chapter 15. Pazuzu

1 For a theoretico-fictive rendition of Pazuzu, see Negarestani, *Cyclonopedia*, 113–21.

2 Taussig, *What Color Is the Sacred?*, 67.

3 Taussig, 47.

Chapter 16. The Red Star

1 Alia Ali describes her video *Mahjar*, accessed September 28, 2022, http:// alia-ali.com/Mahjar-1.

2 See Ali, *Mahjar*.

3 Raffles, *Insectopedia*, 320.

4 Raffles, 320.

5 Cornum, "Radioactive Intimacies," 1.

6 Cornum, 2.

Chapter 17. Narrative Terrorism

1 For the notion of environmental siege, see Stamatopoulou-Robbins, *Waste Siege*.

2 Kedar et al., *Emptied Lands*, 9.

3 Abu El-Haj, *Facts on the Ground*, 3.

4 Kapadia, *Insurgent Aesthetics*, 157.

5 A short list of scholarly explorations of Sansour's work include Hochberg, "'Jerusalem, We Have a Problem'" and *Becoming Palestine*; Robert Duggan, "Larissa Sansour and the Palestinian Ruins of the Future"; and Kapadia, *Insurgent Aesthetic*.

6 For a detailed discussion of the discovery and workings of carbon dating, see Marra, *Hot Carbon*.

7 Frost, *Biocultural Creatures*, 39.

8 Marra, *Hot Carbon*, 33.

9 Marra, 35.

10 Marra, 36.

11 Mitchell, *Carbon Democracy*, 5–6. For further analysis of liquid modernity, see Musiol, "Liquid Modernity.

12 Mitchell, *Carbon Democracy*, 36–39.

13 Mitchell, 36–39.

14 All quotes are from the subtitles in Larissa Sansour's video. I thank the artist's studio for sharing the full version of the video with me.

15 Kosek, "Ecologies of Empire," 664.

16 Kosek, 664.

17 Lockwood, *Six-Legged Soldiers*, 5.

18 See Mark Thompson, "Unleashing the Bugs of War," *Time*, April 18, 2008; Emily Athens, "The Race to Create 'Insect Cyborgs,'" *Observer: Neuroscience*, February 16, 2013; Noah Shachtman, "Pentagon's Cyborg Insects All Grown Up," *Wired*, March 19, 2008; and Sato, "A Cyborg Beetle," 164–67.

19 Schachtman, "Pentagon's Cyborg Insets All Grown Up."

20 Kosek, "Ecologies of Empire," 657.

21 See Mawani, "Insect Wars," 275–95.

22 Mawani, 292.

23 See Russell, "'Speaking of Annihilation.'"

24 Kosek, "Ecologies of Empire," 663.

25 Kosek, 664.

26 Weizman, *Hollow Land*, 190.

27 Kosek, 664.

28 For further elaboration, see Mawani, "Insects, War, Plastic Life," 161.

29 Foucault, *Society Must Be Defended*, 243–45.

30 Foucault, 242.

31 Foucault, 245.

32 Povinelli, *Geontopower*, 19.

33 Massumi, *Ontopower*, 22.

34 Massumi, 22.

35 Eshun, "Further Considerations of Afrofuturism," 291.

36 Foucault, *Society Must Be Defended,* 246.

37 Rana, *Terrifying Muslims*, 6.

38 Massumi, vii.

39 Massumi, viii.

40 Nixon, *Slow Violence*.

41 Nixon, 2.

42 Mbembe, "Necropolitics," 12.

43 Mbembe, 40.

44 Mbembe, 29.

45 Eshun, "Further Considerations of Afrofuturism," 292.

46 Eshun, 292.

Chapter 18. Texas Crude

An earlier version of this chapter appeared in essay form as Sara Mameni, "How Does It Feel to Be an Oil Spill?" *Resilience: A Journal of Environmental Humanities* 8, no. 1 (2020): 82–94.

1   Guidotti, "Hydrogen Sulfide," 569–581; Witter et al., "Occupational Exposures in the Oil and Gas Extraction Industry," 847–56.

2   Guidotti, "Hydrogen Sulfide," 572.

3   Guidotti, 572.

4   Guidotti. 570.

5   Guidotti, 570.

6   Buck-Morss, "Aesthetics and Anaesthetics," 6.

7   Buck-Morss, 6.

8   For a discussion of Kant's categorization of "objective senses," see Derrida and Klein, "Economimesis," 19.

9   Derrida and Klein, 19.

10   On proximal senses, see Marks, "Thinking Multisensory Culture." See also Jones, *Eyesight Alone*.

11   Chen, *Animacies*, 196.

12   Chen, 196.

13   Dickinson, *Anatomic*, 9–10.

14   Dickinson, 9–10.

15   Tsing, *The Mushroom at the End of the World*, 27.

16   Tsing, 28.

17   Stewart, "On the Politics of Cultural Theory," 395.

Chapter 19. A Fire!

1   Jahed, *Directory of World Cinema*, 32.

2   Jahed, 32.

3   Quoted in Jahed, 32.

4   Quoted in Jahed, 32.

5   Rosenbaum, "Radical Humanism and the Coexistence of Film and Poetry in *The House Is Black*," 473–78.

6   Saljoughi, "A New Form for a New People," 4.

7   Saljoughi, 4.

8   For an in-depth study of the Anglo-Iranian Oil Company's operations in Iran, see Shafiee, *Machineries of Oil*, 22.

9   For a discussion of D'Arcy's oil concession, see Shafiee, in particular chapter 1.

10   Shafiee, 167.

11   Shafiee, 175.

12   The overthrow of Mosaddegh in a covert operation known as "Operation Ajax" has been well documented. See, for instance, Marsh, "The United States, Iran and Operation 'Ajax'"; Kim, "The First American Secret War"; and Israeli, "The Circuitous Nature of Operation Ajax."

13   Shafiee, *Machineries of Oil*, 234.

14   Shafiee, 215.

15   For a discussion of the nationalization of oil in Iran and protests by Iranian oil workers, see Khalili, *Sinews of War*, 93 and 181–87.

16   See Shafiee, *Machineries of Oil*, chapter 4. See also Crinson, "Abadan: Planning and Architecture under the Anglo-Iranian Oil Company."

17   Shafiee, 126.

18   Shafiee, 126.

19   Shafiee, 125; Crinson, 342–43.

20   Kinzer, *All the Shah's Men*, 50.

21   Cameron, *Under Sand, Ice and Sea*, 209–10.

22   Shafiee, *Machineries of Oil*, 190.

23   Shafiee, 189 and 309.

24   Kinzer, *All the Shah's Men*, 50. "Anglo-Persian" is the older name for the Anglo-Iranian Oil Company.

25   Damluji, "The Oil City in Focus," 75–88.

26   Damluji, 80.

27   Damluji, 80.

28   Damluji, 79–85

29   Damluji, 79.

30   Jahed, *Directory of World Cinema*, 32.

31   Jahed, 31–32.

32   Naficy, "Iranian Documentary," 41–46.

33   For an overview of the use of media in the Pahlavi era, see Naficy, "Nonfiction Fiction." In the context of media in the 1950s–1970s, Naficy writes, "Most Western film and television programs of this period noted the ancient historical roots of Iran and apprised their audiences of the backwardness of the country, the importance of oil to the West, the strategically important position of Iran, and the valiant efforts of the Shah to modernize his country along Western guidelines" (225).

34   Jahid, *Directory of World Cinema*, 32.

35   Damluji, "The Oil City in Focus," 85.

36   Shams, "The Village in Contemporary Persian Poetry," 455–77.

37   Shams, 459.

38   Cameron, *Under Sand, Ice and Sea*, 206.

39   See "Harriman in Persia," British Pathé, July 26, 1951, http://www.britishpathe.com/video/harriman-in-persia. For a discussion of Harriman's mission to Iran, see Shafiee, 180–88.

40 "Harriman in Persia," British Pathé.

41 *Rig 20* was produced in 1951 by BP, which filmed the fire that erupted at Naft-e Sefid near Ahwaz. This film, along with newsreels and newspapers at the time, all describe Myron Kinley's arrival to put out the fire. In my research and to my knowledge no other fire brought Kinley to Iran. It is my speculation that *A Fire!* references this same fire of 1951 despite the date of 1958 being cited in the film's opening paragraph.

42 Hayles, "Speculative Aesthetics and Object-Oriented Inquiry (OOI)," 159.

43 See Hoover, "Fires Were Lit Inside Them," for an elaboration of this metaphor, 13.

44 Clark and Yusoff, "Queer Fire," 8.

Chapter 20. The Devil's Excrement

1 For an older geological study, see Stone and Zobell, "Bacterial Aspects of the Origin of Petroleum," 2564.

2 Watts, "Oil as Money," 206, 207.

3 Mahdavy, "The Patterns and Problems of Economic Development in Rentier States," 428.

4 Mahdavy, 429.

5 See Wenzel, "How to Read for Oil," 158.

Abu El-Haj, Nadia. *Facts on the Ground: Archeological Practice and Territorial Self-Fashioning in Israeli Society.* Chicago: University of Chicago Press, 2001.

Ahmed, Sara. *Queer Phenomenology: Orientations, Objects, Others.* Durham, NC: Duke University Press, 2006.

Ahuja, Neel. *Bioinsecurities: Disease Interventions, Empire, and the Government of Species.* Durham, NC: Duke University Press, 2016.

Ahuja, Neel. "Intimate Atmospheres: Queer Theory in a Time of Extinction." *GLQ: A Journal of Lesbian and Gay Studies* 21, no. 2–3 (2015): 365–85.

Al-Abbasi, Abeer Abdullah. "The Arabs' Visions of the Upper Realm." *Marburg Journal of Religion* 22, no. 2 (2020): 1–28.

Al-Damkhi, Ali Mohamed. "Expected Scenarios of Environmental Threats in Iraq Compared with Kuwait's Case." *Disaster Prevention and Management* 16, no. 3 (2007): 391–400.

Altabef, William B. "The Legal Man in the Moon: Exploring Environmental Personhood for Celestial Bodies." *Chicago Journal of International Law* 21, no. 2 (2021): 476–512.

Anaïs, Seantel, and Kevin Walby. "Secrecy, Publicity, and the Bomb: Nuclear Publics and Objects of the Nevada Test Site, 1951–1992." *Cultural Studies* 30, no. 6 (2016): 949–68.

Anidjar, Gil. "Terror Right" *CR: The New Centennial Review* 4, no. 3 (Winter 2004): 35–69.

Baggott, Jim. *The First War of Physics: The Secret History of the Atom Bomb, 1939–1949.* New York: Pegasus, 2010.

Barad, Karen. "Transmaterialities: Trans*/Matter/Realities and Queer Political Imaginings." *GLQ: A Journal of Lesbian and Gay Studies* 21, no. 2–3 (2015): 387–422.

Barakat, A. O., A. Mostafa, Y. Qian, M. Kim, and M. C. Kennicutt II. "Organic Geochemistry Indicates Gebel El Zeit, Gulf of Suez, Is a Source of Bitumen Used in Some Egyptian Mummies." *Geoarcheology: An International Journal* 20, no. 3 (2005): 211–28.

Battersby, Christine. *The Sublime, Terror and Human Difference.* New York: Routledge, 2007.

Baucom, Ian. *History 4° Celcius: Search for a Method in the Age of the Anthropocene.* Durham, NC: Duke University Press, 2020.

Beblawi, H., and G. Luciani, eds. *The Rentier State: Nation, State and Integration in the Arab World.* London: Routledge, 1987.

Behdad, Ali. "Orientalist Desire, Desire of the Orient." *French Forum* 15, no. 1 (January 1990): 37–51.

Bein, Amit. "The Istanbul Earthquake of 1984 and Science in Late Ottoman Empire." *Middle Eastern Studies* 44, no. 6 (2008): 909–24.

Belcher, Oliver, Patrick Bigger, Ben Neimark, and Cara Kennelly. "Hidden Carbon Costs of the 'Everywhere War': Logistics, Geopolitical Ecology, and the Carbon Boot-Print of the US Military." *Transactions of the British Institute of Geographers* 44, no. 2 (2019): 65–80.

Benjamin, Walter. "The Work of Art in the Age of Mechanical Production." In *Illuminations*, edited by Hannah Arendt. Translated by Harry Zohn, 1–26. New York: Schocken Books, 1969.

Bennett, Jane. *Vibrant Matter: A Political Ecology of Things.* Durham, NC: Duke University Press, 2010.

Berlekamp, Persis. *Wonder, Image, and Cosmos in Medieval Islam.* New Haven, CT: Yale University Press, 2011.

Biagioli, Mario. *Galileo's Instruments of Credit: Telescopes, Images, Secrecy.* Chicago: University of Chicago Press, 2006.

Biswas, Shampa. *Nuclear Desire: Power and the Postcolonial Nuclear Order.* Minneapolis: University of Minnesota Press, 2014.

Browne, Simone. *Dark Matters: On the Surveillance of Blackness.* Durham, NC: Duke University Press, 2015.

Buck-Morss, Susan. "Aesthetics and Anaesthetics: Walter Benjamin's Artwork Essay Reconsidered." *October* 62 (Autumn 1992): 3–41.

Burbach, David, and Joan Johnson-Freese. "The Outer Space Treaty and the Weaponization of Space." *Bulletin of the Atomic Scientists* 75, no. 4 (2019): 137–41.

Caluya, Gilbert. "Fragments for a Postcolonial Critique of the Anthropocene: Invasion Biology and Environmental Security." In *Rethinking Invasion Ecologies from the Environmental Humanities*, edited by Jodi Frawley and Iain McCalman, 31–45. New York: Routledge, 2014.

Cameron, A. Bryce, *Under Sand, Ice and Sea*. Toronto: Trafford, 1999.

Carboni, Stefano. *The Wonders of Creation and the Singularities of Painting: A Study of the Ilkhanid London Qazvini*. Edinburgh: Edinburgh University Press, 2015.

Cavarero, Adriana. *Horrorism: Naming Contemporary Violence*. New York: Columbia University Press, 2011.

Chakrabarty, Dipesh. "The Climate of History: Four Theses." *Critical Inquiry* 35, no. 2 (Winter 2009): 197–222.

Chakrabarty, Dipesh. "Postcolonial Studies and the Challenge of Climate Change." *New Literary History* 43, no. 1 (2012): 1–18.

Chakrabarty, Dipesh. *Provincializing Europe: Postcolonial Thought and Historical Difference*. Princeton, NJ: Princeton University Press, 2009.

Chen, Mel Y. *Animacies: Biopolitics, Racial Mattering, and Queer Affect*. Durham, NC: Duke University Press, 2012.

Chow, Rey. *The Age of the World Target*. Durham, NC: Duke University Press, 2006.

Chow, Rey. "The Age of the World Target: Atomic Bombs, Alterity, Area Studies." In *Rey Chow Reader*, edited by Paul Bowman, 2–18. New York: Columbia University Press, 2010.

Chuh, Kandice. *The Difference Aesthetics Makes: On the Humanities "After Man."* Durham, NC: Duke University Press, 2019.

Clark, Nigel, and Kathryn Yusoff. "Queer Fire: Ecology, Combustion and Pyrosexual Desire." *Feminist Review* 118 (2018): 7–24.

Clifford, James. *The Predicament of Culture: Twentieth-Century Ethnography, Literature, and Art*. Cambridge, MA: Harvard University Press, 1988.

Cohen, Ed. *A Body Worth Defending: Immunity, Biopolitics, and the Apotheosis of the Modern Body*. Durham, NC: Duke University Press, 2009.

Collins, John. "Terrorism." In *Collateral Language: A User's Guide to America's New War*, edited by John Collins and Ross Glover, 155–74. New York: NYU Press, 2002.

Cornum, Lou. "Radioactive Intimacies: The Making of Worldwide Wastelands in Marie Clements's *Burning Vision*." *Critical Ethnic Studies* 6, no. 1 (2020). https://www.jstor.org/stable/48628949.

Cosgrove, Denis. *Apollo's Eye: A cartographic Genealogy of the Earth in Western Imagination*. Baltimore, MD: Johns Hopkins University Press, 2001.

Crinson, Mark. "Abadan: Planning and Architecture under the Anglo-Iranian Oil Company." *Planning Perspectives* 12 (1997): 341–59.

Cruikshank, Julie. "Invention of Anthropology in British Columbia's Supreme Court: Oral Tradition as Evidence in Delgamuukw v. B.C." *BC Studies* 95 (Autumn 1992): 25–42.

Crutzen, Paul J. "We Live in the Anthropocene, So Will Our Grandchildren." *Herald of the Russian Academy of Sciences* 19, no. 1 (2021): 13–16.

Crutzen, Paul J., John R. McNeill, and Will Steffen. "The Anthropocene: Are Humans Now Overwhelming the Great Forces of Nature?" *Ambio* 36, no. 8 (2007): 614–21.

Crutzen, Paul J., and Eugene F. Stoermer. "The 'Anthropocene.'" *International Geosphere-Biosphere Programme (IGB): Global Change Newsletter* 41 (May 2000): 17–18.

Daggett, Cara New. *The Birth of Energy: Fossil Fuels, Thermodynamics, and the Politics of Work.* Durham, NC: Duke University Press, 2019.

Damluji, Mona. "The Oil City in Focus: The Cinematic Spaces of Abadan in the Anglo-Iranian Oil Company's *Persian Story.*" *Comparative Studies of South Asia and the Middle East* 33, no. 1 (2013): 75–88.

Danrey, Virginie. "Winged Human-Headed Bulls of Nineveh: Genesis of an Iconographic Motif." *Iraq* 66 (2004): 133–39.

Daughtry, Martin J. *Listening to War: Sound, Music, Trauma, and Survival in Wartime Iraq.* New York: Oxford University Press, 2015.

Davidson, Michael. *Concerto for the Left Hand: Disability and the Body.* Ann Arbor: University of Michigan Press, 2008.

Davis, Heather. "The Domestication of Plastic." In *The 3D Additivist Cookbook,* edited by Morehshin Allahyari and Daniel Rourke, 303–5. Amsterdam: Institute of Network Cultures, 2016.

Davis, Heather, and Zoe Todd. "On the Importance of a Date, or Decolonizing the Anthropocene." *ACME: An International Journal for Critical Geographies* 16, no. 4 (January 2017): 761–80.

Davies, Jeremy. *The Birth of the Anthropocene.* Berkeley: University of California Press, 2016.

De la Cadena, Marisol. *Earth Beings: Ecologies of Practice Across Andean Worlds.* Durham, NC: Duke University Press, 2015.

DeLoughrey, Elizabeth M. *Allegories of the Anthropocene.* Durham, NC: Duke University Press, 2019.

Derrida, Jacques, and R. Klein. "Economimesis." *Diacritics* 11, no. 2 (Summer 1981): 2–25.

Dickinson, Adam. *Anatomic.* Toronto: Coach House Books, 2018.

Dimock, Wai Chee. "Deep Time: American Literature and World History." *American Literary History* 13, no. 4 (2001): 755–75.

Dimock, Wai Chee. *Through Other Continents: American Literature across Deep Time.* Princeton, NJ: Princeton University Press, 2006.

Duggan, Robert. "Larissa Sansour and the Palestinian Ruins of the Future." *Journal for Cultural Research* 24, no. 1 (2020): 69–83.

Dupré, Sven. "The Transnational Galileo: A Telescopic View from Somewhere." *Nuncius* 28 (2013): 465–76.

Dyer, Richard. *White: Essays on Race and Culture.* New York: Routledge, 1997.

Eidsheim, Nina Sun. *Sensing Sound: Singing and Listening as Vibrational Practice.* Durham, NC: Duke University Press, 2015.

Eiland, Howard, and Michael W. Jennings. *Walter Benjamin: A Critical Life*. Cambridge, MA: Belknap Press of Harvard University, 2014.

Elden, Stuart. *Terror and Territory: The Spatial Extent of Sovereignty*. Minneapolis: University of Minnesota Press, 2009.

Endres, Danielle. "The Rhetoric of Nuclear Colonialism: Rhetorical Exclusion of American Indian Arguments in the Yucca Mountain Nuclear Waste Siting Decision." *Communication and Critical/Cultural Studies* 6, no. 1 (2009): 39–60.

Eshun, Kodow. "Further Considerations of Afrofuturism." CR: *The Centennial Review* 3, no. 2 (Summer 2003): 287–302.

Falkenberg, Reindert. "Phantom Limb–Phantom View." In *Diana Al-Hadid: Phantom Limb*, edited by Maya Allison, 17–24. Abu Dhabi and Milano: NYU Abu Dhabi Art Gallery and Skira Editore, 2016.

Ferguson, Frances. "The Nuclear Sublime." *Diacritics* 14, no. 2 (Summer 1984): 4–10.

Foucault, Michel. *The Order of Things: An Archeology of the Human Sciences*. New York: Routledge, 2002.

Foucault, Michel. *Society Must Be Defended: Lectures at the College de France, 1975–1976*. New York: Picador, 1997.

Freud, Sigmund. *Beyond the Pleasure Principle*. Translated by James Strachey. New York: W. W. Norton, 1961.

Frost, Samantha. *Biocultural Creatures: Toward a New Theory of the Human*. Durham, NC: Duke University Press, 2016.

Gómez-Barris, Macarena. *The Extractive Zone: Social Ecologies and Decolonial Perspectives*. Durham, NC: Duke University Press, 2017.

González, Zarandona, José Antonio, César Albarrán-Torres, and Benjamin Isakhan. "Digitally Mediated Iconoclasm: The Islamic State and the War on Cultural Heritage." *International Journal of Heritage Studies* 24, no. 6 (2018): 649–71.

Goodman, Steve. *Sonic Warfare: Sound, Affect, and the Ecology of Fear*. Cambridge, MA: MIT Press, 2012.

Grove, Jairus Victor. *Savage Ecology: War and Geopolitics at the End of the World*. Durham, NC: Duke University Press, 2019.

Guidotti, Tee L. "Hydrogen Sulfide: Advances in Understanding Human Toxicity." *International journal of Toxicology* 29, no. 6 (2010): 569–81.

Gusterson, Hugh. *People of the Bomb: Portraits of America's Nuclear Complex*. Minneapolis: University of Minnesota Press, 2004.

Hansen, Svend. "Key Techniques in the Production of Metals in the 6th and 5th Millennia BCE: Prerequisites, Preconditions and Consequences." In *Appropriating Innovations: Entangled Knowledge in Eurasia, 5000–1500 BCE*, edited by Philipp W. Stockhammer and Joseph Maran, 136–48. Oxford and Philadelphia: Oxbow, 2017.

Haraway, Donna J. "Situated Knowledges: The Science Question in Feminism and the Privilege of Partial Perspective." *Feminist Studies* 14, no. 3 (Autumn 1988): 575–99.

Haraway, Donna J. *Staying with the Trouble: Making Kin in the Chthulucene*. Durham, NC: Duke University Press, 2016.

Hayashi, Norihito. "Scientific or Narrative? Tradition of Illustration of the al-Qazwini's

Ajaib al-Makhluqat in the late 15th century Persian Manuscripts." *Advanced Science Letters* 23, no. 5 (2017):4701-4.

Hayles, N. Katherine. *How We Became Posthuman: Virtual Bodies in Cybernetics, Literature, and Informatics.* Chicago: University of Chicago Press, 1999.

Hayles, N. Katherine. "Speculative Aesthetics and Object-Oriented Inquiry (OOI)." *Speculations: A Journal of Speculative Realism* 5 (2014): 158-79.

Henry, J. T. *The Early and Later History of Petroleum.* Philadelphia: Jas. B. Rodgers, 1873.

Hindess, Barry. "Terrortory." *Alternatives* 31 (2006): 243-57.

Hochberg, Gil. *Becoming Palestine: Toward an Archival Imagination of the Future.* Durham, NC: Duke University Press, 2021.

Hochberg, Gil Z. "'Jerusalem, We Have a Problem': Larissa Sansour's Sci-Fi Trilogy and the Impetus of Dystopic Imagination." *Arab Studies Journal* 26, no. 1 (Spring 2018): 34-57.

Hua, Quan, Mike Barbetti, and Andrzej Z. Rakowski. "Atmospheric Radiocarbon for the Period 1950-2010," *Radiocarbon* 55, no. 4 (2013): 2059-72.

Israeli, Ofer. "The Circuitous Nature of Operation Ajax." *Middle Eastern Studies* 49, no. 2 (2013): 246-62.

Jackson, Zakiyyah Iman. *Becoming Human: Matter and Meaning in an Antiblack World.* New York: New York University Press, 2020.

Jahed, Parviz. *Directory of World Cinema: Iran I.* Bristol: Intellect, 2012.

Jones, Caroline A. *Eyesight Alone: Clement Greenberg's Modernism and the Bureaucratization of the Senses.* Chicago: University of Chicago Press, 2005.

Kahn, Douglas. *Earth Sound Earth Signal: Energies and Earth Magnitude in the Arts.* Berkeley: University of California Press, 2013.

Kahn, Douglas. *Noise, Water, Meat: A History of Sound in the Arts.* Cambridge, MA: MIT Press: 1999.

Kant, Immanuel. *Observations on the Feeling of the Beautiful and Sublime.* Translated by John T. Goldthwait. Berkeley: University of California Press, 1960.

Kapadia, Ronak K. *Insurgent Aesthetics: Security and the Queer Life of the Forever War.* Durham, NC: Duke University Press, 2019.

Kedar, Alexandre, Ahmad Amara, and Oren Yiftachel. *Emptied Lands: A Legal Geography of Bedouin Rights in the Negev.* Stanford, CA: Stanford University Press, 2018.

Kelley, Colin P., Shahrzad Mohtadi, Mark A. Caew, Richard Seager, and Yochanan Kushnir. "Climate Change in the Fertile Crescent and Implications of the Recent Syrian Drought." *PNAS* 112, no. 11 (March 2015): 3241-46.

Khalili, Laleh. *Sinews of War and Trade: Shipping and Capitalism in the Arabian Peninsula.* New York: Verso, 2020.

Kheshti, Roshanak. *Wendy Carlos's Switched-On Bach.* New York: Bloomsbury Academic, 2019.

Kim, Jaechun. "The First American Secret War: Assessing the Origins and Consequences of Operation Ajax in Iran." *International Area Review* 9, no. 1 (2006): 195-216.

Kinzer, Stephen. *All the Shah's Men: An American Coup and the Roots of Middle East Terror*. Hoboken, NJ: John Wiley and Sons, 2003.

Klein, Richard. "Climate Change through the Lens of Nuclear Criticism." *Diacritics* 41, no. 3 (Summer 2013): 82–87.

Kosek, Jake. "Ecologies of Empire: On the New Uses of the Honeybee." *Cultural Anthropology* 25, no. 4 (2010): 650–78.

LaDuke, Winona. *All Our Relations: Native Struggles for Land and Life*. Cambridge, MA: South End Press, 1999.

LeMenager, Stephanie. *Living Oil: Petroleum Culture in the American Century*. Oxford: University of Oxford Press, 2014.

Liboiron, Max. *Pollution Is Colonialism*. Durham, NC: Duke University Press, 2021.

Lippit, Akira Mizuta. *Atomic Light (Shadow Optics)*. Minneapolis: University of Minnesota Press, 2005.

Lockwood, Jeffrey A. *Six-Legged Soldiers: Using Insects as Weapons of War*. Oxford: Oxford University Press, 2009.

Mahdavy, Hossein. "The Patterns and Problems of Economic Development in Rentier States: The Case of Iran." In *Studies in the Economic History of the Middle East: From the Rise of Islam to the Present Day*, edited by M. A. Cook, 428–67. London: Oxford University Press, 1970.

Malm, Andreas, and Alf Hornborg, "The Geology of Mankind? A Critique of the Anthropocene Narrative." *Anthropocene Review* 1, no. 1 (2014): 62–69.

Marks, Laura U. "Thinking Multisensory Culture." *Paragraph* 31, no. 2 (July 2008): 123–37.

Marra, John F. *Hot Carbon: Carbon-14 and a Revolution in Science*. New York: Columbia University Press, 2019.

Marsh, Steve. "The United States, Iran and Operation 'Ajax': Inverting Interpretive Orthodoxy." *Middle Eastern Studies* 39, no. 3 (2003): 1–38.

Martin, Emily. *Flexible Bodies: The Role of Immunity in American Culture from the Days of Polio to the Age of AIDS*. Boston: Beacon Press, 1994.

Martin, Randy. *An Empire of Indifference: American War and the Financial Logic of Risk Management*. Durham, NC: Duke University Press, 2007.

Marzec, Paul. *Militarizing the Environment: Climate Change and the Security State*. Minneapolis: University of Minnesota Press, 2015.

Massumi, Brian. *Ontopower: War, Powers, and the State of Perception*. Durham, NC: Duke University Press, 2015.

Mavor, Carol. *Black and Blue: The Bruising Passion of "Camera Lucida," "La Jetée," "San Soleil," and "Hiroshima mon amour."* Durham, NC: Duke University Press, 2012.

Mawani, Renisa. "Insects, War, Plastic Life." In *Plastic Materialities: Politics, Legality, and Metamorphosis in the Work of Catherine Malabou*, edited by Brenna Bhandar and Jonathan Goldberg-Hiller, 159–89. Durham, NC: Duke University Press, 2015.

Mawani, Renisa. "Insect Wars: Bees, Bedbugs and Biopolitics." In *Routledge Handbook of Law and Theory*, edited by Andreas Philippopoulos-Mihalopoulos, 275–95. New York: Routledge, 2018.

Mbembe, Achille. "Necropolitics." *Public Culture* 15, no. 1 (2003): 11–40.

McKittrick, Katherine, ed. *Sylvia Wynter: On Being as Praxis*. Durham, NC: Duke University Press, 2015.

Mentz, Steve. *Break Up the Anthropocene*. Minneapolis: University of Minnesota Press, 2019.

Mignolo, Walter D., and Catherine E. Walsh. *On Decoloniality: Concepts, Analytics, Praxis*. Durham, NC: Duke University Press, 2018.

Miller, David Philip. "The Story of 'Scientist: The Story of a Word.'" *Annals of Science* 74, no. 4 (2017): 255–61.

Mills, Mara, and Jonathan Sterne. "Afterword II: Dismediation—Three Proposals, Six Tactics." In *Disability Media Studies*, edited by Elizabeth Ellcessor and Bill Kirkpatrick, 365–78. New York: New York University Press, 2017.

Mitchell, Timothy. *Carbon Democracy: Political Power in the Age of Oil*. New York and London: Verso, 2011.

Moore, Jason W. *Capitalism in the Web of Life: Ecology and the Accumulation of Capital*. New York: Verso, 2015.

Moore, Jason W. "The Capitalocene, Part I: On the Nature and Origins of Our Ecological Crisis." *Journal of Peasant Studies* 44, no. 3 (2017), 594–630.

Morton, Timothy. *Dark Ecology: For a Logic of Future Coexistence*. New York: Columbia University Press, 2016.

Muñoz, José Esteban. *Cruising Utopia: The Then and There of Queer Futurity*. New York: New York University Press, 2009.

Murty, Katta G. "History of Crude Oil Refining." In *Models for Optimum Decision Making: Crude Oil Production and Refining*, edited by Katta G. Murty, 1–9. Cham, Switzerland: Springer Nature, 2020.

Musiol, Hanna. "Liquid Modernity: Sundown in Pahuska, Oklahoma." In *Oil Culture*, edited by Ross Barrett and Daniel Worden, 129–44. Minneapolis: University of Minnesota Press, 2014.

Myers, David. "The Video Game Aesthetic: Play as Form." In *The Video Game Theory Reader 2*, edited by Bernard Perron and Mark J. P. Wolf, 45–65. London: Routledge, 2009.

Naficy, Hamid. "Iranian Documentary." *Jump Cut: Review of Contemporary Media* 26 (December 1981): 41–46.

Naficy, Hamid. "Nonfiction Fiction: Documentaries on Iran." *Iranian Studies* 12, no. 3/4 (1979): 217–38.

Negarestani, Reza. *Cyclonopedia: Complicity with Anonymous Materials*. Melbourne: re.press, 2008.

Nixon, Rob. *Slow Violence and the Environmentalism of the Poor*. Cambridge, MA: Harvard University Press, 2013.

Pandolfo, Stefania. *Knot of the Soul: Madness, Psychoanalysis, Islam*. Chicago: University of Chicago Press, 2018.

Paris, Michael. "The First Air Wars—North Africa and the Balkans, 1911–13." *Journal of Contemporary History* 26 (1991): 97–109.

Pasquinelli, Matteo. "The Automaton of the Anthropocene: On Carbosilicon Machines and Cyberfossil Capital." *South Atlantic Quarterly* 116, no. 2 (2017): 311–26.

Pinkus, Karen. *Fuel: A Speculative Dictionary*. Minneapolis: University of Minnesota Press, 2016.

Pop, Virgiliu. "The Men Who Sold the Moon: Science Fiction or Legal Nonsense?" *Space Policy* 17 (2001): 195–203.

Povinelli, Elizabeth. *The Cunning of Recognition: Indigenous Alterities and the Making of Australian Multiculturalism*. Durham, NC: Duke University Press, 2002.

Povinelli, Elizabeth. *Geontologies: A Requiem to Late Liberalism*. Durham, NC: Duke University Press, 2016.

Povinelli, Elizabeth. "The Three Figures of Geontology." In *Anthropocene Feminism*, edited by Richard Grusin, 49–64. Minneapolis: University of Minnesota Press, 2017.

Prescod-Weinstein, Chanda. *The Disordered Cosmos: A Journey into Dark Matter, Spacetime, and Dreams Deferred*. New York: Bold Type Books, 2021.

Prior, Daniel G. "Travels of Mount Qaf: From Legend to 42° 0′ N 79° 51′ E." *Oriente Moderno* 89, no. 2 (2009): 425–44.

Puar, Jasbir K. *The Right to Maim: Debility, Capacity, Disability*. Durham, NC: Duke University Press, 2017.

Puar, Jasbir K. *Terrorist Assemblages: Homonationalism in Queer Times*. Durham, NC: Duke University Press, 2007.

Pugliese, Joseph. *Biopolitics of the More-Than-Human: Forensic Ecologies of Violence*. Durham, NC: Duke University Press, 2020.

Pyatt, F. B., G. Gilmore, J. P. Grattan, C. O. Hunt, and S. McLaren. "An Imperial Legacy? An Exploration of the Environmental Impact of Ancient Metal Mining and Smelting in Southern Jordan." *Journal of Archeological Science* 27, no. 9 (2000): 771–78.

Pyne, Stephen J. *Vestal Fire: An Environmental History, Told through Fire, of Europe and Europe's Encounter with the World*. Seattle: University of Washington Press, 2000.

Raffles, Hugh. *Insectopedia*. New York: Pantheon Books, 2010.

Rana, Junaid. "The Racial Infrastructure of the Terror-Industrial Complex." *Social Text* 34, no. 4 (December 2016): 111–38.

Rana, Junaid. *Terrifying Muslims: Race and Labor in the South Asian Diaspora*. Durham, NC: Duke University Press, 2011.

Ray, Gene. *Terror and the Sublime in Art and Critical Theory: From Auschwitz to Hiroshima to September 11*. New York: Palgrave Macmillan, 2005.

Ray, Gene. "Terror and the Sublime in the So-Called Anthropocene." *Liminalities: A Journal of Performance Studies* 19, no. 2 (2020): 1–20.

Raza, Sara. "Diana Al-Hadid: Suspended Informal Architecture in Time and Space." In *Diana Al-Hadid: Phantom Limb*, edited by Maya Allison, 53–61. Abu Dhabi and Milano: Skira Editore, 2016.

Raza Kolb, Anjuli Fatima. *Epidemic Empire: Colonialism, Contagion, and Terror 1817–2020*. Chicago: University of Chicago Press, 2021.

Roads, Curtis. *Microsound*. Cambridge, MA: MIT Press, 2001.

Robbins, Bruce. "The Sweatshop Sublime." *PMLA* 117, no. 1 (January 2002): 84–97.

Rosenbaum, Jonathan. "Radical Humanism and the Coexistence of Film and Poetry in *The House Is Black.*" In *The Documentary Film Reader: History, Theory, Criticism,* edited by Jonathan Kahana, 473–78. New York: Oxford University Press, 2016.

Russell, Edmund P. "'Speaking of Annihilation': Mobilizing for War against Human and Insect Enemies, 1914–1945." *Journal of American History* 82, no. 4 (1996): 1505–29.

Rutkin, H. Darrel. "Celestial Offerings: Astrological Motifs in the Dedicatory Letters of Kepler's *Astronomia Nova* and Galileo's *Sidereus Nuncius.*" In *Secrets of Nature: Astrology and Alchemy in Early Modern Europe,* edited by William R. Newman and Anthony Grafton, 133–73. Cambridge, MA: MIT Press, 2001.

Said, Edward. *Orientalism.* London: Routledge and Kegan Paul, 1978.

Salamanca, Omar Jabary. "Assembling the Fabric of Life." *Journal of Palestine Studies* 45, no. 4 (Summer 2016): 64–80.

Saljoughi, Sara. "A New Form for a New People: Forough Farrokhzad's *The House Is Black.*" *Camera Obscura* 32, no. 1 (2017): 1–31.

Sariyannis, Marinos. "*Aja'ib ve ghara'ib*: Ottoman Collections of *Mirabilia* and Perceptions of the Supernatural." *Der Islam* 92, no. 2 (2015): 442–67.

Sato, H., C. W. Berry, B. E. Casey, G. Lavella, Y. Yao, J. M. VandenBrooks, and M. Maharbiz. "A Cyborg Beetle: Insect Flight Control through an Implantable Tetherless Microsystem," In the *21st IEEE Intl. Conference on Micro Electro Mechanical Systems (MEMS 2008) Technical Digest.* Piscataway, NJ: IEEE Press, 2008.

Scarry, Elaine. *The Body in Pain: The Making and Unmaking of the World.* Oxford: Oxford University Press, 1985.

Scott, Darieck. *Extravagant Abjection: Blackness, Power, and Sexuality in the African American Literary Imagination.* New York: New York University Press, 2010.

Selby, Han. "Climate Change and the Syrian Civil War, Part II: The Jazira'a Agrarian Crisis." *Geoforum* 101 (2019): 260–74.

Seshadri, Kalpana Rahita. *HumAnimal: Race, Law, Language.* Minneapolis: University of Minnesota Press, 2012.

Shachtman, Noah. "Pentagon's Cyborg Insects All Grown Up." *Wired,* March 19, 2008.

Shafiee, Katayoun. *Machineries of Oil: An Infrastructural History of BP in Iran.* Cambridge, MA: MIT Press, 2018.

Shams, Fatemeh. "The Village in Contemporary Persian Poetry." *Iranian Studies* 51, no. 3 (2018): 455–77.

Siebers, Tobin. *Disability Aesthetics.* Ann Arbor: University of Michigan Press, 2010.

Sobchack, Vivian. "Living a 'Phantom Limb': On the Phenomenology of Bodily Integrity." *Body & Society* 16, no. 3 (2010): 51–67.

Sorkhabi, Rasoul. "Pre-modern History of Bitumen, Oil and Gas in Persia." *Oil-Industry History* 6, no. 1 (2005): 153–77.

Spivak, Gayatri Chakravorty. *An Aesthetic Education in the Era of Globalization.* Cambridge, MA: Harvard University Press, 2012.

Spivak, Gayatri Chakrabarty. *A Critique of Postcolonial Reason: Toward a History of the Vanishing Present.* Cambridge, MA: Harvard University Press, 1999.

Spivak, Gayatri Chakravorty. *Death of a Discipline.* New York: Columbia University Press, 2003.

Stamatopoulou-Robbins, Sophia. *Waste Siege: The Life of Infrastructure in Palestine.* Stanford, CA: Stanford University Press, 2020.

Stauffer, Jill. "'You People Talk from Paper': Indigenous Law, Western Legalism, and the Cultural Variability of Law's Materials." *Law Text Culture* 23 (2019): 40–57.

Stewart, Kathleen. "On the Politics of Cultural Theory: A Case for 'Contaminated Cultural Critique." *Social Research* 58, no. 2 (Summer 1991): 395–412.

Stone, Robert W., and Claude E. Zobell. "Bacterial Aspects of the Origin of Petroleum." *Industrial and Engineering Chemistry* 44, no. 11 (1952): 2564–67.

TallBear, Kim. "Beyond the Life/Non-Life Binary: A Feminist-Indigenous Reading of Cryopreservation, Interspecies Thinking, and the New Materialisms." In *Cryopolitics: Frozen Life in a Melting World,* edited by J Radin and E. Kowal, 179–202. Cambridge, MA: MIT Press, 2017.

TallBear, Kim. *Native American DNA: Tribal Belonging and the False Promise of Genetic Science.* Minneapolis: University of Minnesota Press, 2013.

Taneja, Anand Vivek. *Jinnealogy: Time, Islam, and Ecological Thought in the Medieval Ruins of Delhi.* Stanford, CA: Stanford University Press, 2018.

Taussig, Michael. *What Color Is the Sacred?* Chicago: University of Chicago Press, 2009.

Todd, Zoe. "Indigenizing the Anthropocene." In *Art in the Anthropocene: Encounters Among Aesthetics, Politics, Environment and Epistemology,* edited by Heather Davis and Etienne Turpin, 241–54. London: Open Humanities Press, 2015.

Tompkins, Kyla. "Crude Matter, Queer Form." *ASAP/Journal* 2, no. 2 (2017): 264–68.

Trower, Shelley. *Senses of Vibration: A History of the Pleasure and Pain of Sound.* London: Continuum, 2012.

Tsing, Anna Lowenhaupt. *The Mushroom at the End of the World: On the Possibility of Life in Capitalist Ruins.* Princeton, NJ: Princeton University Press, 2015.

Tuck, Eve, and K. Wayne Yang. "Decolonization Is not a Metaphor." *Decolonization: Indigeneity, Education and Society* 1, no. 1 (2012): 1–40.

Turney, Chris S. M., Jonathan Palmer, Mark A. Maslin, Alan Hogg, Christopher J. Fogwill, John Southon, Pavla Fenwick, et al. "Global Peak in Atmospheric Radiocarbon Provides a Potential Definition for the Onset of the Anthropocene Epoch in 1965." *Scientific Reports* 8, no. 3293 (February 2018): 1–9.

Virilio, Paul. *War and Cinema: The Logics of Perception.* Translated by Patrick Camiller. New York: Verso, 1989.

Vomar, Axel. "Listening to the Cold War: The Nuclear Test Ban Negotiations, Seismology, and Psychoacoustics, 1958–1963." *Osiris* 28, no. 1 (2013): 80–102.

Voyles, Traci Brynne. *Wastelanding: Legacies of Uranium Mining in Navajo Country.* Minneapolis: University of Minnesota Press, 2013.

Wald, Priscilla. *Contagious: Cultures, Carriers, and the Outbreak Narrative.* Durham, NC: Duke University Press, 2008.

Wark, McKenzie. "An Inhuman Fiction of Forces." In *Leper Creativity: Cyclonopedia Symposium,* edited by Ed Keller, Nicola Masciandaro, and Eugene Thacker, 39–44. Brooklyn: Punctum Books, 2012.

Watts, Michael J. "Oil as Money: The Devil's Excrement as the Spectacle of Black

Gold." In *Reading Economic Geography*, edited by Trevor J. Barnes, Jamie Peck, Eric Shepperd, and Adam Tickell, 205–19. Hoboken, NJ: Wiley-Blackwell, 2003.

Weizman, Eyal. *Forensic Architecture: Violence at the Threshold of Detectability*. New York: Zone Books, 2018.

Weizman, Eyal. *Hollow Land: Israel's Architecture of Occupation*. New York: Verso, 2007.

Wendt, C. J., and A. Cyphers. "How the Olmec Used Bitumen in Ancient Mesoamerica." *Journal of Anthropological Archeology* 27 (2008): 175–91.

Wenzel, Jennifer. "How to Read for Oil." *Resilience: A Journal of the Environmental Humanities* 1, no. 3 (2014): 156–61.

Wilson, Robert R. "Niels Bohr and the Young Scientists." *Bulletin of the Atomic Scientists* 41, no.7 (1985): 23–26.

Witter, R. Z., L. Tenney, S. Clark, and L. S. Newman. "Occupational Exposures in the Oil and Gas Extraction Industry: State of the Science and Research Recommendations." *American Journal of Industrial Medicine* 57, no. 7 (2014): 847–56.

Wolfe, Patrick. "Settler Colonialism and the Elimination of the Native." *Journal of Genocide Research* 8, no. 4 (2006): 387–409.

Yusoff, Kathryn. *A Billion Black Anthropocenes or None*. Minneapolis: University of Minnesota Press, 2018.

Zakariya, Nasser. *A Final Story: Science, Myth & Beginnings*. Chicago: University of Chicago Press, 2017.

Zalasiewicz, Jan, Colin N. Waters, Mark Williams, Anthony D. Barnosky, Alejandro Cearreta, Paul Crutzen, Erle Ellis, et. al. "When Did the Anthropocene Begin?" *Quaternary International* 383 (October 2015): 196–203.

Zalasiewicz, Jan, Mark Williams, Will Steffen, and Paul Crutzen. "The New World of the Anthropocene." *Environmental Science and Technology* 44, no. 7 (2010): 2228–31.

Anthropocene (*continued*)

militarism and, 25, 117–18; racialization of, 16–17, 30, 48–49; sensing, 52; settler colonialism and, 23–26, 48–49; sublime and, 55; technology and, 23, 196n17; temporality of, 6–7, 14–15, 35, 85–86, 117–18; as work of art, 40–42, 49–52. *See also* climate, climate change; humans, humanism; Terracene

anthropology, 77–80. *See also* ethnography; travel writing

anticolonialism. *See under* settler colonialism

antiquities, 63–64

Arabah, Wadi, 122

Arab Spring, 62

archaeology: future and, 146–51; historiographic narratives of, 114–16; knowledge-production and, 147–51; nation and, 147–48

art, aesthetics, 100, 167–68; Anthropocene and, 40–42, 49–52; climate change and, 27–28, 65–66; crude, 69, 71–72, 79–80, 92, 170; destruction and, 40–45, 94–96; disability and, 58, 66–68; dissent and, 183–84; ethics and, 79–80; gender and, 54–55; humans and, 9, 79, 183; industrialization and, 40–42; materiality and, 69; militarism and, 40–42; oil and, 8, 163–70, 182–84; perception and, 58, 167–69; race and, 60, 72–75, 79–80, 200n12; science and, 27–28; sensing, 53–58, 68–69, 98–99; settler colonialism and, 41–42; sound and, 93–95; Terracene and, 56, 65–67; terror and, 41–42, 54–57, 65–66; toxicity and, 167–70; trauma and, 54–55, 68–69; video games and, 93, 98–99; violence and, 93–96; war and, 65–66, 94–99

art history, 63–64, 67, 100–101

assemblage, 17–18, 21, 154

atomic bomb, 30, 43–45, 56–57, 102. *See also* Anthropocene; explosions; nuclear weapons

autonomy, 56–57, 100, 169–70, 181–82

Bangladesh, 20–21

Barad, Karen, 101

Battersby, Christine, 54–56

Baucom, Ian, 55

beautiful, 54–55. *See also* art, aesthetics; sublime

Behdad, Ali, 76

Benjamin, Walter, 40–42, 96

Bennett, Jane, 65

Biagioli, Mario, 37–38

biodiversity. *See under* ecology

biopolitics, biopower, 47–48, 52, 59–60, 121–23, 155–57; nonhuman animals and, 153; terrorism and, 157–58. *See also* necropolitics

biosecurity. *See* security, securitization

blackness, 16, 29. *See also* race, racialization

blindness, 58, 68. *See also* senses, sensing; vision, visuality

Boas, Franz, 79–80

body, 53, 58–60, 124–25; amputation and, 60–61, 67–68; capitalism and, 59–60; disability and, 66–67; gendering of, 124–25; humans and, 15, 21; immunity and, 19–20; maiming of, 59–60, 66–67; modernity and, 179–80; posthumanism and, 124–25; queerness of, 127–28; racialization of, 124–25; sacred and, 137–39; sensing and, 53–54, 57–60, 66–69, 88; sound and, 87–88, 102–3; temporality and, 144; Terran, 150; terrorism and, 16; war and, 53. *See also* disability; gender; queer, queerness; race, racialization; senses, sensing; trans

Bokova, Irina, 116

Brecht, Bertolt, 33

BRIC (Brazil, Russia, India, China), 25

British Association for the Advancement of Science, 30–31

British Petroleum (BP), 177–78

bronze, 64–65, 122, 205n27. *See also* metals, metallurgy; sculpture

Browne, Simone, 124–25

Buck-Morss, Susan, 54–57, 167–68

Burden, Chris, 66

Bureau of Linguistical Reality, 49–50

Bush, George W., 15–16, 157

Cameron, Bryce, 178–81

capitalism: body and, 59–60; climate change and, 23; extractivism and, 71; matter and, 71–72; sublime and, 55; wastelands and, 48

Capitalocene, 23. *See also* Anthropocene

carbon: Anthropocene and, 23, 25; carbon dating, 148–50, 206n6; carbon democracy, 150; carbon-privileged, 131–33, 206n2; crude oil and, 71–72, 79, 121, 131–33; geopolitics of, 150–51; hot carbon, 150; life and, 121, 150; sacred and, 131–33, 137–39

Cavarero, Adriana, 46–47

Chakrabarty, Dipesh, 15, 22–23, 31–32

Chen, Mel Y., 64–65, 169

Chow, Rey, 42–44, 93

Chuh, Kandice, 56–58

cinema, 171–82; new wave, 172. *See also* documentary; video

Clark, Nigel, 184

class, 97–98, 178–80, 186–87

Clifford, James, 77–78

climate, climate change, 5–6, 13–14, 52–53; art and aesthetics of, 27–28, 65–66; language and, 49–50; life and, 17; militarism and, 20–21, 25, 55; scale and, 14–16; settler colo-

nialism and, 23–26; temporality of, 144; terror and, 20–21; war and, 14, 48, 52–53, 148, 151–53. *See also* Anthropocene; Terracene
Cohen, Ed, 19–20
collectivization, 16–17, 85–86
College Art Association, 116–17
colonialism. *See* settler colonialism
contamination, 52, 59–60, 168–70, 174–76, 182
Cornum, Lou (Navajo), 144
Cosgrove, Denis, 26
cosmology, 25–26, 193n4; Anthropocene and, 25–26, 35–36, 39, 51–52; creation stories, 1–6; Indigenous, 35–36, 114–15, 129–30, 144–45; Islamic, 3–5; science and, 37–38
Crawshay-Williams, Eliot, 78–79
creation stories, 1–6
critical race studies, 23–24, 48–49. *See also* Indigenous studies
crude, crudeness, 71–72, 75, 79–80, 92; racialization of, 72, 75, 79–80
Crutzen, Paul J., 6, 20, 22–23, 30, 32–35, 37–38, 195n3

D'Arcy, William Knox, 78–79, 177, 208n9
Daggett, Cara New, 31
Damluji, Mona, 179–80
DARPA. *See* Defense Advanced Research Projects Agency
data, 2–5, 14–15, 23–26, 45, 124–25. *See also* Anthropocene; knowledge, knowledge-systems
Daughtry, J. Martin, 99–100
Davidson, Michael, 68
Davis, Heather, 23–24
decolonialism. *See under* settler colonialism
Deepwater Horizon oil spill, 123
Defense Advanced Research Projects Agency (DARPA), 152–53
deities, 8, 113–16, 118–21, 124–28, 131–39. *See also* sacred
de la Cadena, Marisol, 48, 199nn10–11
DeLoughrey, Elizabeth, 26
democracy, 150
Derrida, Jacques, 168
Desert Strike: Return to the Gulf (Electronic Arts, 1992), 89–94. *See also* video games
Dickinson, Adam, 169
digital, 123–25. *See also* body
Dimock, Wai Chee, 117–18, 120–21
disability: ableism, 7–8, 15, 67; aesthetics and, 66–68; corrective technologies, 58–59; racialization of, 59–60; sensing and, 58, 66–67; visibility and, 67–68. *See also* body
disability studies, 59
disciplinarity, 20, 29, 37–38. *See also* knowledge, knowledge-systems

displacement, 52–53, 63–64, 68–69, 73–74
dispossession. *See under* settler colonialism
dissent, 48–49, 172, 180–84
divine. *See* deities; sacred
documentary (genre), 9, 106–9, 171–72, 180; political language of editing, 172–77, 180–81
Drake, Edwin L., 72
drones, 7–8, 89, 137, 152–53. *See also* insects; war
Dyer, Richard, 16–17
dystopia, 6, 157–60

earthquakes, 4, 7–8, 83–84, 101–3
ecology, 3–5; biodiversity, 5–6, 14, 35, 46–47, 71, 85–86; injury and, 59–60; race and, 74–75; settler colonialism and, 8–9; sociopolitical disparities and, 13–14; sound and, 101; terror and, 4; of war, 65–66, 85–86, 155–60
economy. *See* capitalism; extractivism
Eidsheim, Nina Sun, 102
ekphrasis, 88–89, 100
Elden, Stuart, 46–47
Electronic Arts (EA), 89–93
El-Haj, Nadia Abu, 147
embodiment. *See* body
entanglement, 4, 18, 56–58, 85–86, 150, 155, 170, 182. *See also* interconnectedness
entomological warfare, 152–54. *See also* insects; war
epic (genre), 6, 33–34, 89
epidemics, 18–19, 134–36, 155–56. *See also* fevers; illness; virus, virology
Eshun, Kodow, 156–57, 159
ethics, 5–6, 32–34, 79–80
Ethiopia, 41–42
ethnography, 77–78. *See also* anthropology; travel writing
Eurocene. *See* Anthropocene
explosions, 4, 7–9, 56, 83–84, 101–3, 158, 173–76; atomic, 43–45, 56–57; sound of, 101–3
extinction, 1–2, 5–6, 17, 35, 46–47, 49–50, 154, 158
extractivism, 1–2, 4–9, 71; aesthetics of, 183–84; crude oil and, 71–72, 78–79, 89; environmental racism and, 74–75; politics of, 163–64, 186; settler colonialism and, 72–75, 78–79; space and, 74; territory and, 46–47; war and, 89, 92, 97, 102, 203n20, 205n25; wastelands, 48

Falkenburg, Reindert, 66–67
fallout. *See under* nuclear weapons
Farrokhzad, Forough, *The House Is Black* (1962), 172
fascism, 41, 96
feminism, 23–24; aesthetics and, 54–55; race and, 28–30; science and, 28–30; speculative knowledge and, 128

military occupation of, 8, 116–17, 157; war
  with Iran, 53–54, 84, 104–5
ISIS. *See* Islamic State of Iraq and Syria
Islam: jinns and, 126–27, 131; pre-Islamic Indigenous religions, 1–5, 113–14, 129–31, 193n4;
  syncretism and, 3; terror and, 17–19
Islamic State of Iraq and Syria (ISIS), 113–16
Ismail, Adam, 35–36
Italy: futurism and, 95–97; Italo-Turkish War
  (1911–12), 96; military aggressions in Ethiopia, 41–42

Japan, 43–45, 56–57
jinns, 8, 131, 193n2; heat and, 127–28; illness
  and, 130–31, 136; memory and, 128; possession and, 2–3, 126–27, 137–39
Jupiter, 38–39

Kahn, Douglas, 95
Kämpfer, Engelbert, 76–78
Kant, Immanuel, 54–56, 79, 167–68, 200n12,
  208n8
Khalil, Mustafa, 35–36
Kheshti, Roshanak, 97
Khoshgozaran, Gelare, 8, 163–66, 169–70,
  174–76, 183; *Crude* (2018), 166–68
Kinley, Myron, 173, 181, 210n41
Klein, Richard, 55
knowledge, knowledge-systems: ancient, 8; archaeology and, 147–49; environment and,
  3; hierarchies of, 3, 6–7, 29–39; Indigenous,
  37–38, 118–19, 128, 193n4; inherited, 1–3, 8,
  131–33; limits of, 5–6; myths and, 137; positivism and, 5–6; racialization of, 29–30; sacred and, 137–39; science and, 27–29, 34–39;
  senses and, 53–54; spatial organization of,
  29–32; speculative, 5–6, 128, 131–33; temporality and, 156–57; unknown, 3–6, 26
Kuwait, 7–8, 93, 106–8

LaDuke, Winona, 74–75
Lamassu (deity), 118–21, 123–24
language: art and, 100; epistemic disobedience
  and, 48–50; future and, 144; inadequacy of,
  7–10; music and, 88–89; poetry and, 172
law: Indigenous sovereignty and, 35–37; territory and, 46–47
Lebanon, 52
legal studies, 37
LeMenager, Stephanie, 121–22
Liboiron, Max (Red River Métis/Michif), 74–75
life, living, 6; Anthropocene and, 17; biopower
  and, 155–56; carbon and, 150; devaluation of,
  48, 153–54; necropolitics and, 158–60; non-

human, 64–66, 121–23, 150, 153–54; precarity
  of, 46–47, 53
Lind, Søren, 146–47
Lippit, Akira Mizuta, 44–45
listening, 85–86, 94–95, 98–99, 103; to earth-
  quakes, 101–2; listening-as-poiesis, 99–100.
  See also senses, sensing; sounds
Lockwood, Jeffrey, 152–53

machines. *See* technology
Mahdavy, Hossein, 187
maiming. *See* disability; injury; terror
Malm, Andreas, 16
Marinetti, Filippo Tommaso, 95–97
Marra, John F., 150
Mars, 35–39, 143–46. *See also* Yemen
Marzec, Robert, 20
Massumi, Brian, 20–21, 124, 156–57
matter, materiality, 1–2; 3D manufacturing and,
  120, 123–24; aesthetics and, 64, 69, 183; capital and, 71–72; crude, 72, 80, 164–68, 183,
  186; dematerialization, 124–25; intelligence
  and, 9; land and, 131–33; life and, 122; metals
  and, 64–65; oil and, 164–68, 183, 186; science
  and, 43–44; softness and, 64, 69; territory and,
  47–48; temporality and, 144, 148–49
Mavor, Carol, 43–44
Mawani, Renisa, 153
Mbembe, Achille, 158–59
McClintock, Anne, 52–53
media, mediation, 96–98, 100, 167–68, 209n33;
  disability and, 59
media studies, 59
Mesopotamia, 63–65, 113–19
metals, metallurgy, 64–66, 97–98, 122, 205n27
Mignolo, Walter D., 25, 48–49
militarism, 4–7; Anthropocene and, 117–18;
  art and, 40–42, 55–56, 96–98; climate change
  and, 20–21, 25, 55; disability and, 59–60; humans and, 18–19; immunity and, 20; insects
  and, 152–54; machines and, 151–53; necropolitics of, 158–60; oil and, 121–22; science
  and, 43–44; wastelands and, 48. *See also* terror; war
Mills, Mara, 59
Mitchell, Timothy, 150
modernity, 72–74, 121–23, 179–82, 187, 206n11
Morton, Timothy, 48–49
Mosaddegh, Mohammad, 177–78
Muñoz, José Esteban, 128
Murty, Katta G., 70–71
museums, museology, 63–64, 95, 113–19
music, 85–89; electronic, 97; extractivism and,
  102–3; war and, 96–99, 102–3

Myers, David, 93
myths. *See under* knowledge, knowledge-systems

Naficy, Hamid, 180
NASA. *See* National Aeronautics and Space
    Administration
nation: archaeology and, 147–48; extractivism
    and, 72–74, 186; history and, 117–18; oil and,
    72–74, 121–22, 128, 150–51, 186; security and,
    119, 124–25. *See also* settler colonialism
National Aeronautics and Space Administration
    (NASA), 35–36, 143–44
National Iranian Oil Company (NIOC), 171–72,
    177–80. *See also* Anglo-Iranian Oil Company;
    Iran
necropolitics, 158–60. *See also* biopolitics,
    biopower
Negarestani, Reza, 8; *Cyclonopedia: Complicity
    with Anonymous Materials*, 136–37
networks, 19, 47–48, 154–55, 158–59
New Orleans, 20–21
NIOC. *See* National Iranian Oil Company
Nixon, Rob, 65–66, 122–23, 158
noise. *See under* sound
nuclear weapons: Anthropocene and, 20, 25;
    bombing of Japan, 43–45; fallout, 17–18, 20, 25,
    56–57; sublime and, 55. *See also* atomic bomb

oil, 8, 72–74, 164–66; 3D printing and, 123–24;
    aesthetics and, 8, 76–79, 182–84; agency of,
    182–84, 186–87; civilization and, 72–74; crude
    (petroleum), 8–9, 70–72, 79, 121, 163–68, 170,
    183; extractivism and, 4–9, 71–72, 75, 78–79,
    163–66; films, 179–81; fires and, 171–77, 180–84,
    210n41; humans and, 70–72; Indigenous peo-
    ple and, 70–76, 128, 131–33, 202nn3–4; intelli-
    gence and, 9; life of, 123; materiality of, 150, 183,
    186; nation and, 128, 150–51; pollution and,
    174–76; racialization of, 74–76, 178–80; sacred
    and, 70–71, 127–28, 131–33; settler colonial-
    ism and, 75, 150–51; spills, 122–23; temporality
    of, 120–23, 128, 185–86; terror and, 186–87; war
    and, 102, 121–23; wastelands and, 9. *See also*
    extractivism
Organization of Petroleum-Exporting Countries
    (OPEC), 185–86
Orientalism, 16, 75–78
Outer Space Treaty (1967), 36–37, 197n45

pain, 54–55, 58, 67–68. *See also* senses, sensing
Pakistan, 19, 157
Palestine, 47–48; biopolitical management of,
    154–56, 159; occupation of, 8–9, 59–60,
    146–51, 154

Pandolfo, Stefania, 126–27
Pazuzu (deity), 134–37
perception, 3, 6–9; aesthetics and, 56–58,
    167–69; Anthropocene and, 14–15; instru-
    mentalization of, 58–59; nonhuman, 9, 183;
    organs of, 57–60. *See also* senses, sensing
pesticides, 153–54
petroleum. *See* oil
petrorefusal, 182–84
petrodollars, 186–87
photography, 43–45, 129–31
picturesque, 54. *See also* art, aesthetics
planetary, 25–26. *See also* Spivak, Gayatri
plastic, 1–2, 120–24. *See also* oil
play, 93–94. *See also* video games
poetry, 1–6, 99–101, 172, 176–77
poiesis, 99. *See also under* listening
politics: aesthetics and, 41–42, 92–93, 96, 100,
    172–73, 176–77; Anthropocene and, 13–14,
    17–21, 25; disparities of, 13–14; of dissent,
    48–49, 172–73, 180–84; of editing, 172–73,
    176–77, 180–81; geopolitics, 13–14, 25, 52–53,
    60, 92–93, 150–51; humans and, 75; of oil,
    121–22, 150–51, 172–73, 176–78, 182–84, 186;
    of science, 30; of terrorist, 17–21, 147–48;
    temporality and, 144, 150–51; of village,
    180–81. *See also* biopolitics, biopower
pollution, 7, 9, 13–14, 48, 74–75, 121–23, 169,
    174–76. *See also* extractivism; toxins, toxicity;
    waste, wastelands
Pop, Virgiliu, 36–37
positivism. *See under* knowledge,
    knowledge-systems
postcolonialism. *See under* settler colonialism
posthumanism, 124–25
Povinelli, Elizabeth, 17–18, 37
Powell, Colin, 14
Prescod-Weinstein, Chanda, 29–30
protection, 59–60, 113–14, 118–24, 153, 155–56.
    See also biopolitics, biopower
Puar, Jasbir, 19, 59
Pugliese, Joseph, 47–48, 59–60

queer, queerness: aesthetics and, 80; body and,
    59, 124–25, 127–28; boundaries and, 119–21,
    124–25; crudeness and, 80; futurism and, 128,
    131–33. *See also* trans

race, racialization, 15, 29–30; aesthetics and, 60,
    200n12; Anthropocene and, 16–17, 21, 48–49;
    body and, 59–60, 124–25; disability and,
    59–60; environmental racism, 74–75; humans
    and, 23, 51–52, 75; labor and, 178–80; matter
    and, 72; oil and, 72–76, 178–80; profiling, 124;